Democracy and Empire

Democracy and Empire

The Athenian Invasion of Sicily, 415–413 BCE

Alexander O. Boulton

Hamilton Books
Lanham • Boulder • New York • Toronto • London

Published by Hamilton Books
An imprint of The Rowman & Littlefield Publishing Group, Inc.
4501 Forbes Boulevard, Suite 200, Lanham, Maryland 20706
Hamilton Books Acquisitions Department (301) 459-3366

86-90 Paul Street, London EC2A 4NE, United Kingdom

Copyright © 2021 by The Rowman & Littlefield Publishing Group, Inc.

All rights reserved. No part of this book may be produced in any form or by any electronic means, including information storage and retrieval systems,without written permission from the publisher, except by a reviewer who may quote passages in a review.

British Library Cataloguing in Publication Information Available

Library of Congress Cataloging-in-Publication Data

Names: Boulton, Alexander O., author.
Title: Democracy and empire : the Athenian invasion of Sicily, 415–413 BCE / Alexander O. Boulton.
Description: Lanham : Hamilton Books, [2021] | Includes bibliographical references and index. | Summary: "This story of Athens' tragic defeat in its attempt to subdue Sicily during the war between Athens and Sparta, discusses the social and political context, the ideas about religion, women, foreigners, and slaves during the great intellectual blossoming of fifth century Athens, and the complex relationship between democracy and empire"—Provided by publisher.
Identifiers: LCCN 2021032050 (print) | LCCN 2021032051 (ebook) | ISBN 9780761872979 (paperback) | ISBN 9780761872986 (epub)
Subjects: LCSH: Sicilian Expedition, Italy, 415–413 B.C. | Greece—History—Peloponnesian War, 431–404 B.C.—Campaigns. | Athens (Greece)—History, Military. | Sparta (Extinct city)—History, Military. | Democracy—Greece—Athens—History—To 1500. | Athens (Greece)—Social life and customs. | Athens (Greece)—Politics and government—To 1500. | Athens (Greece)—Intellectual life.
Classification: LCC DF229.65 .B68 2021 (print) | LCC DF229.65 (ebook) | DDC 938/.05—dc23
LC record available at https://lccn.loc.gov/2021032050
LC ebook record available at https://lccn.loc.gov/2021032051

Contents

Chronology of Ancient Greece and the Sicilian Campaign	vii
List of Maps and Figures	xi
Maps	xiii
Introduction	1
1 To Begin	5
2 The Opening Moves	31
3 The Sicilian Campaign	69
4 The Aftermath	135
Bibliography	151
Index	155
About the Author	161

Chronology of Ancient Greece and the Sicilian Campaign

BCE

776	Traditional date for the first Olympic games.
757	The First Messenian War starts.
c. 750	Greek Alphabet.
632	Cylon seizes Acropolis.
621	Draco establishes law code.
594	Solon becomes Archon in Athens, initiates reforms.
561	Pisistratus takes power in Athens for first time.
555	Pisistratus driven out of Athens.
549	Pisistratus takes power for second time.
546	Croesus of Lydia is captured by Persians.
542	Pisistratus is driven from Athens for second time.
532	Pisistratus regains power in Athens.
527	Pisistratus dies, succeeded by sons Hippias and Hipparchus.
515	Death of Hipparchus.
508	Hippias is forced to leave Athens.
508	Cleisthenes establishes democracy in Athens.
499	Ionian Revolt.

490	Darius of Persia invades Greece; Battle of Marathon.
c. 484	Birth of Herodotus.
480	Xerxes of Persia invades Greece; Battle of Thermopylae; Battle of Salamis.
478	Athens establishes the Delian League; Sparta establishes Peloponnesian League.
476–462	Cimon elected general.
471	Themistocles ostracized.
465	Helots revolt at Sparta.
461	Cimon ostracized. Ephialtes is slain.
460–445	"First Peloponnesian War."
c. 460	Birth of Thucydides.
460–429	"Age of Pericles"; Pericles is reelected as General numerous times.
432	Potidaea revolts from Athens; Corfu declares war on Corinth, Battle of Sybota.
431	Beginning of Peloponnesian War; Pericles delivers funeral oration.
430	Plague in Athens.
429	Death of Pericles.
428	Plato born.
428	Mytilene revolts.
427–425	Laches in Sicily.
427	Mytilene surrenders to Athens; Stasis in Corcyra.
425	Demosthenes and Cleon capture Spartans on Sphacteria.
c. 425	Death of Herodotus.
424	Battle of Delium.
422	Phaeax in Sicily.
422	Battle of Amphipolis; Cleon and Brasidas die; Thucydides is exiled.
421	Peace of Nicias, the "Fifty Year Peace" lasts seven years; Alcibiades forms anti-Sparta alliance.
418	Battle of Mantinea.
416	Melian dialogue.

415	Athens launches armada against Sicily; Mutilation of the Hermai; Alcibiades accused of profaning the Eleusinian mysteries.
414	Alcibiades defects to Sparta; Death of Lamachus.
413	Failure of Sicilian Campaign; Nicias and Demosthenes are slain.
412	Alcibiades is expelled from Sparta.
411	Short-lived "Rule of the Four Hundred"; Thucydides' history ends.
408	Alcibiades returns to Athens in triumph.
407	Alcibiades exiled.
406	Battle of Arginusae.
405	Battle of Aegospotami.
404	Athens capitulates, end of the Peloponnesian War; Rule of the "Thirty Tyrants"; Death of Alcibiades.
c. 404	Death of Thucydides.
399	Death of Socrates.
347	Death of Plato.
342	Aristotle tutor to Alexander, son of Philip II of Macedon.
336	Alexander succeeds his father Philip II of Macedon.
323	Alexander the Great dies.
322	Death of Aristotle.

List of Maps and Figures

Fig. 0.1	Map 1: A Plan of the City of Syracuse besieged by the Athenians with possible locations of walls and counterwalls from a nineteenth-century print.	xiii
Fig. 0.2	Map 2: A Map of the Ancient World during the Peloponnesian War.	xiv
Fig. 1.1	Man and Youth at a Symposium.	15
Fig. 1.2	Pericles.	22
Fig. 1.3	Acropolis and Parthenon.	23
Fig. 2.1	The Battle in the Great Harbor from a nineteenth century print.	32
Fig. 2.2	Nicias.	39
Fig. 2.3	Alcibiades being taught by Socrates, Marcello Bacciarelli, c. 1776.	58
Fig. 3.1	Archaic Marble Herm from Siphnos c. 520 BCE.	82
Fig. 3.2	Hoplite Phalanx, detail from the Chigi Vase.	95
Fig. 3.3	Image of Prothesis (laying out of the dead) and a chariot race.	98

Maps

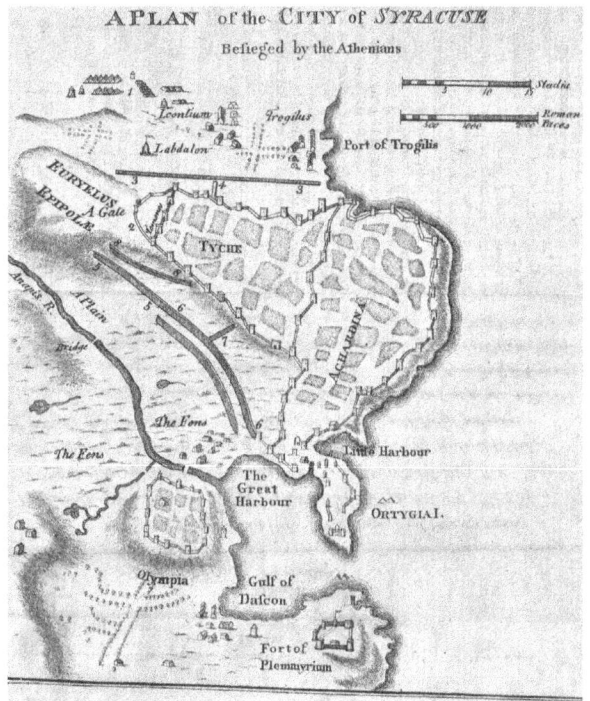

Figure 0.1. Map 1: A Plan of the City of Syracuse besieged by the Athenians with possible locations of walls and counterwalls from a nineteenth-century print. 1 the fortified camps of the Athenians; 2 wall built by the Syracusans facing Epipoli; 3 Athenians' attempted counter-wall north of Epipoli; 4 Syracusans' attempted counter-wall; 5 and 6 The Athenian "double wall" to the Great Harbor; 7 Syracusan palisades; 8 Syracusan wall which prevented the Athenians from encircling the city. *(Alamy stock photo)*

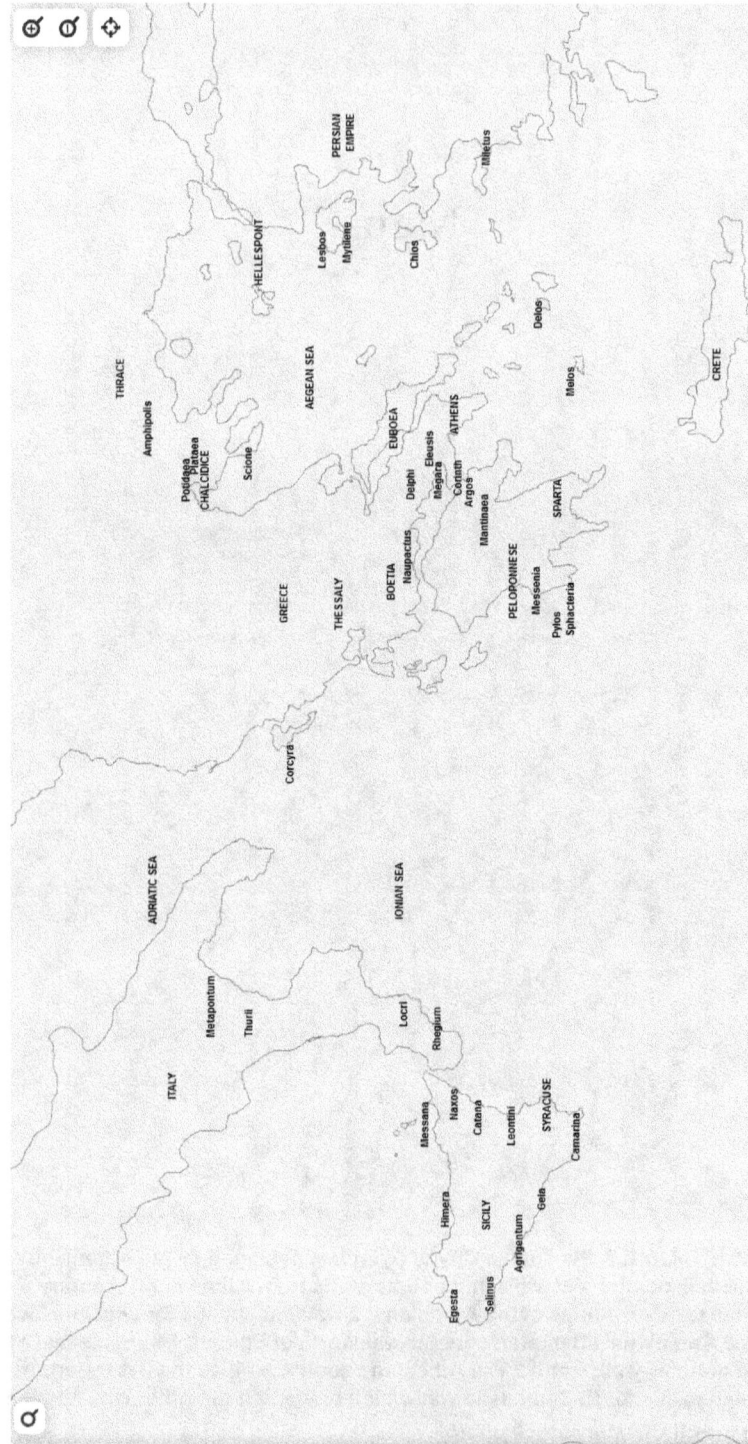

Figure 0.2. Map 2: A Map of the Ancient World during the Peloponnesian War. *(Map by the author)*

Introduction

Athens was at the height of its power when it decided to invade Sicily in 415 BCE.[1] The conquest of Sicily, if it had been successful, might have made Athens the victor in its long war against its enemy, Sparta. It could have cut off Sparta's access to the grain and timber that they imported from the great island in the center of the Mediterranean, and it could have been the first step in Athens' domination of Carthage, Italy, and the Iberian Peninsula.

Three hundred years later, the conquest of Sicily would initiate Rome's subjugation of virtually all the lands surrounding the Mediterranean. And, 2,400 years later, the invasion of Sicily by the Allied Powers during World War II, would be the beginning of the end of the Axis powers. In those cases, the occupation of Sicily initiated two of the greatest epochs in the history of humankind with unprecedented levels of material prosperity, political stability, peace, and artistic and intellectual creativity.

This could have been Athens' destiny. The result of the Athenian campaign, however, was one of the most catastrophic defeats in military history. It was the tipping point in Athens' war against Sparta, which led ultimately to Sparta's victory and the end of the Athenian Empire. This was one of the great turning points in history, whose long-lasting consequences continue to shape who we are and how we think nearly two and a half millennia later.

The story of this tragic event was first told by the Greek historian Thucydides, who was one of Athens's foremost generals in the war. Unfortunately for Thucydides, he failed to prevent Spartan forces from taking an important Athenian outpost in the war, and the Athenian Assembly punished him for this failure by removing him from command and exiling him from Athens. Fortunately for us, this gave Thucydides time to write his great history of the Peloponnesian War (431–404 BCE), named after the large Peloponnesian peninsula at the southernmost tip of mainland Greece and the home of Sparta.

Also fortunately for us, Thucydides spent much of his time in exile behind enemy lines with the Spartan forces. From this unique perspective on the war, Thucydides crafted one of the first, and one of the greatest, historical narratives ever written. His history of the war is the principle source for this retelling of the story of the Sicilian campaign.

My original intention in writing this book was solely to describe the Sicilian Campaign, which I believe is the most important turning point in the war between Athens and Sparta. It is also an exciting story of remarkable personalities and dramatic events. As I wrote and revised this work, however, it became clear that this story could not be told without also considering the complex relationship between the Athenian democracy and the Athenian Empire.

Thucydides gives us the first and the best description of the workings of the world's first democracy. The Athenian ideas that common citizens can make their own laws, that citizens hold the rights of free speech and equality before the law, and that government serves the interests of all its many people without favoring the few who are rich, were all ideas unknown in the world before his time.

Moreover, for many people, including many of America's Founders, Thucydides' story of Athens' failure in the Peloponnesian War and the collapse of its empire is proof of the weakness of a democratic system of government. For them, the Athenian democracy was the cause of the demise of its empire.

Nearly 2,500 years later, we might believe that we see parallels between our situation today and the collapse of the Athenian Empire or the decline and fall of the Roman Empire 1,000 years later. But history is not solely a story of tragic declines and falls. It is also a story of growth and rejuvenation, and one might seem like the other to those who are in the midst of experiencing them.

Thucydides is a wise guide to many of these issues. He has been praised throughout the centuries for his realistic depiction of events and for his objectivity. He saw how the actions and motives of individuals often had great unforeseen consequences, and he saw how small details shaped larger historical patterns. He wrote his narrative of the war between the Athenians and the Spartans[2] during one of the most remarkable periods in human history. Many people who lived in Thucydides' home of Athens and its neighboring territories were beginning to see the world with eyes newly opened. A veil of superstition, of oracles, and of prophecies was slowly being lifted. During most of humankind's history, the physical world and a supernatural realm seemed to coexist without borders. Spiritual forces swirled around, flowing in and out of the material world, and minds perceived things beyond the powers of eyes and ears. Thucydides was one of the first to exclude supernatural forces from his observation of the world in much the same way that we do today. The story of the Sicilian campaign is, thus, many stories, both dark and brilliant, and we can choose one, or we can imagine another, which is more relevant to each of us.

Admittedly, the story of the Sicilian campaign and the Peloponnesian War is not very well known. For most people who have heard of it, it is a story of a long-dead people in a far-away land in an inconsequential war. Part of the blame for this rests with Thucydides himself. As important as his history is, in many places, it is a very dry and boring catalog of places and events which have little clear significance to anyone but the most pedantic scholar. Thucydides admits early on in his book that his goal was not to appeal to everyone. He set out to write about the war as accurately as possible, "as a possession for all time," without any romance or poetry, and purposefully not "to win the applause of the moment." Evidence of his disregard for popular approval is seen in his writing style, which is, according to one of his admirers, "complex," "convoluted," "idiosyncratic," and "obscure."[3]

The awkward style and structure of Thucydides' narrative is partly the result of the conditions of its composition. Thucydides began to write his history near the beginning of the war and continued to write while the war was going on. In most cases, he had no idea as he wrote which events would have a greater or lesser impact on subsequent events, which events he should highlight in his narrative, and which events he should pass over quickly. If he had more time to revise his work, perhaps, it would have been very different.

In addition to all this, Thucydides often assumes that his readers are familiar with the geography of ancient Greece. Who knows today where Amphipolis, Thrace, or Euboea are?—or the thousands of other places that Thucydides names? Often modern historians have only contributed to these problems, themselves getting lost in all the minutia of details, losing sight of the larger picture, and filling voids in Thucydides' narrative with sometimes dubious conjectures.[4]

A close reader of Thucydides' text, however, is likely to be rewarded for the effort. Thucydides' history is a complex tapestry of events in which he tells many overlapping stories simultaneously. Its various threads weave in and out, in a complex and often awe-inspiring pattern. This is often confusing, but it is also part of what gives his history such power. A reader can become emotionally and intellectually engaged as the work unfolds, and as the reader sorts out the many narratives to find meanings in the myriad assortment of details. Much like real life itself.

For those of us who do not have the time to engage with all these issues, this book simplifies Thucydides' monumental history by describing a single, narrowly-focused event in Thucydides' history—the Athenian invasion of Sicily. This was the pivotal event in Thucydides' history, and, as I believe, the single most decisive event in the history of ancient Greece. Critics can argue that the result is a brutal surgery of Thucydides' text, since it leaves out many important events, and dismisses many of the themes that make his book still relevant two millennia later. These criticisms, of course, are appropriate. If this work, however, inspires readers to discover the work of Thucydides on their own, or to delve further into the history of ancient Greece, or stimulates thinking about the interrelated natures of democracy and empire, then some of the purpose of this book will have been accomplished.

NOTES

1. A note on terms: In this work I generally have used the words "Sparta" and "Spartans" to refer to "Sparta and their allies," or less frequently, "Lacedemonians," or "Peloponnesians"; and the same with the use of "Athens" and "Athenians" where the words often refer to "Athens and their allies." In both cases, the "allies" often included mercenaries. In addition, I have used the most common spellings of names such as Nicias and Alcibiades (not the perhaps more correct Nikias, and Alkibiades). I have often used, as well, the most common English equivalents of common Greek words. For example: "city" or "city-state" for *polis*, "Council" for the *boule*, and "Assembly" for the *ecclesia/ekklesia*. All years refer to BCE, unless otherwise noted.

2. Thucydides did not give the work a title, it is most commonly titled The History of the Peloponnesian War, completed c. 411 and consisted of 8 vols./books.

3. Emily Greenwood, *Thucydides and the Shaping of History* (London: Duckworth, 2006), 5.

4. A very incomplete general bibliography of relevant works: Perez Zagorin, *Thucydides: An Introduction for the Common Reader* (Princeton, NJ: Princeton University Press, 2005); Donald Kagan, *Thucydides: The Reinvention of History* (New York: Penguin Books, 2009); Kagan, *The Outbreak of the Peloponnesian War* (Ithaca, NY: Cornell University Press, 1969); Kagan, *The Archidamian War* (Ithaca, NY: Cornell University Press, 1974); Kagan, *The Peace of Nicias and the Sicilian Expedition* (Ithaca, NY: Cornell University Press, 1981); Kagan, *The Fall of the Athenian Empire* (Ithaca, NY: Cornell University Press, 1987); Victor Davis Hanson, *A War Like No Other: How the Athenians and Spartans Fought the Peloponnesian War* (New York: Random House, 2005); A. W. Gomme, A. Andrewes, and K. J. Dover, *A Historical Commentary on Thucydides* (New York: Oxford University Press, 1945–1981), in 5 vols.; Simon Hornblower, *Thucydides* (London: Duckworth, 1987); Hornblower, *Commentary on Thucydides* (New York: Oxford University Press, 1991–2008), in 3 vols.; G. E. M. [Geoffrey Ernest Maurice] de Ste. Croix, *The Origins of the Peloponnesian War* (London, Duckworth, 1972); de Ste. Croix, *The Class Struggle in the Ancient Greek World: From the Archaic Age to the Arab Conquests* (Ithaca, NY: Cornell University Press, 1981); and Peter Green, *Armada from Athens* (Garden City, NY: Doubleday, 1970). In addition to these works, an excellent guide and introduction to all things Thucydides and the Peloponnesian war is Robert B. Strassler, editor, *The Landmark Thucydides: A Comprehensive Guide to the Peloponnesian War* (New York: Free Press, 1996).

Chapter One

To Begin

One way to begin to think about ancient Greek history is by comparing it with the history of the United States. Both histories begin with a revolution. The history of the United States begins with the American Revolution of 1775 to 1783. The history of ancient Greece, for our purposes, begins with the revolt of the Greeks states from Persia, which led to the Persian Wars of 490 and 480 BCE. In both cases, small, culturally backward states on the periphery of a great empire revolted, and during the ensuing war, they united and shaped their own unique identity as a united, independent, and freedom-loving people. The major personalities and battles became embedded in their national folklore, and the great leaders became the iconic paradigms of wisdom and virtue.

Leonidas, who led the three hundred Spartans who held off the Persian advance at the Battle of Thermopylae, was hardly George Washington. Nor was Themistocles, who persuaded the Athenians to build a navy, which defeated the Persians at Salamis, a Thomas Jefferson or an Alexander Hamilton. But these heroes of the Persian wars had an influence similar to that of Washington, Jefferson, and Hamilton to set the models for leadership and to define the values that inspired their societies for years to come.

Continuing the analogy: after the wars of independence were over, the individual colonies of North America united, and the city-states of Greece cemented their unions. The United States of 1787, which established a federal government, had its parallel in the Delian League, which formed a strong alliance of Greek states led by Athens in 478. In both cases, a commercial system protected trade and established a common currency that united the independent states and brought prosperity and security to the whole.

In the case of Greece, Athens organized the Delian League as a mutual defense against further Persian aggression. Each city contributed ships or money to the League, which got its name because its' treasury was on the island of Delos. Over time, the Delian League ceased being a voluntary association of independent states, and participation became mandatory. The treasury was moved to Athens, and the contributions of the states became forced tribute. Similarly, in the United States, the new nation was gradually recognized as a "perpetual union" of the states, with open commercial borders, and a centralized system of government and taxation.

In both Greece and North America, however, the joining of what were once independent states into a single large body was soon tested as the differences between their cultures, institutions, and economies became increasingly apparent, and a war broke out that threatened the fragile union.

In the United States, the conflict erupted with the Civil War of the Northern against the Southern states. In ancient Greece, the conflict between the northern city-state of Athens and the southern city-state of Sparta erupted in the Peloponnesian War (Sparta being located in the Peloponnese, the large peninsula at the southern extremity of Greece [see map 2]). In both of these cases, separated in time by over two millennia, a northern, commercially-dynamic, and individualistic population (the North/Athens) fought against a southern, agrarian, slave-based society (the South/Sparta).

We should be careful, here, in thinking about cycles of history because there are important differences between ancient Greece and modern America, that in their own way may contain lessons for us.

The outcomes of these civil wars were clearly different. In the United States, the North won and, despite the numerous unhealed wounds of the war, was able to maintain a relatively stable balance between a centralized government and local and state power. In ancient Greece, Athens, never considered fully incorporating its "allies" into its political system, and after a long contest, was defeated by its southern neighbor, Sparta. This book is the story of the different path that the Greek city-states took, and particularly the critical turning point in the Athenian defeat—the invasion of Sicily in 415.

The analogy of the histories of ancient Athens and the United States is, of course, a great over-simplification. By looking closely into the cloudy mirror of ancient Greece, however, we may see ourselves a little more clearly. We might gain some insight into our own history, and even perhaps take a small uncertain peek into our future.

The conflict between Athens and Sparta offers, as well, a deeper look into a past that was already ancient before those city-states were born. Much of human history is the story of the sometimes harmonious and sometimes conflicted relations between cities and the agricultural areas that provide them with food and natural resources. In the Old Testament of the Bible, we can read about the pastoral patriarchs and the rise and fall of their urban kingdoms.[1] We can see this history recapitulated in the transition from the highly urban, centralized Roman empire to the decentralized, agrarian societies of the Middle Ages, and again, perhaps, in the relationship between the red states and the blue states in the United States at the beginning of the twenty-first century. The differences between these urban and agricultural societies were not and are not just economic and political; they shaped the everyday life, the culture, the thought, and the individual character and morals of their members.

Thucydides noted some of the differences between urban Athens and agricultural Sparta. On the eve of the Peloponnesian War, he described the "great contrast between the two national characters."[2] Thucydides said the Athenians were "addicted to innovation." They were quick to imagine new plans and quick to put them into action. The Spartans, in contrast, only wanted to preserve what they already had. The Athenians threw themselves into every new adventure without considering the dangers, and when their plans fell apart, they remained optimistic. The Spartans, conversely, were unreasonably cautious. They avoided all new endeavors, and even after deciding on a course of action, they continued to procrastinate. The Athenians never stayed in one place but were constantly moving from place to place. The Spartans were reluctant to leave home. The Athenians were never content with any new success, seeing only their failures, and any failure was quickly followed by new hopes and renewed action.

> Thus they toil on in trouble and danger all the days of their life, with little opportunity for enjoying, being ever engaged in getting: their only idea of a holiday is to do what the occasion demands, and to them laborious occupation is less of a misfortune than the peace of a quiet life. To describe their character in a word, one might truly say that they were born into the world to take no rest themselves and to give none to others.[3]

Despite the differences between Athens and Sparta, they had much in common. A distinctive Greek culture which was shared by Athens, Sparta, and the hundreds of other communities around the eastern Mediterranean emerged in the critical eighth century BCE. After a three-hundred-year dark age following the collapse of Mycenaean culture, a new civilization blossomed. Agriculture expanded into newly cultivated areas. The population doubled in a hundred years. Small villages coalesced to form the unique political and social structure of the *polis*—a city-state composed of an urban center surrounded by its villages and farms. Trading networks expanded and Greek settlers followed merchants to establish new colonies in Sicily and around the Mediterranean. In the eighth century, the Greeks built monumental temples and created new styles in art. During this time, as well, some unknown scribes adapted the Phoenician writing system, which consisted only of consonants, by adding symbols for vowels thus creating the world's first true alphabet. The great epics of Homer and the works of Hesiod were now written down and large numbers of Greeks learned to read and write. In

776, Greeks from around the Mediterranean competed in the first Olympic games.

Most importantly for the purposes of this book, the Greeks in the eighth century created a new military structure. The ancient way of fighting described by Homer of warriors fighting in individual combat, was replaced by the *hoplite* phalanx. The hoplites were soldiers named after the Greek word for their round shields. Their most distinctive feature was the phalanx in which the soldiers fought shoulder-to-shoulder and shield-to-shield in tightly massed formations.

This new military structure had large consequences for the whole of Greek society. Every male citizen who could afford the heavy hoplite armor was a soldier in the army of his polis where success in battle depended, not on individual initiative or on cunning, but on strict discipline. A single hoplite who lost courage and broke rank could cause the defeat of the army and the destruction of his homeland. Honor, courage, devotion, and submission to the traditions, rituals, and the gods of the polis were consequently the greatest virtues.

All of these innovations that marked the eighth century were probably in some way related to each other, and each in their own way helped to bring the Greek city-states together in a common culture. But this did not mean that relations between the *poleis* (plural of polis) were harmonious. Although they shared devotion to the Olympian gods, they each worshiped their local gods and heroes. The god Apollo watched over and protected Sparta, as Athena did the same in Athens. The Spartans, as well, revered their great mythical hero Heracles, and the Athenians revered Theseus. In addition, although the Greeks were defined by their common language, there were many dialects. The Spartans spoke in a distinctive Doric dialect common to their neighbors in the Peloponnese, while the Athenians shared the dialect of the Ionians who spread out in the islands and around coast of the Aegean. These differences contributed to giving each polis its distinctive character, and also contributed to a state of near constant warfare between the Greek poleis.

SPARTA

Sparta's unique path, not surprisingly, was shaped by a war with their neighbors to the west, the Messenians, in the eighth and seventh centuries BCE. The Spartans, once they had finally conquered the Messenians, perhaps could have colonized them and assimilated them into their own population. They decided instead to enslave them and force them to labor on their agricultural estates. The practical problem with this was that once the Messenians were subjugated, the Spartans had to keep them subjugated. The entire structure of

Spartan society, consequently, was shaped by the necessity of maintaining their power over their Messenian slaves. To keep them at their work and to protect against uprisings of their slaves, called *helots*, Sparta became a thoroughly militarized society, and Spartans learned from an early age to revere the martial values of strength, courage, and indifference to physical pain or emotional distress.

The German philosopher, Georg Wilhelm Friedrich Hegel described this dialectic between master and slave.[4] The slave continually strives for freedom, while the master continually enforces his control. The struggle between master and slave, thus, requires great energy from both parties, and, in the process, both are fundamentally changed. In this way, the personalities and the cultures of the slave and of the master create each other.

Spartan society is the perfect illustration of this.

Very early in Sparta's history, a semi-mythical law-giver named Lycurgus established the basic structure and rules, which would govern Spartan society for five hundred years, and which molded the Spartans into the fiercest warriors in the ancient world.

We should be careful when we discuss the nature of ancient Spartan society since the Spartans left few written documents, and outsiders who might have added to the historical record were prohibited from entering Sparta, because they might introduce new ideas and customs.

Much of what we know about the Spartans, consequently, comes from the writings of the historian Plutarch, who wrote over three hundred years after the age of classical Greece. Plutarch helped to shape a very romanticized image of Sparta that was nourished over the years by historians and philosophers, and which has persisted in many quarters of the popular culture to this day.

Nevertheless, from Plutarch and other sources, including Thucydides, we can understand many of the unique characteristics of Spartan society. One of the first things to note is the unique Spartan political order. Lycurgus's laws provided for a dual kingship. The two kings most likely came from the two leading families in Sparta, but they generally had little power. Their position was largely ceremonial, except during war, when one of them would remain at home in Sparta, while the other would lead the Spartan army in battle, when his command would be absolute.

Like many other political systems (including our own), Sparta had three principle bodies: an executive, and an upper, and a lower legislative body. The executive was represented by the two kings. The upper body in Sparta was the *gerousia*, a council of Spartan men over the age of sixty. The lower house was the assembly, or *apella*, in which all male Spartans over thirty years old participated. Here the citizens would make their decisions on issues before them by shouting or beating on their shields to indicate approval or disapproval of a proposal. The real power in Sparta, however, was held by the five *ephors*, male full citizens who were elected annually, and who determined what issues should be considered by the assembly.

It is often said that Lycurgus created a government based on the equality of all Spartans.[5] One of his first acts was to distribute the lands of the Spartans and the Messenians equally among the Spartans. In addition, he banned the use of gold or silver, to prevent the accumulation of wealth, and with it, the spirits of arrogance and of luxury among the populace.

Spartan "equality," however, did not mean freedom. Spartans lived all of their lives in a militaristic totalitarian system that shaped every aspect of their lives. At birth, they were each carefully inspected by officials of the state. If an infant showed any weakness or deformity, they were thrown off a promontory of Mount Taygetus. At the age of seven, a Spartan boy was separated from his mother and joined a military-style barracks. He would eat and sleep with his unit until he was thirty years old, when he could join the apella. He could marry, but would see his wife only at night, and would be back in his barracks before daybreak. Throughout his life he participated in rigorous physical exercise and military training, and he would be expected to fight and, if necessary, to die for his polis, until he was sixty years old.

All this time he was taught to despise physical comforts, to ignore pain, and to reject individual pleasures and comforts. In the winter, he walked barefoot and slept on the ground with only his red cloak as a blanket. His principle diet was an ill-tasting black broth of pork, blood, and vinegar. One visitor to Sparta who tasted it remarked, "Now I understand why Spartans are so willing to die."

An annual ritual sent young boys to steal cheese at the altar of Artemis Orthia, which was defended by older boys who whipped the boys until they bled. Any boy who showed weakness or a lack of courage was deemed a social outcast.

Plutarch tells the story of a young Spartan who stole a weasel, but before he was able to kill and eat the weasel, he was called to a muster. He knew that if he were caught stealing, he would be punished, but not for stealing (which was actually encouraged), but for being caught. To avoid this, the boy hid the weasel under his cloak, where it ate its way through the boys' bowels, killing him.

As a rite of passage and a test of courage (and to strike terror among the helots) select young Spartans enrolled in a unit called the *krypteia*. They were instructed to scatter through the countryside armed only with knives, and at night to kill any helots they found on the roads.

In all of these ways, Spartan society demonstrated its primary goal of building an all-powerful fighting force. In this social environment, Spartans had few opportunities and apparently little desire for expressing personal or independent ideas, and they became famous for their laconic speech, named after the Spartan home territory of Lacedaemonia. The Spartans expressed themselves in a pattern of minimalist speech that compressed meaning into the fewest possible words. The famous example of this was a Spartan's reply to Philip II of Macedon. The Macedonian king threatened to invade the Peloponnese and warned Spartans, saying "if I bring my army to your land, I will destroy your farms, slay your people, and raze your city." The one Spartan reply was a single word, "if."

THE BIRTH OF DEMOCRACY

Athens

The mythical figure of Heracles in Sparta had its parallel in the Athenian hero, Theseus, who was credited with the founding of Athens. He did this by uniting the several villages, called *demes* (from which we get the word democracy), around Athens into a single body. The small farmers now became citizens of the polis who had a voice in the laws and policies of the polis. Their rights, however, were tied to their obligations. The most important of these obligations was service in the Athenian army. Every farmer who could afford the heavy armor of shield, spear, sword, bronze helmet, breastplate, and leg armor served as a hoplite in the Athenian army, and participated in the Athenian assembly.

This era also marked the beginning of an explosion of ideas in politics, art, architecture, drama, and philosophy that would reach its peak in Athens three centuries later and which have ever since influenced nearly every society in the world. It also marked the beginning of a new social structure as large landowners consolidated their holdings at the expense of smaller landholders. This growing inequality inevitably led to conflict between the powerful few, the *oligos* (the origin of the word oligarchy), and the many *demos*, those who lived in the demes. This conflict would be a driving force in much of the subsequent history of Greece.

Solon

The erratic history of Athens' search for a just system of government begins with Draco, the Athenian aristocrat who wrote Athens' first written law code around 621. It was commonly said that his laws were written not in ink, but in blood. Under Draco's laws, the punishment for almost every crime was death. Nevertheless, his draconian laws can be seen as a step toward a more just legal system because, as a written code, they limited the powers of a wealthy few to arbitrarily decide guilt or innocence and to determine the punishment for crimes.

Unfortunately, Draco's laws had little effect on stemming the increasing wealth of the great landowners and their growing power over their poorer neighbors. By the beginning of the seventh century, a breaking point was reached, and Athens' impoverished farmers were on the verge of revolt. For years, poor tenant farmers, plagued by poor harvests and crushed by debts, were often forced to the extreme of selling their family members and even themselves into slavery to pay their debts to wealthy landholders. In response to this crisis, the "many"—the common citizens of Athens, and the "few," the oligarchs, came together to appoint Solon, who was a general in the Athenian army and a poet, as the chief magistrate of Athens and gave him great powers to make fundamental changes (594 BCE). Because of his wisdom and virtue, Solon was trusted by both the rich and the poor. In his position as a magistrate, he passed a series of reforms that forever made his name synonymous with wisdom and justice. Most importantly, he ended the practice of debt slavery. A person could no longer offer himself as collateral for a loan. The implications of this reform were huge. After the passage of this law, an Athenian citizen could not be a slave. To be a member of the Athenian polis was now a mark of honor. Regardless of one's material condition, an Athenian could claim the status of a free person. This was a radical step that would have extraordinary and enduring consequences. For most of human history, the line between a free person and a slave was very fluid, and there were many indistinct degrees on the spectrum between freedom and slavery. Solon's laws began a long history of the celebration of freedom and of the degradation of slavery.

Along with ending the practice of enslavement for debts, Solon canceled many of the debts that small farmers owed to the great landowners. In addition, his laws encouraged the diversification of the economy by encouraging the production of olives—one of the great staples of the ancient Greek economy. Olive oil was used in cooking and as well as for lighting. As part of his plan to stimulate the economy, Solon standardized the system of weights and measures and welcomed artisans from all of Greece into Athens. At the same time, he laid the basic foundations for the structure of the Athenian government. He established the Athenian upper legislative body, the council, called the *boule*, which consisted of 400 of the wealthiest citizens of Athens He also created the assembly, called the *ecclesia*, where citizen of Athens could speak and vote.

Having done all of this, Solon prohibited any revision to his laws for a period of ten years and, believing that his work was done, he left Athens and traveled around the Mediterranean to Egypt, Cyprus, and Lydia. In this way, he prevented anyone from pressuring him to make any alteration in his laws.

Pisistratus

Solons' fears for the survival of his reforms were well-founded. In 561, an Athenian nobleman named Pisistratus, a distant relative of Solon, seized power and became the tyrant of Athens. At this time, the word *tyrant* did not carry all of the associations of arbitrary and brutal power that later generations have attached to the term. A tyrant was simply someone who used unorthodox methods to gain power. In early Greek history, this was seen as neither a good thing nor a bad thing, and historians have described some tyrants as wise and virtuous rulers.

Pisistratus is generally considered as an example of a "good tyrant." Although Pisistratus was from one of the great aristocratic families in Athens, he was the leader of a faction that represented the interests of some of the poorest people in Attica. His followers raised sheep in the hills around Athens and traded with their more affluent neighbors on the coast and the plains, exchanging wool and honey for iron tools. Pisistratus stood in opposition to Megacles, who led a faction of wealthy landholders and merchants who lived near the coast, and Lycurgus, who was the leader of another faction of even wealthier landholders who lived on the fertile plains.

The Greek historian Herodotus tells the story of how Pisistratus three times attempted to gain power in Athens by deceit, cunning, and finally by force before finally gaining and keeping power on his third try.[6] Pisistratus' first attempt to seize control began when he wounded himself and drove his chariot into the center of Athens claiming that he had been attacked by his enemies. He pleaded for protection and the credulous Athenians granted him a bodyguard. With this force, Pisistratus took over the Acropolis and claimed power over the city.

His rule lasted only a short time. His enemies, Lycurgus and Megacles, soon joined forces and drove him from the city. Pisistratus then devised another plan even more outrageous than the first. Herodotus described it as "the silliest scheme I ever heard of." One day Pisistratus arrived in Athens accompanied by a tall, strikingly beautiful woman who was dressed in military armor. He claimed that she was the goddess Athena and that she was welcoming Pisistratus back into the city. Incredibly, this ruse worked, and Pisistratus gained power for a second time.

Unknown to the city's population, Pisistratus had made a deal with Megacles, who had turned against Lycurgus, and supported Pisistratus's rule. In exchange for his support, Pisistratus cemented the alliance by marrying Megacles' daughter. Megacles hoped by this that a grandchild of his might gain power in his own right in Athens. Pisistratus, however, wished to ensure that power in Athens would stay within his own family line, and refused to consummate his marriage with Megacles' daughter. As Herodotus delicately described it, Pisistratus "had intercourse with her in an indecent way." When Megacles' daughter told her father of this, Megacles was enraged, and united again with Lycurgus, and drove Pisistratus from Athens for a second time.

Pisistratus made his third, final, and successful attempt with the help of an army of his friends from nearby cities, and with a body of mercenaries. When this force appeared before Athens' walls, an Athenian force came out to defend the city. For a few hours, both armies waited for the other to move. After a while, the Athenians decided to take their mid-day meal and soon after eating some of them dozed off while others played games of dice. Pisistratus now saw his opportunity and attacked, driving the disorganized Athenian army from the field.

Pisistratus quickly consolidated his power over the city by appealing to the poorer class of citizens. He expelled his enemies and confiscated the land of the great landholders and distributed it to the poor. He reduced the taxes on the poorest citizens and provided jobs for many of them in numerous public works projects. He built roads and an aqueduct and public fountains, which for the first time ensured a consistent water supply to the growing city.

In addition, he established public festivals, including the great festival of the Panathenaea, which celebrated the goddess Athena and the founding of the city. He encouraged the arts and sponsored the composition of the definitive versions of Homer's *Iliad* and *Odyssey*. In these ways, he fostered a sense of civic identity and patriotism. His contemporaries and modern historians generally consider him a wise and humane leader, who, although he was a tyrant, opened the way for democracy by improving the lot of the lower classes and by reducing the power of the wealthy families.

Unfortunately, Pisistratus' sons did not follow his example. After Pisistratus died at an advanced age, his two sons, Hippias and Hipparchus, assumed power. For a short time, the brothers followed their father's benign policies, but a lovers' triangle, a murder, and the execution of the assassins ended the short-lived Pisistratid's dynasty and opened the way for democracy.

The trouble began when Pisistratus' son, Hipparchus, made sexual overtures to an Athenian youth named Harmodius. Harmodius was the *eromenos* of Aristogeiton. This was an example of a relationship typical in ancient Greece between two men, a young eromenos and an older man, the *erastes*, in which the erastes was a lover, friend, and mentor to the young eromenos. Numerous paintings on ancient Greek pottery depicted in explicit detail such relationships in which an older man with a beard is aroused by a beardless youth.

Harmodius, according to Thucydides, was "in the flower of youthful beauty" when Hipparchus twice made advances toward him. Both times, Harmodius rejected the tyrant's advances. This turned Hipparchus' desire into anger, and he initially decided to force himself on the youth. Hipparchus, though, changed his mind and devised a plan to humiliate and dishonor Harmodius. Hipparchus invited Harmodius' sister to carry a sacred basket through the city in the annual procession of the Panathenaea, but before the event, he abruptly cancelled the invitation and announced that she was unworthy of carrying the religious object and was prohibited from the procession. As Athenians interpreted this, Hipparchus implicitly proclaimed that

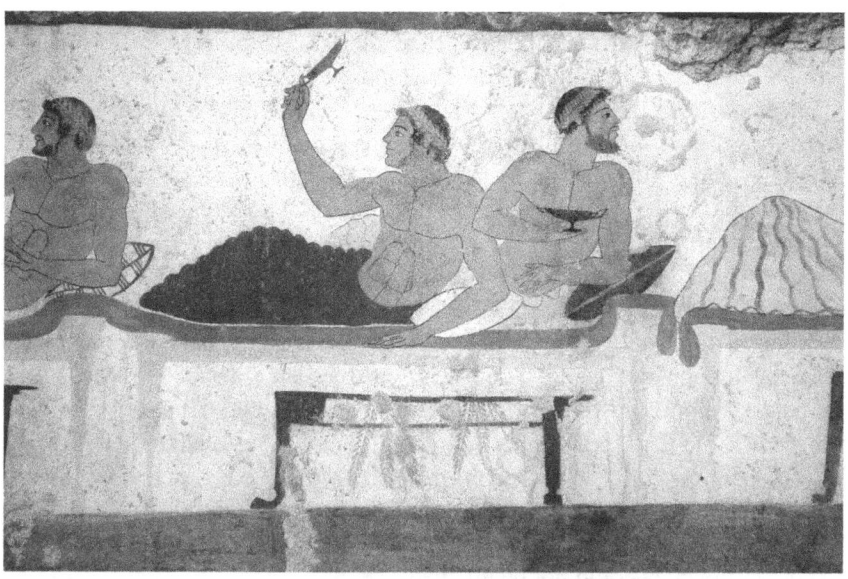

Figure 1.1. Man and Youth at a Symposium. From Tomb of the Diver, c. 489 BCE. *(Paestum Archaeological Museum, Italy/Alamy stock photo)*

Harmodius' sister was not a virgin. This dishonored the girl as well as the whole family.

In response to this insult, the two lovers Harmodius and Aristogeiton, plotted to take revenge. When the procession of the Panathenaea occurred, and all of Athens came out to celebrate the goddess of the city, Harmodius and Aristogeiton hid daggers beneath their cloaks and as Hipparchus walked in the procession near the temple of the twelve gods, Harmodius and Aristogeiton rushed at him and, with quick thrusts of their daggers, slew him. Hipparchus' guards reacted swiftly. They seized Harmodius and instantly killed him. Aristogeiton, ran off into the crowd, only to soon be captured, tortured, and killed.

After Hipparchus' assassination, his brother Hippias, who was now the sole ruler of Athens, became progressively isolated, paranoid, and cruel. Within months, he was soon forced out of the city. With Hippias gone, Harmodius and Aristogeiton were celebrated throughout Athens as the tyrannicides who liberated Athens from their oppressors, and statues of the two lovers were prominently placed in the *agora*. In this public marketplace in the center of Athens, they remained as symbols of Athenian freedom for over five hundred years.[7]

Cleisthenes

Hippias' departure from Athens opened the way to power of Cleisthenes, who is often called "the father of Athenian democracy." Cleisthenes was a member of the noble Alcmaeonid family, which included some of the most illustrious figures in the history of ancient Athens. We have already met Megacles and will soon meet Pericles and Alcibiades. This family was associated with the people of Athens and its commercial port, and often competed for power with the factions representing the hills and the plains.

The Alcmaeonids traced their ancestry back to Nestor, who sailed with Jason to find the golden fleece and who fought alongside Agamemnon and Achilles to recover Helen from Troy. All of the Alcmaeonids, however, suffered under a dark curse. About a hundred years earlier in 632, Megacles' grandson, who was also named Megacles, was the leader of a group who held power in Athens, when, a rebel aristocrat, named Cylon, attempted to seize power. When Cylon's coup collapsed, the angry Athenians chased Cylon and his supporters to the Acropolis where they found safety in the temple of Athena and claimed to be protected by the goddess. As long as they remained in her temple, they could not be touched.

The Athenians persuaded them that they could leave the temple and stand trial in the city if they tied a rope to Athena's statue, and held on to one end of it. This, they believed, would maintain the goddesses' protection. With this understanding, the rebels left the temple, holding on to the rope, and came down to the city. Unfortunately for Cylon, the rope broke, or perhaps it was cut, and the Athenians, led by Megacles, saw that Athena's protection had vanished, and set on the rebels, stoning them to death.

The populace of Athens soon regretted their actions, and they blamed Megacles for the sacrilege, and they believed that he and all his family were cursed. This curse became a powerful tool used by the enemies of the Alcmaeonids for years to come. Despite the curse, some of the Alcmaeonids were among the most brilliant Athenians who would shape its history in the following years.

When Hippias fled Athens, Sparta briefly installed their own puppet government in Athens. This led the people of Athens to revolt and give power to Cleisthenes, who promised to give the common people, according to Aristotle, "the control of the state."[8] The system of government, which Cleisthenes established, is recognized as the world's first democracy. It survived in Athens in its essential form, with only minor breaks, for nearly 200 years, and it influenced the formation of democratic governments around the world, and especially in the United States.

The major problem Cleisthenes faced was the same as that faced by the founding fathers of the United States. Then, as now, powerful factions competed for power and continually threatened the stability of the state. In 1787,

James Madison, the principal architect of the US Constitution, argued in the Federalist Papers, that an intricate system of checks and balances would neutralize competing factions and prevent any one faction from becoming dominant. This was the same stratagem devised two thousand years earlier by Cleisthenes. For Cleisthenes, the major factions were the four powerful tribes who controlled large territories throughout Attica. Their networks of related families and kin were led by great landholders who traced their power back to the dark ages before the rise of the poleis, and they claimed descent from a mythical hero who was the offspring of a human and a god. Each family and region of Attica, therefore, had its own gods and goddesses, and its unique religious rituals and traditions. The leading families of each tribe were supported by its local religious practices. They built temples and offered gifts in honor of the local deities. They sponsored feasts and celebrations. In this way, they cemented their association with a divine order that permeated all social relations in a world without currency or writing.

Cleisthenes' radical solution to reduce the power of Athens tribes was to invent ten new tribes; each new tribe was composed of members from each of the three major areas of Attica: the plains, the coast, and the hills. Each tribe would send fifty members, chosen by lot, to a newly created Council of five hundred, replacing Solons' Council of four hundred. The Council would propose motions that the Assembly would debate and vote on. Each new tribe would have its new hero, and a statue of each of the ten heroes was prominently placed in the agora. In addition, henceforth, all men would be named after the local deme to which they belonged, rather than by their father's name (a reform that was only partly effective).

Also, recognizing the continual threat that a strong man could arise and destroy the democratic government, the Athenians created the system of ostracism. Annually, the Assembly could vote to expel any citizen who appeared to be too powerful. Citizens would scratch the name of an individual on a broken shard of pottery, called an *ostracon*, and anyone with sufficient votes would be exiled from Athens for ten years on pain of death. He would still retain all of his property, and after the ten years had passed, he could return without further penalties. By that time, however, his political power would have been restrained.

In addition, all major public offices were filled by a process of chance selection. This process, called sortition, could elevate any citizen for a short time into a member of a jury, or the chief officer of the Assembly for a single day. This was not a representative system of government, such as in the United States in which a member of Congress or a Senator votes for the interests of his or her constituents. Athenian democracy is typically described as a direct democracy, since all male citizens could participate in the Athenian Assembly.

ORIGINS OF THE ATHENIAN EMPIRE

Themistocles

Persia's attempt to dominate Greece and its invasions of the Greek mainland in 490 and in 480 marks the beginning of the most dynamic era of ancient Greek history. The successful resistance of Greek states to Persian dominance helped to shape a fragile sense of Greek unity and cultural identity; it saw the triumph of democratic states powered by ideas of citizen participation, free speech, and the equality of rights. It marked the rise of the Athenian empire and its dramatic collapse, and the flowering of philosophic and aesthetic traditions that still shape our perception and understanding of the world.

The historian Herodotus tells the story of how Persia attempted to subdue the Greeks, and how Greece, led by some of its most illustrious heroes, fought to save Greek independence. The most famous of them was Leonidas, the Spartan king whose band of three hundred held off a Persian advance at the pass of Thermopylae. We can see in his character and actions the fundamental Spartan values of self-sacrifice and of courage in the face of death.

Less well known is the Athenian general in the war against the Persians who embodies many of the characteristic values of the Athenians. Themistocles of Athens had two controlling passions—his opposition to Sparta and his opposition to the oligarchs who dominated much of Athens society and politics. In the years after Persia's first invasion of the Greek mainland, Themistocles saw that Greek independence from Persia depended on control of the waters of the Aegean, and he convinced the Athenians to build up its navy. When the Persians invaded a second time, Themistocles' navy was victorious over the Persians in the straits of Salamis (480 BCE). Following the Greek victory over the Persians, the Athenian navy allowed Athens to dominate many of the poleis of Greece. The power of Athens, however, depended to a large degree, on the growing political power of the rowers in their ships who came from the lowest class of Athenian citizens. As Athens' empire grew, so did its democracy.

In Athens and in much of ancient Greece, heroes often saw their stars fall as dramatically as they rose. As the Persian threat receded, Themistocles' many enemies among the Athenian oligarchs with the help of Sparta turned the Athenian people against him, and he was forced to flee the city. Ironically, Themistocles found refuge in Persia where he served as a governor of a province under the Persian king Artaxerxes.

Pausanias

Despite the fact that the Athenians had led the major victories of the Greeks over the Persians (at Marathon in 490 and at Salamis in 480 BCE), Sparta was the leader of the Greek alliance that ultimately defeated the Persians. Their army was the acknowledged supreme power in Greece, and the leader of the Spartan forces, Pausanias, won a stunning victory over the Persians in the last land battle of the war at Plataea (479 BCE). Pausanias, motivated by this success, then went on to capture the large island of Cyprus and also Byzantium, guarding the gates to the Black Sea. Pausanias, however, became intoxicated by his power and thereby became ambitious for more.

Pausanias had amassed a fortune from the spoils of his battles and began to enjoy the luxuries that, as a Spartan, he could never have dreamed of. Soon he began to conspire with his enemies, the Persians. He adopted Persian customs and dress. No more meals of black broth. He now enjoyed elaborate banquets of the finest delicacies.

Back in Sparta, when people heard reports of Pausanias' new lifestyle and stories of his arrogance and violent temper, they decided to recall Pausanias to Sparta. When he returned, a rumor spread that Pausanias was scheming to lead an uprising of the helots—the Spartans greatest fear—and a group of angry Spartans moved to arrest him. Someone, however, alerted Pausanias and he ran to the temple of Athena on the Spartan acropolis. As long as he remained in the temple he was protected by the goddess and he could not be touched. The Spartans, therefore, left him there, but they built a wall around the temple so that he could not leave. Pausanias remained in the temple without food or water until he was just on the edge of death from starvation. The Spartans, in order to avoid pollution of the temple, then broke down a section of the wall and pulled his limp body out and watched him expire. After these events, the Spartans returned to their traditional isolation on the Peloponnesian peninsula, continuing to resist any further change to their way of life.

With the collapse of Spartan leadership, many of the Greek states now turned to the Athenians. Still afraid that the Persians might return, they formed an alliance and pledged contributions of money or ships to defend themselves, and they established a treasury for this purpose on the sacred island of Delos. In the beginning, each member of the Delian League had an equal vote in their regularly scheduled conferences. Over time, the influence of the Athenians over the Delian League expanded. When the powerful and wealthy polis of Naxos, an island in the center of the Aegean, was either unwilling or unable to supply ships to the League and attempted to leave the alliance (c. 476), Athens sent out an army that subdued the city, destroyed their navy, and forced them to stay in the League. A few years later, Thasos, an island in the north Aegean, also attempted to revolt, and the Athenians laid siege for two years. When the Athenians overcame them, they destroyed their walls took control of their mines, and forced the Thasians to pay compensation. By then, what had once been the voluntary contributions of equal partners in the League had evolved into compulsory taxes, which some now called "tribute."

The most prominent leader in Athens at the end of the Persian Wars was the oligarch, Cimon, who resisted Athens' growing power over its former allies. He sought to build friendships among all the Greek states, and especially with Sparta. Cimon was the son of Miltiades, the leader of the victorious Greek forces at Marathon. He was a successful general, as well, who was generally admired by the Athenian people. His popularity with the Athenians increased when he found the bones of Theseus on the island of Skyros and brought them back to Athens. Like most of the landed aristocrats in Athens, Cimon was not a friend to democracy, but he had better reasons than some for his opposition to democracy. Several years earlier, the popular Assembly at Athens had accused his father, Miltiades, the victor at Marathon, of treason when Miltiades had failed to capture a Persian stronghold on the island of Paros. The Athenians imprisoned Miltiades, where he soon died from wounds suffered in the battle against the Persians.

Like many Athenian aristocrats, Cimon admired the austerity and strict regimen of the Spartan way of life, which was so unlike that of Athens. Sparta reciprocated by naming Cimon a *proxenos*, an unofficial ambassador to the Spartans. As a proxenos, he advocated for Spartan interests at Athens, and he endorsed a policy of sharing a dual hegemony between Athens and Sparta over the Greek states. To explain what he believed should be Athens' relationship with Sparta, Cimon turned to a metaphor of oxen yoked together to plow the hard Greek soil. Athens and Sparta, he declared, were "yoke fellows."

This mirage of friendship between Athens and Sparta prevailed for only a short time. In 462, an earthquake in Sparta precipitated a chain of events that ended Cimon's political power and set the course of enmity between the two powers. In that year, an earthquake rumbled through much of the Peloponnese and gave a large number of helots an opportunity to revolt against their Spartan masters.

The helots established a stronghold on Mount Ithome, where they were able for months to hold off a Spartan army. The Spartans ultimately called out to their fellow Greeks for help. Cimon responded to the Spartan call by leading a troop of 4,000 Athenian hoplites to Sparta. The Spartans were not pleased by the arrival of the Athenians. Watching the Athenians and their strange ways, the Spartans became afraid that the Athenians would infect Sparta with radical ideas, and they sent them away. When Cimon returned to Athens with his troops, the populace of the city became angry at Cimon and the Spartans for rejecting Athenian aid and they ostracized Cimon.

Pericles

The popular party in Athens during this time was led by Ephialtes and his protégé, Pericles. They had been working for months to discredit the oligarch Cimon, and with Cimon's political downfall, they became the major powers in the city. Ephialtes and Pericles now began an ambitious project to limit the power of the oligarchs, when Ephialtes was murdered (461 BCE), most likely by his aristocratic enemies, leaving Pericles the primary center of power in the city.

For nearly forty years, Pericles was the most powerful person in Athens. In his position as one of the ten generals (the *strategoi*) who were elected each year from one of the ten tribes in Athens, Pericles, through his political acumen and the force of his personality, was mostly able to hold in check the competing political factions in Athens. According to Thucydides, "by his rank, ability, and known integrity, [Pericles] was enabled to exercise an independent control over the multitude—in short to lead them instead of being led by them. . . . In short, what was nominally a democracy became in his hands government by the first citizen."[9]

Pericles political power stemmed largely from his recognition that the military and economic superiority of Athens depended on its navy, and its navy depended on the *thetes*, the poorest class of citizens in Athens, who maned the oars of the merchant ships and warships. The thetes owned no land and were unable to afford the armor of the hoplites. As Athens military strategy became increasingly reliant on its navy, the polis became increasingly dependent on the brute strength of the thetes to power their ships. To tie their affections and interests to those of the state, and to counter-balance the power of the aristocrats, Pericles gave the thetes new rights. Pericles' reforms allowed thetes to attend the Assembly, and, if they were chosen by sortition like other Athenian citizens, they could serve on juries and even on the Council. These positions had previously been held only by the hoplites and the higher classes of citizens who were moved by their sense of civic duty to serve in these positions without pay. Now, the thetes and all citizens would be paid to serve in these offices. The thetes at the same time benefited from working for pay on the numerous building projects sponsored by Pericles. These included the construction of new roads, sanitation systems, and the monumental buildings, which were rising on the Acropolis.

Aristocratic Athenians, who had mostly been content with the moderate democracy of Cleisthenes and Cimon, found these radical reforms bitter pills to swallow. Like many political conservatives ever since, they believed that public money was being used to give advantages to a class of people who did not deserve them and who were morally corrupted by them. The philosopher Plato was a typical critic of Pericles, claiming that Pericles "was the first who

Figure 1.2. Pericles. *(Alamy Stock Photo)*

Figure 1.3. Acropolis and Parthenon. Acropolis and Parthenon as imagined during the Age of Pericles by Friedrich Thiersch 1880. *(Alamy Stock Photo)*

gave the people pay, and made them idle and cowardly, and encouraged them in the love of talk and of money."[10]

Despite these criticisms, the ideas of democracy and equality have endured, and Pericles deserves some credit for them. At a funeral for the Athenian soldiers who gave their lives in the first year of the war with Sparta, Pericles defined the basic characteristics of a liberal democratic state that have remained virtually unchanged ever since.

Part of this famous oration reads,

> Our constitution does not copy the laws of neighboring states; we are rather a pattern to others than imitators ourselves. Its administration favors the many instead of the few; this is why it is called a democracy. If we look to the laws, they afford equal justice to all in their private differences; if to social standing, advancement in public life falls to reputation for capacity, class considerations not being allowed to interfere with merit; nor again does poverty bar the way, if a man is able to serve the state, he is not hindered by the obscurity of his condition.[11]

Pericles believed that these ideas of equality under the law, along with ideas of free speech, and of an open and tolerant government, inspired all the poleis of ancient Greece, making Athens "the school of Hellas." Although the ideas of democracy and equality were never fully realized in ancient Athens, these, along with the ideas of rationalism, humanism, and secularism, accompanied a cultural blossoming in the arts, architecture, philosophy, and politics, which emerged during the Age of Pericles, and have continued to shape the life of the Western world for over two millennia.

Pericles was an aristocrat from the Alcmaeonid family, and, like many of his class, he was influenced by the new ideas of the early Greek philosophers who were moving away from mythological explanations of the world and toward more materialistic explanations. One of these was Pericles' friend, Anaxagoras, who is said to have brought philosophy and scientific inquiry from Ionia to Athens, and to have taught Pericles self-control. Anaxagoras' ideas, however, were not welcomed by the common people in Athens, and they forced him to flee the city.

Pericles was also influenced by the sophist, Protagoras, who taught that "Man is the measure of all things," and who claimed, according to Aristotle, that with his methods of rhetoric, he could "make the weaker argument the stronger."[12] Protagoras' assertion was echoed by a rival of Pericles who said that Pericles was the better fighter because even when he lost, he claimed that he had won and was able to convince others that he had won.

Pericles' unconventional thinking extended to his domestic life. He divorced his Athenian wife with whom he had two children and lived openly with a foreigner *hetaera*, named Aspasia, with whom he had another child. The hetaera were highly educated prostitutes who could entertain clients with lofty conversations and with music. She was a friend of Socrates and was famous for hosting gatherings of some of Athens' most notable political and intellectual figures.

Aspasia's reputation as a prostitute and the owner of a brothel inevitably made her a target for critics of Pericles. At one time, Aspasia was charged with impiety and brought before an Athenian jury. Her accusers claimed that Aspasia had procured Athenian women to satisfy Pericles' sexual perversions. This was a serious crime because the women in question were Athenian citizens and not the common prostitutes of the streets. Pericles took the unusual step of appearing at her trial, and openly weeping while defending her. His performance convinced the jury to acquit her of all charges.

Another friend of Pericles who was accused of impiety was Phidias, the acknowledged master of classical Greek sculpture. Phidias created the colossal forty-foot tall statue of Athena made of bronze, gold, and ivory, which stood in the central chamber of the Parthenon. In her hand, she held a shield that was alleged to depict both Pericles and Phidias himself. This was considered a sacrilege so shocking that the Athenian populace brought Phidias to trial for his crime. This time, Pericles' defense of his friend was ineffective. Phidias was found guilty and imprisoned, where he soon died.

As the stories of Anaxagoras, Aspasia, and Phidias illustrate, it was dangerous to be a friend of Pericles. His enemies never tired of spreading stories and rumors about Pericles and everyone in his circle. Some spread rumors that that Pericles murdered his mentor, Ephialtes, and that he started the Peloponnesian War merely to satisfy a whim of Aspasia.

In the first year of the war with Sparta, Pericles' enemies pressed their case against him, charging him with military setbacks and financial improprieties. Early in the war, they were briefly able to remove him from his position as general and fine him a large sum of money. Thucydides notes that "not long afterwards, however, according to the way of the multitude, they again elected him general."[13]

In his time and in ours, Pericles has been blamed for a host of "sins." They have criticized him for his policy that brought Athens into the Peloponnesian War, and they have criticized his strategy in the war. They have criticized him for diverting money from the Delian Leagues' treasury to fund public works projects in Athens, and they and have accused him of being an imperialist who "enslaved" Athens' allies.[14]

Despite these criticisms of Pericles, it must be admitted that he deserves much of his reputation for wise leadership that has continued from the ancient world to our own. For thirty years, he held in balance the competing factions that would ultimately tear Athens apart. During that time, Athens indeed became the "school of Hellas." Greek culture flourished. The Parthenon and the great buildings on the Acropolis were built. Phidias, Socrates, Aeschylus, Euripides, and Sophocles produced their greatest work. The poorest classes prospered. The first democracy recognized the rights of all its citizens, and the basic foundations of Western civilization were laid. Athens dominance over its allies, which was tied to its navy and the political power of the thetes, moreover benefited the entire empire by promoting commerce by establishing a standardized currency and protecting shipping in the Aegean from pirates. At the same time, Athens defended local democratic governments among its allies.[15]

It is true, however, that Athenian democracy was no utopia. Our admiration for the democracy of ancient Athens should be tempered by our recognition that slaves, women, and noncitizens were not able to fully participate in Athens' society and its government.[16]

Approximately one third of ancient Athens' total population of about 250,000 people were slaves. We can tell from the few ancient sources that mention them, that their living conditions and statuses varied widely. A few slaves were owned by the Athenian polis and lived in relative comfort, serving in administrative jobs or in Athens' token police force. Other slaves were domestic workers, living in the households and often eating at the same table with their masters. Many of these also worked in the fields or in craft shops alongside free laborers. At the other end of the spectrum, large numbers of slaves worked in brutal conditions as miners extracting silver from underground tunnels beneath Laurium. These mines provided the foundation of Athens' great wealth, allowing Athens to become the greatest power in the

Aegean. Whatever the condition of individual slaves, none of them enjoyed the same rights as free Athenian citizens. They could be savagely beaten at the whim of their masters, and in court hearings, their testimony was compelled by torture. Slaves were, at least in theory, as well, non-Greeks. They each carried, therefore, the double stigmas of being a slave and a barbarian—so called because their language seemed to consist only of a series of sounds, "bar, bar, bar." While traditional textbooks used to spend little ink discussing slavery, modern scholars recognize that slaves and their labor shaped the world of ancient Athens, both economically and culturally. One consequence of this was that ideas of slavery and of freedom provided the fundamental language for thinking about social and political relations among all the Greek poleis.

Some scholars have compared Greek attitudes toward slaves and toward non-Greeks to modern-day racism in America. Some scholars detect racism even in the attitudes and relations among the Greeks whose linguistic dialects reflect the distinct ethnic groups of Ionians, Dorians, and Aeolians.[17] Ideas about race and racial relations in America, however, should probably be seen more correctly as unique to the modern era. Racism is one thing that is not a legacy of the ancient world. It is the idiosyncratic product of the tumultuous cultural history of the West from the seventeenth century to the present.

Athenian society was divided not only between slave and free, but also between citizens and non-citizens, or *metics*. These were the many people who had come to Athens attracted by the opportunities that a wealthy, commercial metropolis offered. They worked in shops and as merchants and played an important role in keeping Athens' economy buzzing. They shared none of the rights, however, that were common to Athenian citizens. They could not participate in the Assembly or hold civic offices, which were often sources of income for Athenian citizens. If accused of a serious crime, they could be sold into slavery. In addition, they could not own land; they had to pay taxes that citizens did not have to pay; and they were compelled to serve in Athens' army.

Again, the difference with the United States is worth noting. In the United States, the middle class of people who are producers and consumers, and who are workers in businesses, industry, and commerce, are the engines of the economy. Their active political participation ameliorates the potential conflicts between the wealthy and the poorer classes, and their values and aspirations help to shape a relatively stable political and social system. The metics of Athens could have fulfilled a similar role. Instead, the political divisions of rich and of poor shaped much of Athens' and the Greek states' history.

Another excluded group in Athens society, and generally in much of human history, were women. Here we can see that ancient Athens arguably marks the nadir of a misogyny in the West that has been characterized by ups and downs over the centuries. The women and men who were citizens of Athens lived separate lives. An Athenian woman did not participate in politics and was not to be seen in public places.

While an Athenian man gathered in the agora to discuss public events, his wife or daughter remained at home, which one scholar described was generally "dark, squalid, and unsanitary."[18] A man did the shopping for the household, believing that his wife would easily be cheated by crafty merchants in the marketplace. A woman could not own property, but yet, was herself imagined as the property of her father, brother, or husband. A girl as young as fourteen years could be married off to man who was twice her age.[19] Above all, a woman was modest and submissive toward her menfolk. Pericles famously summed up women's status in Athenian society when he declared that it was a woman's greatest glory is to be "least talked of among men whether for good or for bad."[20]

All of these attitudes and restrictions, however, refer only to the women who were citizens of Athens. Women who were not citizens lived much different lives. They could be seen in public places, and sometimes engaged in trade. Numbers of them, as well, worked in the sex trade, and the most liberated women in ancient Athens were probably the few *hetaera*, whose beauty and intellect attracted wealthy clients, and who enjoyed high status, and themselves became fairly wealthy. One Athenian man explained the various roles of women in Athenian society: "We have mistresses for our enjoyment, concubines to serve our person, and wives for the bearing of legitimate offspring."[21]

Despite restrictions on their activities, both citizen and noncitizen women played an important role in the cultural life of ancient Athens. Women were the most active participants in the religious rites and cults that played a central role in the life of the polis. We can get some sense of their importance in Athenian society from the representations of strong-willed women like Clytemnestra, Medea, and Antigone who populated the tragedies of Aeschylus, Euripides, and Sophocles, and many of these plays reveal the strong underlying tensions between the sexes in ancient Athens.

The social roles of women in Athens contrasts sharply with those of their opposite numbers in Sparta. In Sparta, women's first duty, like that of all Spartan men, was to the state. Spartan women were expected to be physically fit, to bear strong children, and perhaps even to fight. Spartan women exercised in public alongside Spartan men, according to some sources in the nude. In addition, unlike Athenian women, Spartan women could own property in their own names.

The "First Peloponnesian War"

Athens and Sparta were at the furthest ends of a chain of powerful states that stretched from mainland Greece across the narrow isthmus to the Peloponnese (see map 2). In the north, Athens was the homeland of those who lived on the islands and around the coasts of the Aegean, and who spoke an Ionian dialect of Greek. These states were tied to Athens by their legendary descent, by their maritime interests, and by their participation in the Delian League. In the south, Sparta was the leader of a league of Peloponnesians who spoke a Dorian dialect of Greek. Between them were the powerful states of Megara, Corinth, and Argos.

The balance of power in the Greek world shifted dramatically in 461 when Megara decided to leave the Peloponnesian League and become an ally of Athens. This set-in motion a chain of events that led to what has become known as the "First Peloponnesian War," from 459 through 446, and was a precursor to the great Peloponnesian War of 431 through 404. Athens welcomed the alliance with Megara because Megara's position at the northern end of the isthmus connecting Attica and the Peloponnese protected her from potential invasion from its southern neighbors. Corinth, however, saw the expansion of Athenian power as a threat to their own interests, and when Athens constructed a wall around Megara, it caused Corinth, according to Thucydides, to have "a deadly hatred against Athens."[22]

For fifteen years, a series of battles pitted the forces of Athens, Megara, and Argos against those of Sparta, Corinth, and Thebes. Very early in this war, Athens inexplicably sent an expedition of 250 ships to Egypt to liberate it from Persian rule. The utter destruction of these forces should have warned Athens to avoid fighting wars simultaneously in two places, one of which was across hundreds of miles of the water. Any lesson that the Athenians might have learned from this was forgotten forty-six years later when Athens decided to launch a similar expedition to Sicily.

In Greece, the First Peloponnesian War saw Athens gain and then loose the vast territory of northern mainland Greece, and the war ultimately ended inconclusively when Megara rejoined the Peloponnesian League and all parties agreed to a peace treaty that prohibited hostilities for thirty years. The "Thirty Years Peace" between all the belligerents in the First Peloponnesian War implicitly recognized a balance of power between Athens and Sparta. Henceforth, Sparta and its hoplite warriors would be the dominant power on land, and Athens with its warships and merchant vessels, would be dominant on the sea.

Although the results of the battles of the First Peloponnesian War were inconclusive, Athens during this time cemented the final steps in the creation of its empire. In 454, Athens declared that the treasury on Delos was unprotected if the Persians took the opportunity to attack and moved the treasury to

Athens. Soon Athens was using funds from the League for a variety of purposes that built is own power and prestige. Athens by this time held virtually irresistible power over its previous allies, who were now, in many peoples' minds, subject states.

Athens' military power and cultural influence was arguably at its peak during the fifteen years that the Thirty Years Peace lasted. Under Pericles' administration, Athens welcomed people and products from around its empire. Athens became home to philosophers, artists, architects, and dramatists. The architectural monuments and statues on the Acropolis were built, the empire eliminated piracy in the Aegean, and it created a relatively stable economic network of states with a standardized coinage, weights, and measurements.

Not everyone appreciated the rise of Athenian power, however.

When Naxos, and then Thasos, attempted to revolt and were subdued, opposition to Athenian power increased. According to Thucydides, Athenian hegemony over their "allies" in the Delian League was now "slavery."[23] Thucydides apparently agreed with the Spartans, when they claimed that they fought to save all of Greece from "Athenian slavery," and many Greeks indeed saw Athenian domination as oppression. But many did not. Many of the common people who lived under the harsh rule of oligarchs throughout the Greek world looked to Athens to liberate them from the tyranny of local aristocrats and to establish democratic governments.

At the same time as Athenian power grew, a polarization between classes seems to have affected nearly all of the Greek poleis. Factions in nearly every city supported either a democracy or an oligarchy, and looked respectively to either Athens or Sparta for support. In this increasingly polarized environment, every polis in Greece seemed ripe for a revolution in government.

NOTES

1. James K. Aitken and Hillary F. Marlow, eds., *The City in the Hebrew Bible: Critical, Literary and Exegetical Approaches* (London: T&T Clark, 2018).

2. Thucydides, 1.70: Passages are from Thucydides, *The History of the Peloponnesian War*, translated by Richard Crawley in 1874 (hereafter cited Thucydides), unless otherwise noted.

3. "When we contemplate the great contrast between the two national characters [of Athens and Sparta]; a contrast of which as far as we can see, you have little perception, having never yet considered what sort of antagonists you will encounter in the Athenians, how widely, how absolutely different from yourselves. The Athenians are addicted to innovation, and their designs are characterized by swiftness alike in conception and execution; you have a genius for keeping what you have got, accompanied by a total want of invention, and when forced to act you never go far enough. Again they are adventurous beyond their power, and daring beyond their judgment, and in danger they are sanguine; your wont is to attempt less than is justified by your power, to mistrust even what is sanctioned by your judgment, and to fancy that from danger there is no release. Further, there is promptitude on their side against procrastination on yours; they are never at home, you are never from it for they hope by their absence to extend

their acquisitions, you fear by your advance to endanger what you have left behind" (Thucydides, 1.70).

4. A. V. Miller, Translator, *Hegel's Phenomenology of Spirit* (New York, Oxford University Press, 1977), 111–19.

5. But see John V. A. Fine, *The Ancient Greeks: A Critical History* (Cambridge, MA: Harvard University Press, 1983), 137–75.

6. Herodotus, *The Landmark Herodotus: The Histories*, ed. Robert B. Strassler, trans. Andrea L. Purvis (New York: Anchor Books, 2009), 1.59–1.61 (hereafter cited Herodotus).

7. The story of Harmodius and Aristogeiton is told by Thucydides, 6.56–59, and in *The Constitution of Athens*, attributed to Aristotle, see J. M. Moore, "Introduction," in *Aristotle and Xenophon on Democracy and Oligarchy*, trans., intro., and commentary by J. M. Moore (Berkeley: University of California Press, 1975), xviii.

8. Arisitole, "The Athenian Constitution," in *Arisitole: The Politics and the Constitution of Athens, Aristotle*, ed. Stephen Everson (New York: Cambridge University Press, 1996), 209–64, at 225.

9. Thucydides, 2.65.

10. Benjamin Jowett, Translator, *The Dialogues of Plato* (New York, Oxford University Press, 1920), *Gorgias*, 515, vol. 1, 577.

11. Thucydides, 2.37.

12. But see, Robert W. Wallace, "Plato's Sophists, Intellectual History after 450, and Sokrates," in *The Cambridge Companion to the Age of Pericles*, ed. Loren J. Samons II (Cambridge: Cambridge University Press, 2007), 215–37, at 216.

13. Thucydides, 2.65.

14. See, for example, Loren J. Samons II, "Conclusion: Pericles and Athens," in *The Cambridge Companion to the Age of Pericles*, ed. Loren J. Samons II (Cambridge: Cambridge University Press, 2007), 282–307.

15. G. E. M. Ste. de Croix, *The Origins of the Peloponnesian War* (London: Duckworth, 1972); G. E. M. Ste. de Croix, *The Class Struggle in the Ancient Greek World: From the Archaic Age to the Arab Conquests* (Ithaca, NY: Cornell University Press, 1981); P. J. Rhodes, "Democracy and Empire," in *The Cambridge Companion to the Age of Pericles*, ed. Loren J. Samons II (Cambridge: Cambridge University Press, 2007), 24–45.

16. On these subjects, see for example: Cynthia Patterson, "Other Sorts: Slaves, Foreigners, and Women in Periclean Athens," in *The Cambridge Companion to the Age of Pericles*, ed. Loren J. Samons II (Cambridge: Cambridge University Press, 2007), 153–78.

17. Benjamin Isaac, *The Invention of Racism in Classical Antiquity* (Princeton, NJ: Princeton University Press, 2004); Rebecca F. Kennedy, C. Sydnor Roy, and Max L. Goldman, trans., *Race and Ethnicity in the Classical World: An Anthology of Primary Sources in Translation* (Indianapolis, IN: Hackett, 2013); and Jonathan M. Hall, *Ethnic Identity in Greek Antiquity* (Cambridge: Cambridge University Press, 1997).

18. Sarah Pomeroy, *Goddesses, Whores, Wives, and Slaves: Women in Classical Antiquity* (New York: Schocken Books, Random House, 1975), 79.

19. Pomeroy, *Goddesses, Whores*, 64.

20. Thucydides, 2.45.

21. Pomeroy, *Goddesses, Whores*, 8.

22. Thucydides, 1.103.4.

23. Thucydides, 1.98. This event was perhaps in 471 BCE.

Chapter Two

The Opening Moves

THE CAUSES OF WAR

The agreed upon "Thirty Years Peace" did not last for half that time. Soon, many of Athens' neighbors became alarmed by Athens' growing power, and numerous small conflicts threatened a renewed outbreak of war.

The first of these was a democratic revolution in Epidamnus, in the northwest corner of Greece. Epidamnus was a colony of Corcyra (modern Corfu), which was strategically located on the route from Greece to the heel of the Italian boot and from there to the wealthy cities in Sicily.

When Corinth came to the aid of the oligarchs at Epidamnus, a war between Corcyra and Corinth, the two greatest sea powers after Athens, seemed imminent. Athens initially wanted to avoid any involvement in this conflict, knowing that anything they did might break the "Thirty Years Peace," and pull them into a larger war. Athens recognized, however, that if Corinth defeated Corcyra, then Corinth could also threaten Athenian naval dominance in the Aegean. The Athenians could not allow this. When the Corcyreans appealed to Athens for help, Athens decided, therefore, to send ten triremes to defend Corcyra. The Athenian triremes were the ultimate weapon of the ancient world and the key to Athenian dominance in the Aegean. They were ships that were over one hundred feet long, with three levels of oarsmen. They were light, incredibly fast, and highly maneuverable. With their skilled crews, they could drive across the oars of enemy ships, or they could outflank them and ram them broadside, piercing their hulls with their bronze ramming prows.[1]

The captains of Athenian triremes, in this case, were given strict instructions not to fight but to act only as a show of force. The ten Athenian triremes joined 110 Corinthian ships facing the enemy's fleet of 150 ships in the

Figure 2.1. The Battle in the Great Harbor from a nineteenth century print. This inaccurately shows the triremes with their masts and sails up during the battle. In actuality, they would have been removed beforehand and stored onshore to make the ships lighter and more maneuverable. *(Alamy Stock Photo)*

straits of Sybota between Corcyra and mainland Greece. This was the greatest number of ships in sea battle in ancient Greece up to that time.

When the Corinthian and the Corcyrean ships advanced toward each other, the Athenians, as they were instructed, remained in place. Neither the Corcyreans nor the Corinthians had the skill or the knowledge of tactics that the Athenians possessed, and the ships on both sides came together without plan or discipline. The Corcyreans initially gained the advantage on their left flank, but the Corinthians dominated on the other end of the line and began to butcher every enemy and even some of their own men in the confusion. Up to then, the Athenians had stayed in place watching the battle unfold, but now, against their instructions, they joined the Corcyreans in the fight. As the Corinthians reorganized their lines and began a renewed attack, they saw on the horizon a fleet of Athenian ships which had recently been sent out from Athens as reinforcements. The Corinthians now began to back water, abandoning their attack. By now, the sun was setting, and the battle ended as neither side, in the darkness, could see either the enemy's or their own ships. The next day, neither side renewed the fight, and each side claimed victory.[2]

The escalating conflict between Athens and Corinth led Athens to tighten its control over Potidaea which was in the unusual position of being both a member of the Athenian-led Delian League and a colony of Corinth. Potidaea, the southernmost finger of the Chalcidian peninsula in the northern Aegean, resented Athens' new restrictions and revolted, and Athens sent a force to subdue Potidaea, which was only accomplished after a two-year siege. One of the common foot soldiers who was in the Athenian force was the philosopher, Socrates, who, during the battle, saved the life of his young friend, Alcibiades (about whom we will hear much more later). The battle was inconclusive, and the Athenians were forced to lay siege to the city for two years before the Potidaeans finally capitulated.[3]

THE DECISION TO GO TO WAR

As tensions among the Greek poleis increased, Athens accused Megara of encroaching on land on the boarder near Athens, which was sacred to the goddesses Demeter and Persephone. Athens, as well, charged that the Megarians were encouraging their slaves to flee Athens and to join Megara. In response to these insults, Athens passed a decree prohibiting the merchants of Megara from entering Athenian harbors and the agora—potentially crippling the Megarian economy.

Athens had now antagonized both of the states, Megara and Corinth, which sat on the isthmus separating Athens from the armies of the Peloponnese. To this point in time (432 BCE), Sparta had observed the terms of the "Thirty Years Truce," and had stayed out of the fighting, but this could not last. In response to these events, the Corinthians called all of the Peloponnesian allies to gather in Sparta for a conference. When they met, the Corinthians had a long list of complaints against Athens. Instead of condemning Athens, however, the Corinthians criticized the Spartans for their continued inaction. The Spartans, they said, had done nothing all the time that Athens' power was increasing. They argued that Sparta should have "crushed [Athenian power] in its infancy."[4] Sparta, they said, must stop delaying and lead their allies in a war against Athens.

It happened that some Athenians were in Sparta on some other business on the day of this meeting, and they spoke defending Athens' actions and its growing power. They claimed that it was not Athens' intention to become the dominant power in Greece. The Athenians reminded the Peloponnesians that after the Persian Wars and the recall of Pausanias, the Greek allies had asked Athens to lead them. Now that Athens had an empire, it would not be safe for Athens to give it up. Athens' allies would perceive any change in policy as weakness and this would be a signal to revolt. Athens thus was compelled to protect and increase their empire. They explained that,

> Fear being our principal motive, though honor and interest afterwards came in. . . . It was not a very wonderful action, or contrary to the common practice of mankind, if we did accept an empire that was offered to us and refused to give it up under pressure of three of the strongest motives, fear, honor and interest. And it was not we who set the example, for it has always been the law that the weaker should be subject to the stronger.[5]

For Thucydides, the strongest of these motives was fear. It was fear that gave Athens its empire, and fear that led Sparta to resist it. The "truest cause" of the war between the Athenians and the Peloponnesians, Thucydides said, was "the growth of the power of Athens, and the fear which this inspired in Sparta [which] made war inevitable."[6]

The ideas that fear, along with honor and interest, were fundamental human motives, and that the weak must submit to the strong has become known to modern political theorists as the "Athenian thesis." These ideas will recur at critical points in Thucydides' narrative and have shaped many discussions of political relations ever since.[7]

The Spartan king, Archidamus, listened carefully to the words of the Athenians and the Corinthians, and, although he understood the strong emotions of Sparta's allies, he resisted the call for war. He knew that a war with Athens would not be short. The Athenians had a much larger population from which it could draw a large force of *hoplites*. Athens had more horses, and ships, and a much superior navy. In addition, Athens had many allies who would support Athens throughout a long war with men, money, and ships.

Archidamus said that the qualities of "slowness and procrastination," which the Spartans were famous for, were not defects but signs of the Spartans' "wisdom and moderation." "We are wise," he said, "because we are educated with too little learning to despise the laws, and with too harsh discipline to disobey them."

Archidamus noted that the Athenians had offered to submit the issues between them to arbitration, as required by the truce of the "Thirty Years Peace," and said that the Spartans should make use of the time while they were negotiating to prepare for war. He did not say, and it did not need to be said, that war, as well, might precipitate an uprising of helots, forcing Sparta to fight two wars at once, one at home against their slaves and another in the field against Athens.

Archidamus' words, however, did not convince the Spartans. The Assembly demanded that Athens must dissolve the Delian League and lift the siege of Potidaea. Athens must, as well, revoke the Megarian decree and remove the curse of the Alcmaeonidae. This last demand was directed at Pericles, the descendent of the Megacles, who was responsible for the violation of Cylon's supplication at the temple of Athena. In plain terms, Pericles must leave the city.

Inevitably, Athens rejected these demands. Pericles was resolute. He would not yield to any demands. He would not leave Athens. The Delian League would remain intact. The Megarian decree would not be lifted. The siege of Potidaea would not end. And Athens would vigorously defend itself against Sparta.

In the summer of 432, Sparta voted to declare war against Athens. Neither side was eager to start hostilities, however. Athens was determined that they would not be responsible for starting the war.[8] Sparta, for its part, sent three missions to Athens offering to negotiate a resolution of issues, but Athens rejected them.

PLATAEA

The *polis* of Thebes, to the north of Athens, made the first move in the spring of 431 by invading the Athenian ally, Plataea, which was situated between the two much larger city-states. The Thebans had prepared by plotting with some citizens of Plataea to betray their city by opening the city gates in the middle of the night. On the appointed night, three hundred Theban hoplites rushed through the gates of the city and into the marketplace. Once there, they surprisingly announced that their intentions were friendly. They wanted to establish an alliance with the city, and they lay down their arms in the marketplace as a show of their good intentions. The conspirators in the city who had opened the gates for the Thebans were amazed by this. They had hoped that the Thebans would slay their enemies and place themselves in power.

The Theban plan for a peaceful take-over of the city at first seemed to work, but soon the Plataeans realized that the Theban force had no reserves to support them. Working throughout the night, the citizens of the city quietly and quickly organized a resistance. To avoid being seen by the Thebans, the Plataeans broke through the interior walls of their houses to make passages so that their movements could be detected by the Thebans. The Plataeans then closed the city gates and placed wagons as barricades at key points in the city. Just before dawn, the Plataean citizens attacked. They quickly scattered the Theban forces who ran wildly in different directions looking for an exit, all the while the women and slaves in the city shouted curses at the Thebans and threw stones and roofing tiles at them from the tops of buildings. The panic-stricken Thebans, at last, rushed into a large building that they mistakenly believed led to another city gate. There they were trapped and massacred.[9]

PERICLES' STRATEGY

Pericles' strategy was straightforward. He knew that Athens could not win a conventional land war against Sparta. Sparta had proved during the Persian war that their hoplite army was virtually invincible on land. As long as Athens had a naval fleet, however, and had access to its port, the Piraeus, Athenian ships could support its population within its walls. Food, supplies, and money would continue to stream into the city.

Pericles, therefore, convinced the citizens of Attica's *demes*, the many small villages and towns surrounding Athens, to abandon their homes and come within the walls of Athens for protection. Accordingly, the farmers of Attica sent their cattle and sheep off to Euboea, the large island to the north of Athens, and gathered all of their household possessions, even stripping parts of their houses, to bring them into the city. The swarms of people pouring into the city crowded into every available plot of land, even settling on the sacred land at the base of the Acropolis.

Meanwhile, Archidamus slowly led his army across the isthmus toward Athens. By mid-summer, when the corn was ripe, his troops appeared on the outskirts of Attica. There, they set up a camp from which they launched raids into the countryside, destroying crops and houses. The Athenians watched from the walls of the city as the Spartans destroyed their homes. Not happy doing nothing, many of them wanted to go out and meet the Spartans in the field, and they began to grumble against Pericles. Most Athenians knew that Pericles and Archidamus were friends and believed that Archidamus would spare Pericles' own property. Pericles, in response to these rumors, gave all of his property outside Athens' walls to the people of Athens.

At the same time, Pericles sent a hundred ships to sail around the coast of the Peloponnese, making raids on the countryside. This was perhaps as much a sign of resistance to satisfy the citizens of Athens for action than for any practical strategic reason. Meanwhile, Pericles continued to urge that the Athenians avoid a land battle against the Spartan hoplites, and resist any temptation to expand the war. He argued that eventually the Spartans would lose their enthusiasm for the war when they saw that their raids had no effect. Pericles urged the Athenians "to wait quietly, to pay attention to their navy, to attempt no new conquests, and to expose the city to no hazards during the war."[10] If the Athenians agreed "not to combine schemes of fresh conquest with the conduct of war, and will abstain from willfully involving yourselves in other dangers," then Athens would prevail, adding (prophetically) "indeed, I am more afraid of our own blunders than of the enemy's devices."[11]

THE PLAGUE

The Spartans' first invasion of Attica lasted only a few weeks. The Spartans were satisfied to make raids on the countryside and made no attempt on the city itself. Despite the many Spartans who criticized Archidamus for not being more aggressive, the Spartan army came back across the isthmus to spend the winter months at home.

This may have given Athens hope that Pericles' strategy would be successful, and indeed it might have succeeded if it had not been for something that no one could have foreseen.

The large numbers of people who crowded within Athens' city walls during the hot summer created unsanitary conditions that were ideal for the spread of disease.

In 430, the second year of the war, an outbreak of a plague erupted in the city that persisted for several years, killing nearly half the population.

The plague appeared first at the Piraeus, arriving in ships from Egypt, Libya, and Persia. It attacked everyone—the strong as well as the weak. First came headaches and fevers, followed by redness and inflammation of the eyes and throat. Victims sneezed and coughed. The tongue began to bleed. The disease then moved to the chest and stomach. By then, the body was wracked by violent spasms. Streams of fluid were expelled from red pustules and ulcers that erupted on the skin. Half-dead people wandered through the city, seeking relief from their fevers. Some threw themselves into the city's wells and fountains, polluting the water supply. After about a week, the victim usually died. Those who survived often succumbed shortly afterward from weaknesses brought on by the disease.

As long as the plague raged, the usual funeral rites were abandoned. Dead bodies piled up in the streets and around the sanctuaries, where suffering people had gone seeking divine protection. Some people threw the corpses of their family members on the funeral pyres of strangers. Birds and animals, which normally would feed on human flesh, stayed away from the decaying bodies, and the few that did feed on the corpses died soon after.

All norms of behavior were forgotten. Many who were so far spared from the disease looted the property of the dead and dying. Others gave in to despair, abandoning all hope. They sought relief in pleasures of the moment, expecting neither to live nor if they survived, to be punished.

One hundred thousand Athenians may have perished from the plague. Both Pericles and Thucydides suffered from the plague. Thucydides fortunately recovered, but Pericles did not.

The death of Pericles marked a great turning point in Athens' fortunes. Thucydides records that, "As long as [Pericles] was at the head of the state during the peace, he pursued a moderate and conservative policy; and in his time [Athens'] greatness was at its height."[12] Following Pericles' death, inept and corrupt politicians filled the great vacuum in leadership. These were a new generation of men, whose wealth generally came not from their landed estates, but from commerce. As Thucydides saw it, these politicians used exorbitant rhetoric to lead the ignorant, gullible, and emotional population of Athens to their eventual downfall. These greedy and ambitious demagogues (literally, the "leaders of the people") led the Athenians to follow policies exactly contrary to those of Pericles. Thucydides described them as "more on a level with one another, and each grasping at supremacy. They ended by committing even the conduct of the state affairs to the whims of the multitude. This, as might be expected in a great and sovereign state, produced a host of blunders, and amongst them the Sicilian expedition."[13]

NICIAS

The first person who came to the fore following Pericles' death was the Athenian general, Nicias. At first, Nicias seemed an exception to Thucydides' judgment that the successors to Pericles were second-rate figures. Nicias was a wise and moderate leader who appeared to be a natural successor to Pericles. Like Pericles, Nicias was from an aristocratic family. His great wealth, however, came not from his agricultural lands like that of other aristocratic families, but from his silver mines, which employed over a thousand slaves. He lacked the eloquence and charisma of Pericles but made up for these deficiencies by spending huge sums on religious and theatrical events to win the approval of the masses.

It is likely that Nicias shared the sentiments of the unknown Athenian aristocrat, known to scholars as "the Old Oligarch," who described the Athenian polis during the early years of the Peloponnesian War. Like many of his fellow aristocrats, the Old Oligarch had mixed feelings about the Athenian democracy. He recognized the justice in giving political rights, free speech, and material rewards to the poor people in Athens. He said that "the commons which mans the fleet and has brought the state her power, and the steersmen and the boatswains and the shipmasters and the lookout-men and the ship-builders – these have brought the state her power much rather than the infantry and the well-born and the good citizens."[14] The lowest class of people serving in the navy, he said, brought every good thing to Athens: the delicacies of Sicily, Italy, Cyprus, Egypt, and the Peloponnese. As a result, the city took from each of these places something of their way of life, their language, their food, and their dress.

The Old Oligarch, however, loathed the idea of equality. He complained that in Athens, even slaves and *metics* had rights, and aristocrats, like himself, were prohibited from striking a slave or a metic who refused to step aside when passing on the street.

Figure 2.2. Nicias. *(Alamy Stock Photo)*

The Old Oligarch contended that "In every land the best element is opposed to democracy. Among the best elements there is very little license and injustice, very great discrimination as to what is worthy, while among the commons there is very great ignorance, disorderliness and rascality."[15] He complained that the common citizens preferred bad government in which they were free, to good government in which they were not.

The Old Oligarch noted that the social structure, which pitted aristocrats against democrats in Athens, influenced Athens relations with other Greek states. Whenever civil unrest erupted in a city, the Athenian people sided with the lower classes, and the aristocrats sided with the aristocrats. "For like is well disposed to like." As a consequence, when the Athenians conquered a city, "they disfranchise the good citizens, rob them of their wealth, drive them into exile, or put them to death."[16]

Nicias was perhaps a little less skeptical of democracy than the Old Oligarch, but he lacked the common touch. He made up for this with his ostentatious generosity and philanthropy. He supported religious festivals, dramatic and gymnastic exhibitions, and contributed money to a statue of Pallas Athene on the Acropolis. After the plague devastated Athens, Nicias organized and financed the purification of the sacred island of Delos. He built a bridge of gilded boats, painted and strewn with garlands, and led a procession across the channel to Delos. There, dressed in a splendid robe, he offered sacrifices and joined in ritual chanting. After this, he hosted a great banquet dedicated to Apollo and gave an estate worth 10,000 drachmas for a temple to the god Apollo. At the same time, to prevent anyone from claiming a right to property on the island based on the birth or death of a family member, he had the graves on the island dug up and the bodies removed, and passed a law prohibiting women from giving birth or anyone from dying on the island.[17] It is not clear how this last provision was enforced.

Nicias' generosity reflected his deep convictions—his strong patriotic spirit, his deep religious devotion, and his desire to be liked. These sentiments influenced his actions as a successful general through most of his life. He brought a soothsayer with him on military campaigns who would give him insights on his strategy from reading the entrails of sacrificed fowl.

Usually, he was successful in his campaigns against Athens' enemies at Cythera, Minoa, Corinth, and Thyres. His greatest success, however, might have come from avoiding failures rather than winning victories. He no doubt shared the Old Oligarch's criticism that the Athenians banished, ostracized, or even killed its best people. Cimon, the hero of Marathon, as mentioned earlier, is one example. The most famous example, though, is probably Themistocles, who convinced the Athenians to use the silver from the newly-found mines in Laurium to build a navy before the second invasion of the Persians and then used the navy to win a victory over the Persians at the Battle of Salamis. Renown as the "savior of Greece" and the architect of the

Athenian empire, Themistocles was exiled from Athens and ended his days in a province of Persia. Stories like these led the philosopher, Heraclitus, to claim that it was a common sentiment among the Greeks to "have none who is best among us; if there be any such, let him be so elsewhere and among others."[18]

Nicias seems to have had this always in mind. Cautious by nature, in order to avoid controversy or envy, he kept his opinions to himself, and gave all credit for his good fortune to the gods. As a general, according to Plutarch, Nicias "played for safety."[19] He avoided battle when he could, and whenever possible, he used inside informers to turn over a besieged city to his forces without bloodshed. This did not endear him to everyone in Athens. In the comedy *The Knights* (424 BCE), Aristophanes has one character say of another that he was "not one to cringe and creep about like Nicias." Thucydides' opinion was that Nicias wanted to "hand down to posterity a name as an ever-successful statesman and thought the way to do this was to keep out of danger and commit himself as little as possible to fortune . . . peace alone made this possible."[20]

Thucydides describes an incident that illustrates both the Greek customs of warfare and also gives insight into Nicias' character. After intense fighting against the Corinthians in 425, Nicias won a victory in which 212 Corinthians were killed, and fewer than fifty Athenians died. As was the custom, the victorious Athenians stripped the armor from the bodies of their dead enemies and piled the armor into a *trophy*. Then they took their own dead and their spoils to their ships and set sail. These acts were the traditional signs by which a victory was marked. Later, Nicias discovered that the Athenians had left the bodies of two soldiers behind. He returned to the battlefield, and sent a herald to the Corinthians, asking permission for a truce to take up the bodies. This was traditionally interpreted as a recognition of defeat, and by doing this, Nicias implicitly gave the victory, which he had won, to the Corinthians.[21] Nicias judged that he would more likely be criticized for returning without all the Athenian dead than for losing a battle. Later events would prove Nicias' decision was correct.[22]

CLEON

Nicias' moderate conservative leadership in Athens was challenged by Cleon—the opposite of Nicias in almost every aspect. Where Nicias was cautious, Cleon was daring. Nicias was devout, Cleon was worldly. Nicias lacked the common touch, Cleon appealed to the populace. Nicias was an aristocrat, Cleon was a leather merchant and the son of a tanner.

Cleon was one of the "new men," who filled the vacuum left by Pericles. While Pericles was alive, Cleon was a fierce critic of Pericles and his policies. He was probably responsible for bringing the charges against Pericles that led to Pericles' fine and his temporary removal from office. At that time, Cleon was in the oligarchic faction opposed to Pericles' populism. After Pericles' death, however, Cleon took on the mantle of the popular faction in opposition to the policies of Nicias.

Cleon and other "new men," like Hyperbolus and Eucrates, were not aristocrats, as were the previous leaders of Athens. They were from the merchant class. Their power stemmed, not from their breeding or their noble character, but from their ability to move the Athenian people by the force of their words. These demagogues generally urged swift and violent action against their enemies, usually with little understanding or deliberation or consideration of the consequences. They inflamed passions and manipulated social divisions creating crises, which they claimed only they could resolve. They disregarded the usual political process and the rule of law and attacked their political rivals using lies and exaggerations to paint them as corrupt and unpatriotic. Men like Cleon had no consistent political philosophy and were guided only by their craving for political power. When they gained power, they established strict authoritarian regimes, which ultimately collapsed from their own excesses.

Thucydides and Aristophanes are our only contemporary sources of knowledge about Cleon. Neither of them liked him. Thucydides described Cleon as "the most violent man in Athens and at that time the most powerful with the [people]."[23] Aristophanes, in his comedy, *The Knights*, created a character based on Cleon, who was "the biggest rogue and liar hereabouts." The character was a bully who "hurled" "portentous, mountainous, volcanic words" against "dark Conspirators." Those who made masks for the characters in Athenian dramas refused to make a mask for Cleon's character out of fear of his temper.

Thucydides and Aristophanes had good reason to dislike Cleon. Cleon was likely responsible for Thucydides' banishment, and initiated the prosecution of Aristophanes for his earlier play, *The Babylonians*, which Cleon claimed was unpatriotic.

The Roman historian, Plutarch, added to the criticisms of Cleon, describing Cleon's "intolerable arrogance," and his "audacity which none could restrain." Plutarch claims that Cleon, "broke down all the conventions of decent behavior in the Assembly. It was he who first introduced shouting and abuse in his speeches, as well as the habit of slapping his thigh, throwing open his dress and striding up and down the platform as he spoke, and his habits produced among the politicians an irresponsibility and a disregard for propriety which before long were to throw the affairs of Athens into chaos."[24]

Cleon's character is probably most clearly revealed during the famous debate over the fate of Mytilene. Mytilene was the principal city on the island of Lesbos and was a semi-independent state within the Athenian empire. It had a considerable navy and thus contributed ships, rather than money to the Athenian dominated Delian League. Based on this, it could claim status as an autonomous state.

When Mytilene revolted from the League and asked Sparta for aid in the autumn of 428, Athens responded by sending out a hundred ships, and a thousand infantry, and laid siege to the city.[25] By spring, food supplies in the city were running low. Reinforcements and supplies from Sparta failed to arrive, and the city prepared for a final assault from the Athenians. Alcidas, the Spartan general at Mytilene, in these dire circumstances, consequently made the fatal decision to arm the population of the city with full hoplite armor. Once the citizens of city were armed, however, they refused to obey Alcidas and the oligarchs, and they compelled them to negotiate with the Athenians.

Paches, the Athenian general at the scene who negotiated with them, promised that no one would be enslaved or put to death before a messenger was sent out to Athens and had returned with instructions. The Mytilenian oligarchs who had instigated the revolt were skeptical of the Athenian's promises, and, afraid for their lives, they fled to the city's sacred altars for sanctuary. Paches, nevertheless, arrested them, promising them, once again, that no harm would come to them while the Athenian Assembly decided on a course of action.

When word of these events came to Athens, Cleon proposed to the Assembly that the entire male population should be slain, and the women and children should be sold into slavery. The Assembly approved these drastic measures and sent a warship with instructions to Paches to begin the mass executions.

On the next day, however, some members of the Assembly had second thoughts, and at the request of ambassadors from Mytilene, they met again to reconsider the previous day's decision.[26] Cleon vehemently responded to the Athenians' indecision with a withering criticism of the Athenian democracy. A democracy, he said, was incapable of maintaining an empire unless it recognized that it was, in essence, a tyranny and that all of its subjects at any time were eager to revolt. Athens subjects had no loyalty to Athens, but only feared its power. To submit now to any sentiments of compassion, Cleon claimed, would be suicidal. Athens, if it would hold onto its empire must have consistent policies and must not constantly question its decisions, claiming that "bad laws which are never changed are better for a city than good ones that have no authority."[27]

Cleon warned the Athenians citizens that they must not be persuaded "by cleverness," by "new-fangled arguments," or by "elaborate sophisms." He claimed that "ordinary men usually manage public affairs better than their more gifted fellows."[28] Those people who now wanted clemency for the

Mytilenians, he claimed, must have been bribed by the Mytilenian envoys to change their minds.

The whole population of Mytilene, Cleon argued, required swift justice. They deserved the severest punishment because they enjoyed special privileges within the empire. They were independent states within the empire, who, because they had a large navy, paid no tribute to Athens. Despite their privileged position, they chose to side with Athens' bitterest enemies. The Mytilenians, Cleon claimed, did not revolt, since revolt implies that they were oppressed, instead, the Mytilenians committed "deliberate and wanton aggression."[29] If they were not punished for it, Athens' other allies would also revolt on the smallest pretext, believing that if they succeeded, they would win their freedom, and if they failed, they would not be punished and would not be any worse off than before. Cleon urged, as well, that the Athenians make no distinction between the aristocrats who started the rebellion, and the populace, claiming (incorrectly) that the populace had joined the aristocracy against the Athenians.

Cleon concluded by urging, once again, that the Assembly be steadfast, and not reverse its decision. There are three failings, he said, most fatal to empire "pity, sentiment, and indulgence." Compassion, he said, was due only "to those who can reciprocate the feeling."[30] The punishment of the Mytilenians was not a question of right or wrong, "you must carry out your principle and punish the Mytilenians as your interest requires; or else you must give up your empire and cultivate honesty without danger."[31]

In this speech, as recorded by Thucydides, Cleon reiterated the key concepts of the "Athenian thesis"—that the will of the strong must be obeyed, that compassion is due only to those who are equal in power, and that ideas of justice and of morality must be disregarded by empires. They are signs of weakness that can only lead to ruin, and that states must act only in regard to their self-interest.

When Cleon was finished, Diodotus, the son of Eucrates, rose to speak. We know virtually nothing about Diodotus. His name appears nowhere else in the historical record, and we might conclude that his argument reflects Thucydides' own ideas. Diodotus addressed Cleon's arguments point by point. In response to Cleon's opposition to reopening the debate on the fate of Mytilene, Diodotus argued that great decisions should not be made in haste or in anger but required calm deliberation. "The two things most opposed to good counsel are haste and passion; haste usually goes hand in hand with folly, passion with coarseness and narrowness of mind."[32] Diodotus argued that accusing opponents with bribery, and implicating them with corruption or conspiracy, as Cleon had done, deterred wise men from expressing alternative opinions, which were necessary for the wise deliberation that was essential in a democracy. In speeches to the Assembly, Diodotus said, let the people decide between a good speaker who advocates a bad cause, and a bad speaker who advocates a good cause.

In his argument, although Diodotus strongly disagreed with Cleon that the Mytilenians should be put to death, he agreed with him that the Assembly should disregard ideas of justice or of compassion. The Assembly should consider only what was the most effective way to advance Athens' real interests. The Assembly, he said, should not consider the past offenses of the Mytilenians but should only consider what was best for Athens in the future. "We are not in a court of justice, but in a political Assembly, and the question is not justice, but how to make the Mitylenians useful to Athens."[33]

Diodotus argued that putting all the Mytilenian men to death, as Cleon argued, would not be an effective deterrent because desperate men, who are driven either by necessity or by ambition, do not consider the consequences of failure. Athens should have good policies, therefore, that would prevent rebellions before they can start, rather than turn to violence after the fact. Diodotus argued that the common people in every polis supported Athens. To destroy them in Mytilene, would alienate the common people in all of Greece. A humane policy, on the other hand, Diodotus claimed, would foster friendship with Athens' allies. Athens, therefore, should follow a lenient policy, even if it meant ignoring minor offenses. Diodotus, furthermore, asked the Assembly to imagine a hypothetical city that was in revolt. Would it surrender to Athens, knowing that it might lead to their death, or would its citizens, seeing that death would be the result of either surrender or defeat, fight on until the end?

At the conclusion of Diodotus' speech, the Assembly held a vote by a show of hands and decided very narrowly to rescind the order of execution.

A ship was quickly outfitted and sent out that evening with the hope that it could get to Mytilene before the ship that had been sent out the previous day could perform its awful mission. The Mytilenian ambassadors who were in Athens provided the ship's crew with wine and barley cakes and promised great rewards to the rowers if they arrived in time to stop the executions. The ship's crew rowed throughout the night, eating meals at their oars, and taking turns sleeping. Fortunately, the ship that had been sent out the previous day was in no hurry to carry out its orders and proceeded slowly toward Lesbos. The second ship from Athens, aided by a favorable wind, arrived at Mytilene shortly after the first ship had arrived, just as Paches was reading the orders for execution.

In the days that followed, with the general massacre of the Mytilenians adverted, Cleon successfully persuaded the Assembly to put to death only a thousand of the leaders of the revolt.

THE CORCYREAN REVOLUTION

While these events were occurring, back at Corcyra, the little island that started it all, several hundred oligarchs who had been captured by the Corinthians in the earlier conflict, returned to the island. The common people of Corcyra believed that the friends or families of the aristocrats had paid a ransom for their release, but, in fact, the Corinthians had carefully selected the Corcyrean aristocrats, and instructed them to overthrow the democracy and to bring Corcyra into an alliance with Corinth and the Peloponnesians.

Shortly after their arrival, the aristocrats proposed to the Corcyrean Assembly that Corcyra end its alliance with Athens. The Corcyreans rejected this proposal and voted to remain allies with Athens, but also to be friends with Corinth and the powers on the Peloponnese. The returning oligarchs, who were in league with the Corinthians, were not satisfied with this compromise and accused Peithias, who was the leader of the common people, with enslaving Corcyra to Athens. Peithias was thus brought to trial and was acquitted of the charge. Peithias then retaliated by accusing five of the oligarchs of desecrating land sacred to Zeus and Alcinous. Shortly afterward, as Peithias was speaking before the Corcyrean Council advocating a stronger alliance with Athens, the oligarchic conspirators broke into the meeting and killed Peithias and sixty of his followers.

All-out conflict then erupted between the people and the oligarchs, which ended when a Spartan force arrived and forced the leaders of the popular faction to take refuge on the Corcyrean Acropolis. The following day, skirmishing erupted again as both sides sought help from the neighboring countryside and offered freedom to any slaves who joined them. Overwhelmingly, slaves poured into the city to join the popular forces. Their numbers were offset, however, by a force of mercenaries who were hired by the oligarchs and the Spartans. On the third day, fighting intensified. Even the women of the town joined in, from the rooftops of their homes, throwing pots and roofing tiles down on the foreign fighters. In the face of this resistance, the oligarchs and their forces set fire to the city as they fled.

The next day, an Athenian fleet of twelve ships with five hundred Messenian hoplites arrived under the command of the Athenian general, Nicostratus, and established an unstable truce. Within a week, another Spartan force arrived in a fleet of fifty-three ships and confronted the Athenians. The Corcyreans joined the Athenians with sixty ships but were unable to coordinate with the Athenians. The Corcyreans (as they had earlier) lacked a plan for battle and rushed out to sea with little order. The twelve Athenian ships tried vainly to divert the Peloponnesians as they attacked the disorganized Corcyreans. By sunset, however, the Peloponnesians had taken thirteen Corcyrean ships and claimed victory.

That night, the two Spartan officers who were on the scene, Alcidas, the most timid general in the Spartan army, and Brasidas, the most aggressive general in the Spartan army, argued about what to do the following day. Brasidas (of whom we will hear much more later) urged immediately advancing on the demoralized and defeated city. The timid Alcidas, however, was his superior officer, and he made the decision to sail away.

The following day, an Athenian force of sixty ships led by the Athenian general, Eurymedon, arrived. The people of Corcyra, suddenly freed from their fears after weeks of attacks and counterattacks, now began to take revenge on their enemies. They were able to convince fifty of the oligarchs, who had taken sanctuary in the temple of Hera, to come out and stand trial. All of them were promptly condemned to death and killed. Others who had taken sanctuary, now saw their fate, and rather than allow themselves to be slaughtered by the Corcyreans, killed themselves, some by hanging themselves from trees, others by the sword.

For seven days, the killing continued as the Corcyrean populace slaughtered their enemies in the city. The killing escalated as some citizens killed others over personal grudges, and as debtors killed those who had lent them money. As Thucydides noted, "death thus raged in every shape . . . there was no length to which violence did not go; sons were killed by their fathers, and suppliants dragged from the altar or slain upon it."[34] For seven days, the Athenian general, Eurymedon, stayed in the harbor with his fleet of sixty ships and did nothing as the butchery continued.

This conflict in Corcyra was the first great *"stasis"* of the Peloponnesian War, a catastrophic internal social conflict, that would become increasingly common as the war continued. In peacetime, Thucydides wrote, when all of the peoples' needs are met, harmony reigns. In a period of stasis, however, factions are magnified, as popular parties and oligarchic parties appealed to outside forces. Generally (but not always), democratic factions appealed to democratic Athens, and oligarchies appealed to Sparta. In such times, when the comforts of peacetime are removed, humans are reduced by circumstances to their base nature. "War," Thucydides declares, "is a violent master."[35]

In such times as these, Thucydides wrote, words changed their meanings as each side used "fair phrases to arrive at guilty ends."

> Reckless audacity came to be considered the courage of a loyal ally; prudent hesitation, specious cowardice; moderation was held to be a cloak for unmanliness; ability to see all sides of a question inaptness to act on any. Frantic violence became the attribute of manliness; cautious plotting, a justifiable means of self-defense. The advocate of extreme measures was always trustworthy; his opponent a man to be suspected. To succeed in a plot was to have a shrewd head, to divine a plot still shrewder; but to try to provide against

having to do either was to break up your party and to be afraid of your adversaries.[36]

DEMOSTHENES

An opportunity to end the Peloponnesian War appeared in 425, when Athens captured a Spartan army on the island of Sphacteria, near Pylos on the west coast of the Peloponnese. This Spartan army included the sons of many of the finest families in Sparta, and many Athenians hoped to use these hostages to force Sparta to end hostilities. The credit for the Athenian victory went to the demagogue, Cleon. The victory, however, was largely the work of Demosthenes. This Demosthenes is not as well known as the famous orator of the same name from the following century, but he deserves equal praise. The Demosthenes of the Peloponnesian War was one of the best generals that Athens ever had. He combined an aggressive instinct with intelligence and cunning. In addition, he pursued a strategy, which, if consistently followed, might have prevented Athens' ultimate defeat.

Demosthenes plans, however, were not initially promising. He abandoned Pericles' policy of avoiding land battles, believing that he could cut the Peloponnesian connection with mainland Greece by forming alliances with the Acarnians and the Messenians. Fortifying a line across the southern tier of mainland Greece, and connecting Acarnania with Boeotia, would protect Athens' northern border while preventing Sparta from receiving aid from the tribes in the northwest (see map 2).

The Messenians had good reasons for joining Demosthenes' forces against the Spartans. They were among the slaves of the Spartans who revolted during the earthquake of 462. For ten years, the Messenians fought for their freedom in a stronghold on the rocky slopes of Mount Ithome. They were ultimately able to negotiate a truce that allowed them passage, under Athenian protection, to Naupactus, a strategically crucial position guarding access to the Gulf of Corinth. Here they established a thriving colony and welcomed other slaves who were fleeing Sparta.

Demosthenes put his plan in motion in 426 when, with his Messenian allies, he invaded the territory of the Aetolians. Demosthenes, no doubt, felt that conquering the Aetolians would not be difficult. They were a barbarous people, living in dispersed villages without walls. They spoke a foreign tongue and they ate the raw flesh of animals. In addition, the Aetolians could not afford the heavy armor of the Greek hoplites.

Demosthenes' plans quickly collapsed, however, when the Aetolians united and appeared before him en masse, and the Aetolians' lack of heavy armor turned out to give them an advantage. As the Athenian line of hoplites moved toward them, the Aetolians ran forward to meet them with no formation, individually throwing spears, rocks, and anything at hand. As the Athenians moved forward, the Aetolians ran back, reformed, and ran at them again. The Athenians in their helmets, which restricted their sight, and in their heavy hoplite armor, were too slow to engage them. Again and again, the Aetolians attacked and retreated until the Athenian lines broke and the Athenians fled the field in disarray. Then the hunting began. The Aetolians tracked them down in the roads and fields. Some of the Athenians hid in the forests, but the Aetolians set them on fire and slaughtered the Athenians as they fled the flames. The combined forces of Athenians and Messenians were utterly defeated. One hundred and twenty Athenians were killed in the battle. These were "the best men in the city of Athens," according to Thucydides.[37]

Demosthenes, afraid of the reaction of the Athenian Assembly, stayed in Naupactus for months rather than return to an angry assembly at Athens. Demosthenes had learned some important lessons, however, that he would use in the future.

Demosthenes was able to redeem himself a few months later with a series of victories against a Spartan army and their allies at Amphilochia, in northwest Greece (see map 2).[38] Demosthenes' forces were seriously outnumbered by the Spartan forces. Anticipating that the Spartans could easily turn his right flank, Demosthenes hid some elite soldiers in a sunken road overgrown with bushes near this weak spot. As Demosthenes expected, when the battle started, the Athenian right flank began to yield before the Spartan forces. Suddenly, Demosthenes' elite troops broke out from their hiding place. They pushed back the Spartan advance, and the whole of the Spartan army, who, seeing their best forces retreat, panicked and fled the field, and were soon captured by Demosthenes' forces.

In the truce after the battle, Demosthenes prohibited the allies of the Spartans from leaving the field, but he secretly allowed the Peloponnesian troops to leave. While the allies of the Spartans were busy retrieving their dead, the Peloponnesian troops in groups of two and three pretended that they were gathering herbs and firewood. Slowly at first and then in a run, the Peloponnesians rushed out of the camp, leaving their allies behind. In this way, Demosthenes had not only won the battle but succeeded in shaming the Peloponnesians and discrediting them in the eyes of their allies.

A short while after this, Demosthenes led his army on an overnight march and attacked a Spartan camp at dawn. Demosthenes placed his Messenian allies in the front rank, instructing them to call out in the Doric dialect, which they shared in common with the Peloponnesians. The Peloponnesians, hearing their native tongue, did not realize that they were being attacked, and were cut down as they awoke from sleep and before they could put on their hoplite armor.

These victories in the northwest allowed Demosthenes to form treaties with the rival factions in the area and pacified the region for much of the duration of the war. After these triumphs, Demosthenes felt that he could safely return to Athens. He brought with him 300 *panoplies* (the captured weapons and armor of his enemies), which filled the treasuries of temples throughout Attica.

The following year, in 425, Demosthenes and two other Athenian generals sailed from Athens to reinforce an Athenian army in Sicily. Their orders, however, were unclear, and Demosthenes was informed by his Messenian friends that Pylos, in the southwest corner of the Peloponnese, was undefended by the Spartans. This was in the homeland of the Spartan helots and Demosthenes knew that if he could take Pylos, he could attract runaway slaves from Sparta and establish Athenian control of the area (see map 2). Demosthenes argued with the other generals in the fleet about this plan, which was ultimately decided when a squall came up, forcing the whole fleet into the great bay at Pylos. As the weather continued to prevent sailing, as Thucydides tells it, the soldiers, having nothing else to do, without orders on their own initiative, began to fortify the site.

The Spartans at the time were celebrating a religious festival and, at first, did not recognize the danger that the Athenians on their frontier represented, and so they did nothing. When the Spartans finally recognized the danger that the Athenian base posed, they sent out a fleet of ships. A battle in the harbor at Pylos concluded quickly with the much superior Athenian fleet destroying the Spartan ships. The Spartans then sent out infantry troops by land, but they were unable to breach the hastily-built Athenian fortifications.

Despite these setbacks, the Spartans were able to capture the island of Sphacteria, which lay at the opening of the harbor. Sphacteria, however, became their prison. The Athenian fleet prevented the Spartans from supplying their forces on the island, and 420 Spartans (plus their helot slaves) were trapped on the island without food or water.[39] The Spartans on the island were forced to ask the Athenians for a truce, halting all aggression, during which they sent envoys to Athens to negotiate a permanent peace.

In Athens, the Spartan envoys, the representatives of the greatest fighting force in the ancient world, gave one of the earliest and best anti-war speeches in history. The Spartans argued that great conflicts cannot be settled merely by military victories. Fortune is fickle, they argued, and the future uncertain. Athens was successful thus far only through good luck, and it would not be wise to seek a greater victory.[40] It was now possible, they said, to establish a lasting peace. Athens should "be guided by gentler feelings," and should conquer their rivals with "generosity." The Athenians should accept the Spartan plea for peace immediately and avoid fostering a never-ending hatred between the states. Therefore, "let us be reconciled, and for ourselves, choose peace instead of war."

When Cleon, who was still the most influential man in Athens, heard these words, he reacted vehemently. He saw that the Athenians had gained a superior position and could move against the Spartans on Sphacteria any time they chose, and he chose to take full advantage of the situation. When the Spartans asked to negotiate with Athenian commissioners in a closed session, rather than before the volatile Assembly, Cleon accused them of wanting to negotiate in secret. Cleon exclaimed, "No! if they meant anything honest, let them say it out before all."[41]

The Spartans now faced a "catch-22," if they appealed for peace before a public assembly, their allies would feel betrayed and abandon them. If the Athenians rejected their offer of peace, the Spartans would then be alone and at the mercy of Athens. The Spartan ambassadors, realizing that their mission was a failure, left Athens without an agreement. The truce at Sphacteria ended, and the Athenian siege of the island continued.[42]

The Spartan forces on Sphacteria were now desperate. Without food, they faced starvation. In this extremity, they paid slaves to risk sailing across the harbor in small boats at night to get grain, wine, and cheese. Other slaves avoided the watchful eyes of the Athenians by swimming, pulling animal skins filled with poppy-seeds, linseed, and honey. Those who succeeded without being caught by the Athenians received high prices for their goods and promises of freedom from the Spartans.[43]

Word soon reached Athens that Demosthenes' forces were unable to prevent the smuggling of food to the Spartan soldiers, and the Athenians became afraid that the Spartans might yet escape from the island. Soon, the citizens of Athens turned against Cleon and regretted that he had rejected the Spartan offer of peace.

Cleon responded to his criticism by claiming that the bad news from Pylos were all lies. In response to these claims and counter-claims, the Assembly appointed a commission to go to Pylos and observe for themselves the actual state of affairs. Cleon was not pleased with this. He was afraid that a commission might prove that he was wrong, and he argued that it would be a waste of time. He argued that if the Assembly believed these reports, they should immediately send a force to capture the island. Cleon pointed his finger at Nicias, the "general, whom he hated, [and] he tauntingly said that it would be easy, if they had men for generals, to sail with a force and take those in the island, and that if he had himself been in command, he would have done it."[44]

Nicias replied to this taunt, saying that if Cleon thought it would be so easy, he should indeed do it, and offered to give his office as a general to Cleon. Cleon at first thought that this was a joke, but when he found that Nicias was serious, he quickly declined. Nicias then repeated the offer, and Cleon again rejected it. The more that Cleon backed down, the more the Assembly encouraged him to take the position, until Cleon finally saw that he had no choice and agreed to lead an expedition to Pylos. As he departed Athens, Cleon bragged that in twenty days, he would either take all of the Spartans alive or he would kill them on the spot.

Men of good sense, according to Thucydides, approved the decision to send Cleon to Pylos, thinking that if Cleon succeeded, it would be good, and if he failed, they would at least be rid of him.[45]

By the time that Cleon, with his force, ultimately arrived at Pylos, Demosthenes had nearly broken the siege with his own troops. Some of his troops had made a campfire on the island, which quickly got out of control and burned through the previously lush forest on the island—revealing the positions of the Spartans. Demosthenes forces, now aided by Cleon's detachment, as well as by the Messenian light infantry, closed in on the Spartan forces.

Following Demosthenes' plan of battle, the Athenians surrounded the Spartans but did not move against them. Instead, they sent their Messenian allies against the Spartans. The Messenians lacked heavy armor and were not trained to fight in the tight formations of a *phalanx*, but they were inspired by their hatred of their former masters. They ran toward the Spartan positions, throwing stones and spears at the enemy. When the Spartans, in their heavy armor, marched to meet them, the Messenians ran away and regrouped to charge again. At the beginning of the battle, the Messenians were cautious, knowing the reputation of the Spartans. As the conflict continued, however, they lost their fear and fought the Spartans with increasing ferocity. In the battle, the Spartans could not see the spears and arrows of the Messenians through the swirling dust and ashes flying up from the dry ground, and they could not hear the commands of their officers over the loud cries of the Messenians. Finally, some Messenians found a route behind the Spartan lines and gained the high ground behind the enemy. When a general slaughter of Spartans was imminent, Cleon and Demosthenes called off the Messenians and offered a truce to the surviving Spartans, who meekly lowered their shields and waved to indicate their surrender.

Before twenty days had passed, Cleon's promise to finish the work at Sphacteria had been fulfilled, and Cleon triumphantly led 290 captive Spartans into the prisons in Athens.[46]

In Athens, the populace was surprised to see the captured Spartan hoplites who were reputed to prefer death to the shame of surrender. Some Athenians taunted the Spartans as they marched into the city. One Athenian citizen asked a Spartan whether those who had fallen were men of honor, implying that the living prisoners were dishonored. The Spartan replied that an arrow "would be worth a great deal if it could tell men of honor from the rest."[47]

In 425, Cleon was now at the peak of his powers in Athens. The hostage Spartans, some of them from the best families in Sparta, were protection from any future attack on Athens. The Spartans understood that their soldiers could be slain by the Athenians at the slightest provocation. Meanwhile, the Athenian victory at Pylos encouraged Athens' allies to make raids in the Peloponnese, freeing scores of helots. The Athenians soon occupied critical locations in the Peloponnese, and Athenian fleets continued to ravage the coast. As Athenian spirits soared, the Spartans' morale was at its lowest point in the war as they faced the destruction of their hoplites, the loss of control of their allies, and the likelihood of a revolt of their helots.

Sparta's fortunes were saved at this point by what scholars in another context have called "victory disease." The Athenians who had been so fortunate to this point believed that nothing that they wished was impossible and that their strength was invincible.

> So thoroughly had the present prosperity persuaded the citizens [of Athens] that nothing could withstand them, and that they could achieve what was possible and impracticable alike, with means ample or inadequate it mattered not. The secret of this was their general extraordinary success, which made them confuse their strength with their hopes.[48]

BRASIDAS

Athens' euphoria did not last long. One Spartan who was not discouraged was Brasidas, one of the greatest of Sparta's generals. He had already distinguished himself in battles at Methone,[49] Megara,[50] and Pylos (where he received a wound and had to be carried off the field of battle). No longer satisfied with simply defending the Peloponnese against Athenian raids, and the Spartans' annual invasions of Attica, Brasidas conceived a bold plan to bring a Spartan army to Thrace in northern Greece, from which he could cut off Athenian supply routes to the Black Sea and to the rich agricultural and mining resources of the area.

In the summer of 424, Brasidas moved his army to Thrace and the three-fingered Chalcidice peninsula, where, through a combination of force and of persuasion., he captured several cities from the Athenians (see map 2).[51] Atypical of most Spartans, Brasidas combined military daring with diplomacy. Unlike the majority of his countrymen, Brasidas was also an articulate and persuasive speaker. He assured the Athenian cities that if they revolted and became allies of Sparta, they could keep their independence and their constitutions. Although the popular factions were suspicious of these promises, he assured them that his purpose was neither to support the local aristocrats nor to "enslave the many to the few or the few to the many." He told the citizens that if they rejected his appeals to join Sparta, he was prepared to use force to compel them. He denied, however, that Sparta wanted to have an empire like that of Athens. Sparta, he asserted, was motivated solely by the desire to free all of Greece from Athenian slavery. Faced with the prospect of fighting a Spartan army or agreeing to these mild terms, one polis after another—first Acanthus, followed soon by Scione and Mende—revolted from Athens.

Athens' optimism, which was now deflated by Brasidas' success in Thrace, was further depressed later that year with two major defeats. At the Battle of Delium, Athens' northern neighbor of Boeotia, an ally of Sparta, defeated a large Athenian army. The battle is famous to military historians for the Boeotians' unorthodox use of a twenty-five-man deep phalanx instead of the traditional eight. In a sign of the advancing complexity of Greek warfare, the Boeotians used this force, along with an elite force of 300 hoplites and its cavalry, to break the Athenian lines.[52] The battle is famous, as well, to cultural historians since among the hoplites who fled the battle was the philosopher Socrates, who calmly walked, while others ran in panic, as if he was merely walking on the streets of Athens, rather than on a bloody battlefield. Over a thousand Athenians died that day, which ended with Athens' enemies only a day's march from the city.[53]

Shortly after these events, Brasidas in the north marched through a snowstorm at night to take the important Thracian colony of Amphipolis. The loss of Amphipolis meant that Athens no longer had access to the gold and silver mines of the region, as well as to the timber and agricultural produce that came from northern Greece. The historian, Thucydides, who happened to be the Athenian general nearest to the city, quickly sailed with seven ships to Amphipolis, but arrived too late to prevent its capture. For this failure, the Athenian Assembly, probably at Cleon's direction, punished Thucydides by exiling him for twenty years. These events were catastrophes for Athens, which lost both a strategic position and an effective general, but they are a blessing for us since Thucydides was now able to spend his time in exile writing his history of the war.

By this time, Athens was finally ready to discuss peace with Sparta, and the Assembly appointed Nicias to draft an agreement between Athens and Sparta and their allies for an armistice to last for one year as a preliminary for a hoped-for lasting agreement (423 BCE). The hopes for peace almost instantly dissolved, however, when two days after the treaty was signed, Brasidas succeeded in convincing the Athenian allies of Scione and Mende to revolt. When Athens demanded that these towns be returned to them, as the armistice demanded, Brasidas refused to give the towns up.

Athens responded to this by sending Nicias with an army to retake the two cities. In an initial assault on Mende, Nicias was wounded, and his troops withdrew. Inside Mende, however, the people of the city had second thoughts about revolting from Athens. When the Spartan general in command of the city called upon its citizens to fight against the Athenians, one of them told the Spartan general that the people did not want a war and would not fight. The Spartan general was not used to a commoner talking to him like this, and violently struck the citizen. The common people of the city were outraged by this, and they attacked the Spartan guards and the city's oligarchs. Nicias, learning of this, seized the opportunity and renewed his assault on the city. This time he succeeded, and the city returned to Athenian control.

Following this victory in Mende, Nicias was unable to take Scione where a siege lasted throughout the fall, winter, and spring of the next year, when the city finally fell to the Athenians in 422.

When the agreed-upon one-year armistice ended, Cleon, looking for a climactic showdown against Brasidas, set out with a force from Athens to find the Spartan general.[54] The two men and their armies soon came face-to-face at Amphipolis, where both sides encamped, and prepared for what they knew would be a decisive battle. In preparation, the Athenians and the Spartans both sent out messengers in all directions, seeking allies and mercenaries from all the neighboring tribes and towns.

Thucydides, who likely blamed Cleon for his dismissal, is merciless in his description of Cleon's actions at Amphipolis. Cleon, he says, was inexperienced, incompetent, and over-confident in his limited abilities. Every soldier in the Athenian army recognized Cleon's shortcomings and questioned the general's authority. Meanwhile, Cleon acted erratically, moving the army from one place to another without reason.

While his army waited for reinforcements, Cleon walked up a hill that separated the two enemies' camps. From this vantage point, he could peer under the gates of the Spartan camp, and he could see soldiers' feet and horse's hooves moving about. Misinterpreting this, Cleon concluded that the Spartans were as unprepared for battle as he was, and he gave orders for his army to withdraw. Brasidas now saw his opportunity and struck quickly. Spartan hoplites rushed out of the main gate of their camp and ran at top speed into the center of Cleon's ill-formed line. Simultaneously, another Spartan force rushed out from second gate of their camp. Cleon's army, seeing that they were being attacked from two sides, fled the field in a panic. Cleon, himself, led the flight of his fleeing army but was quickly overtaken and slain.

Brasidas' army was victorious, but Brasidas had received a serious wound in the battle. He was carried off the battlefield and brought into Amphipolis, where he heard the news of his army's victory and soon afterward died from his wounds. The people of Amphipolis, relieved from the Athenian yoke, as Thucydides says, acclaimed Brasidas as their savior. They claimed him as the founder of their city, and in later years, they held sacrifices, offerings, and games in his honor.[55]

With the deaths of both Cleon and Brasidas, Athens and Sparta were finally ready for serious peace talks. With the strongest advocates for war in Athens and in Sparta gone, the peace parties in both cities now found their voices.

Among the Athenians, their defeats at Delium and Amphipolis had badly shaken their confidence. In addition, the loss of her colonies in Chalcidice made the Athenians afraid that more of their allies might revolt, and they now looked back on their previous rejections of peace offers as a mistake.

Meanwhile, many in Sparta were also anxious to discuss peace. They were anxious to bring home the Spartan soldiers who had been captured on Sphacteria, and they watched anxiously as the Athenians plundered their country from Pylos and Cythera, while every day more of their helots deserted. They shared the fears of Athenians, in addition, that their allies might desert them.

In addition to all this, a thirty-year truce between Sparta and Argos, one of Sparta's greatest rivals on the Peloponnese, was soon to expire. If Argos joined with Athens, Sparta might face their combined forces. Argos had remained neutral all the time that Athens and Sparta had been fighting for the past ten years, and during that time Argos' prosperity and its ambitions had grown. As Athens and Sparta continued to deplete their resources in their war, Argos saw an opportunity to become the dominant power in Greece. In these circumstances, both Athens and Sparta were now ready to talk peace.

With Cleon gone, Nicias was now recognized as the most successful general of his day and was at the height of his popularity. With his fellow general, Laches (about whom we will hear more later), they led the Athenian negotiators of a treaty of peace.

Nicias' Spartan counterpart in desiring peace was the Spartan king Pleistonax,[56] the son of the disgraced Pausanias, the Spartan general who had grasped for power at the end of the Persian War and who met his death outside of the temple of Athena in Sparta. Pleistonax had a history only slightly less complicated than that of his disgraced father. Around 445, during the so-called First Peloponnesian War, he led an invasion into Attica, but he inexplicably withdrew his forces and returned to Sparta without engaging in battle. His enemies accused Pleistonax of accepting a bribe from Pericles to withdraw his troops, and they forced him into exile. While he was away from Sparta, his enemies continued to criticize him, charging him with building a house on ground consecrated to Zeus.[57] Pleistonax was only able to come back to Sparta, his rivals charged, because he bribed the Delphic oracle to advocate for his return.[58] The Spartans were known for their religious devotion, and they believed that Pleistonax was cursed for these acts, and that his curse was the cause of all the disasters that Sparta had recently suffered during the war. Pleistonax, in these circumstances, was eager to restore his reputation and absolve himself of any curse by agreeing to a peace treaty.

The resulting "Peace of Nicias" ended the first act of the Peloponnesian War. This has also been called the "Ten Years War" after the length of time from its beginning in 431 to 421, and it is also sometimes called the "Archidamian War," after the Spartan king who unsuccessfully tried to prevent it. According to the provisions of the Peace of Nicias, each party would free its hostages and restore its conquests. Only Nisaea, the principal port of Megara, was excepted from this provision and would remain under Athenian control. In addition, the parties agreed to a mutual defense treaty. Athens and Sparta would come to each others' aid if either was invaded, and Athens would help Sparta in the event of a helot revolt.

The peace parties in both poleis had great hopes that this would be a first step in a lasting peace. Athens and Sparta decided in a single stroke to put aside all of their differences. If the Peace of Nicias had succeeded, a very different history than this one could have been written. Athens might have continued to grow culturally and commercially, gradually expanding its power over the populations of the Aegean and of the Mediterranean. Sparta, embracing its isolation from the rest of the world, would slowly fade into virtual insignificance, becoming merely a footnote in our ancient history textbooks. But this alternative history was not to be.

Almost immediately, serious issues threatened the fragile peace. The signing of a peace treaty did little to quiet the ambitions of the war parties or the conflicts that continued between the rival factions in either Athens and Sparta. Anger, suspicion, and distrust, nourished during ten years of war, did not easily dissipate. In both Athens and Sparta, numerous factions did everything they could to scuttle the agreement. In this uneasy environment, despite the terms of the treaty, Athens refused to give up Pylos, and the Spartan commander at Amphipolis refused to return that city to Athens. In addition, within months of the signing of the treaty, Athens' siege of Scione was finally successful, and the Athenians put to death every man in the city and enslaved the women and children.

Further threatening the Peace, Sparta's principal allies—the Corinthians, Boeotians, Eleans, Megarians—felt that the Spartans had abandoned them and decided not to recognize the Peace. Argos now saw the treaty between Athens and Sparta, as an opportunity to expand its power, and sent envoys to all of the Greek poleis who might conceivably have a grievance against Sparta proposing an alliance. After a confused scramble for allies among the Greek poleis, each of whom had their own specific interests, Argos ultimately succeeded in forming a new, anti-Spartan, Peloponnesian league consisting primarily of Sparta's neighbors Corinth, Mantinea, and Elis.

ALCIBIADES

In 420, Sparta, seeing the dangers that they now faced, sent envoys to Athens, hoping to strengthen the tenuous peaceful ties between the two former enemies. Once there, they met with members of the Athenian Council of five hundred—the administrative arm of the Athenian democracy. The major figure in the Council that day was Alcibiades, the leader of the war party in

Athens and one of the most fascinating, charismatic, and enigmatic figures in all of history. It is impossible in this day to unravel the tangled stories and fables that attach to his name and to uncover the true nature and motives of the man.[59] More than anyone else, his brilliant and erratic personality shaped the erratic trajectory of Athens' fortunes following the Peace of Nicias.

Alcibiades was the orphan of a war hero, Cleinias, who died in the Battle of Coronea during the First Peloponnesian War.[60] As an infant, Alcibiades was taken into the household of his uncle Pericles, where he was raised. As a youth, he was one of many young men who gathered around Socrates in the agora and listened as the philosopher questioned Athens' noblest citizens about the nature of justice, virtue, and courage. Alcibiades, however, was not born to be a philosopher like Socrates. Alcibiades embodied the best and the worst characteristics of a wealthy Greek youth of the classical era. He was extraordinarily beautiful and exceedingly wealthy, and found more joy in training his horses, which won prizes in the Olympic games, than in the sober pursuit of wisdom. Born under the curse of the Alcmaeonidae, he became known for his extravagant and dissolute lifestyle, which were soon overshadowed by his powerful driving ambition.

Figure 2.3. Alcibiades being taught by Socrates, Marcello Bacciarelli, c. 1776. *(Alamy Stock Photo)*

After Cleon's death, Alcibiades took on Cleon's role as the principal advocate for an aggressive policy toward Sparta, and he became Nicias' most prominent rival. Alcibiades resented that he had been excluded from the negotiations with Sparta that culminated in the Peace of Nicias. As a war hawk who had friendly relations with the Spartans, he believed that he was in a unique position to negotiate with them. Alcibiades declared that his family's relationship with Sparta dated back to even before Pericles' friendship with the Spartan king Archidamus II. Furthermore, Alcibiades had befriended the Spartan captives from Sphacteria who were imprisoned in Athens. Adding to all of this, Alcibiades likely saw himself as a natural successor to Pericles who was destined to lead Athens as Pericles had done. He had only been denied his rightful place at the treaty table, he believed, because, at thirty years old, he was perceived as too young for such an important role.

Harboring these resentments, when the treaty to ratify the Peace of Nicias first came before Assembly, Alcibiades spoke against it. He charged that the Spartans could not be trusted and that Sparta only wanted to make peace with Athens, while they fought against Argos, after which they would turn once again against Athens.

When the Spartan envoys arrived in Athens, in 420 in an attempt to strengthen the fraying ties between the two states, they met with the Athenian Council and announced that they came with full powers to negotiate all the remaining issues with Athens. Alcibiades led the discussions with the Spartan envoys in the Council. Feigning friendship with the Spartans, Alcibiades promised to help them and advised them to tell the Athenian Assembly that they did not have the authority to negotiate the status of Pylos, Amphipolis, and the Spartan alliance with Boeotia. The Spartans agreed to this, and the following day, before the Assembly, they denied having full negotiating powers, as Alcibiades had advised them. At this, Alcibiades now charged the Spartans with trying to deceive the Athenians, accusing the Spartans of saying one thing one day and something else the next. The Assembly was incensed by this news and was about to consider forming an alliance with Sparta's enemy, Argos, when an earthquake struck and ended the Assembly.

The following day, Nicias tried to repair the damage that Alcibiades' ploy had inflicted on the cause of peace. Nicias, in the Assembly, argued that friendship with Sparta continued to be in Athens' best interests and urged the Assembly to send a mission to Sparta to discuss the continuing issues between them. The Assembly agreed to this and appointed Nicias to lead a commission to Sparta. When Nicias arrived at Sparta, the Spartans were still incensed over the treatment of their envoys and refused Nicias' pleas. Nicias then returned to Athens with nothing to show for his efforts, and the Assembly "flew into a passion." Nicias was disgraced for the failure of the mission, and the Assembly agreed, at Alcibiades' urging, to a one hundred-year alliance with Argos, Mantinea, and Elis. Despite these events, neither the Athenians nor the Spartans rejected the treaty of peace established by Nicias the previous year. At least in theory, the Peace of Nicias still held.[61]

Sparta's fortunes, at this time, were at their lowest point during the Peloponnesian War. The Spartans' reputation as invincible fighters had been severely tarnished by the capture of their hoplites on Sphacteria. The treaty of peace with Athens and the subsequent treaty between Athens, Argos, Mantinea, and Elis, were seen by many throughout the Greek world as proof that Sparta had been soundly defeated. To add further insult, the polis of Elis, where the Olympic games were held, accused Sparta of breaking a treaty and banned all Spartans from competing in the Olympic games in 420, and when a Spartan illegally entered a team in the chariot races, and won, he was publicly whipped by one of the Olympic referees.

Throughout the summers of 419 and 418, Argive and Athenian forces marched through the Peloponnese while the Spartans did nothing. Both of Sparta's kings at this time had a reputation for avoiding battle. The Spartan king, Pleistonax, had negotiated the "Thirty Years Peace" with Nicias, and his counterpart, King Agis II, had twice set out with his army to face the Argive and Athenian armies, and twice turned back when his sacrifices gave unfavorable signs. Agis set out a third time, but before a battle began, he met with Thrasylus, the leader of the Argive forces, and the two men agreed to a truce. This enraged the soldiers in both armies. Everyone was ready for battle, and everyone believed that they were in the superior position and would be the victors. When Thrasylus returned home with his army, he was stoned by the angry citizens of Argos, and he was only able to save his life by fleeing to an altar. In Sparta, meanwhile, the populace initially decided to destroy Agis' house and fine him ten thousand drachmas, but ultimately chose to appoint ten monitors who were to attend the Spartan king and advise him in all future battles.

Agis' opportunity to redeem his reputation came in the final months of the summer of 418 at the Battle of Mantinea. Alcibiades had persuaded the Athenians to send an army of a thousand Athenian hoplites to join a larger Argive army. The united Argive and Athenian forces faced an army of Spartans and their few remaining Peloponnesian allies. The Spartans were veterans who had fought alongside Brasidas, along with a number of *neodamodeis*—helots who were freed by the Spartans in reward for serving in the army. Thucydides claims that these were the largest forces to engage in battle during the Peloponnesian War.[62]

Both armies drew up in battle formation, coming within a stone's throw from each other. The Spartans, led by Agis, were ready to attack when an old veteran in his army, seeing that the Argives were in the stronger position, called out to the king and warned him that he should not attempt to "cure one evil with another"—that is, he could not correct his poor past decisions with another poor and probably disastrous decision.[63] For a fourth time, Agis led a Spartan army off the field of battle in face of the enemy.

Agis spent the next day on a new plan. He ordered his soldiers to divert a river that marked a boundary between the Mantineans and their rivals the Tegeans. The Argives consequently came down from their high ground to prevent the diversion of the river. Agis' plan succeeded sooner than expected. The Spartans, just returning from the work of diverting the river, were surprised the following day when the Argive army suddenly appeared. The Spartan line, however, quickly formed.[64] Neither side had the time for the customary sacrifices before battle.

The Spartans, as we have seen, were famously reluctant to fight, despite their reputation as the most formidable warriors of the ancient world. Once engaged, the courage of the individual soldiers and their years of training and their battlefield order made them invincible. Spartan kings, although they had little power in deliberations in Sparta, once on the battlefield, their commands were absolute. Barking commands to his hierarchy of officers, his orders passed quickly from his warlords, to his captains, to the company commanders.

Typically, the first to engage the enemy were the *peltasts*. These were light infantry, named after their crescent-shaped shields. They had little armor other than their shields and had only javelins or, in some cases, only slings and arrows or stones which they threw at the enemy, and then ran quickly away. They were followed by the slow-moving heavily armed hoplites, named after their circular shields—called hoplites—which each one held on their left arm. The shield protected his left side and the right side of the man next to him. Each man thus crowded as closely as possible to the man on his right. Behind them were as many as eight more lines of hoplites, who pushed the lines in front of them forward. As the Spartans advanced slowly across the field of battle in their red cloaks, flute players followed behind playing tunes that kept each man at the pace and kept the lines from becoming uneven and disarranged.

Each army put their best units on their right flank—the position of most honor. These troops led the attack while the left flank held their defensive positions. As a result, two armies in battle typically revolved around each other in a counterclockwise direction. In battle, spears and swords clashed against defenders' shields, as the lines pushed forward and were pushed from behind. The critical moment in battle occurred when one army's right flank succeeded in overpowering their enemy's left flank, sparking a general rout of the defeated troops. Military cohesion was essential. A single individual who lost his courage and broke the line could cause the defeat of the whole army and the destruction of their city, the deaths of all the men, and the rape and sale into slavery of their wives and daughters.

Within this usual pattern of battle, anything might happen. On this day in Mantinea, the Argives ran straight into the Spartan line. They broke through the center and continued pushing as far as the Spartan supply wagons in their rear, which were defended only by old men. At the same time, the Spartan left flank fell back. Agis, however, moved his forces to close the hole in the line, and the Spartans were able to reform their lines. The Spartans soon gained the advantage and pushed against the Argives until the Argive line broke and fled in a panic. The Spartans pursued a short distance and then withdrew—avoiding the classic mistake of pursuing a defeated enemy, which might reform and turn on the advancing scattered army and turn their victory into a defeat.

As was the custom after battle, the Spartans, stripped their slain enemies of their shields and armor and pilled it all in a trophy, and they carried their dead off the field either to be buried or to be placed on a funeral pyre and their bones returned to their home cities. Typically, a battle was only over when one side signified their defeat by sending a herald to the other side asking permission for a truce to gather their dead.

If the Argives and the Athenians had won a victory at Mantinea, it would have given the Athenians an invincible position in Greece, permanently ending their conflict with their nemesis, the Spartans. Instead, the Battle of Mantinea essentially restored the status quo as it was established by the Peace of Nicias. Despite the fighting at Mantinea, the so-called Peace of Nicias still held. Following the Spartan victory, the Athenian alliance with Argos, which Alcibiades had put together, fell apart, and Sparta and Argos now signed their own treaty; Sparta's spirits and its reputation were revived; and the war between Athens and Sparta would continue for another fourteen years.

MELOS

Melos is an island in a strategic position about halfway between Athens and Crete in the Aegean Sea. As the war raged between Athens and Sparta, Melos claimed to be a neutral power. This, however, was unacceptable to the Athenians who, in 416, sent thirty-eight warships with 2,700 hoplites on board, to the island to compel it to join the Athenian empire.

When they arrived, the Athenian generals and the Melian magistrates held a conference at which the Athenians tried to convince the Melians to submit peacefully to Athenian rule. This confrontation between the Athenians and the Melians, as reported by Thucydides, is one of the most famous passages in his history of the Peloponnesian War. It has been excerpted in numerous college history textbooks and has provided the subject matter for generations of philosophers and political theorists. Its complex maze of logical and ethical conundrums serves as a foreshadowing to the next major event in Thucydides' narrative—Athens' invasion of the much larger island of Sicily.

The Athenians were blunt. The Athenians noted that the common people of Melos, who might be persuaded by an emotional speech, were not present. The Athenians, therefore, would not make an elaborate speech to the Melian magistrates. They told the Melians flatly that they must submit to Athens, or they would be destroyed.

The Melian magistrates were told that they must choose between submission or destruction based solely on the facts that they could see before them. Their decision should be based upon what was most practical, and they should not by persuaded by either flowery language or on abstractions of what was right or just. The Athenians told the Melians, "you know as well as we do that right, as the world goes, is only in question between equals in power, while the strong do what they can and the weak suffer what they must."[65]

The Melians were not persuaded by these words and told the Athenians that someday the tables might be turned, and Athens might be forced to make a similar decision, would they not then appeal to justice? The Athenians ignored this and claimed that a swift submission to their will would be best for both the Athenians and the Melians since neither side would then have to endure the hardships of a long siege. The Melians, especially, would not have to endure months of deprivation and starvation, which would inevitably end in their surrender to the stronger forces of the Athenians.

The Athenians justified their actions by saying that if they allowed Melos to remain neutral, Athens would appear weak, and any perception of weakness might lead Athens' allies to revolt. The choice was stark. Every state must be either a friend or an enemy. No state and no one could remain neutral.

The Melians countered this argument by saying that if Athens forced the Melians to submit to Athenian domination then all of the independent poleis in Greece would turn against Athens, fearing that eventually, Athens would turn on them and try to force their submission also. The Melians argued, as well, that in a war, nothing is certain. In the confusion of war, anything can happen, and while there was any possibility of remaining free, they should resist being enslaved by the Athenians.

The Athenians replied that the Melian's hopes were a delusion. Hope, they said was "danger's comforter." It was an emotion that is common to those who ignore what is before their eyes and put their faith in what is invisible. Only the vulgar riffraff believed in "prophecies and oracles, and other such inventions that delude men with hopes to their destruction."

The Melians persisted in their argument. They would trust that the gods would come to their aid since they were "just men fighting against unjust men."

The Athenians believed that this argument was ludicrous. They reiterated that justice was not at issue:

> Of the gods we believe, and of men we know, that by a necessary law of their nature they rule wherever they can. And it is not as if we were the first to make this law, or to act upon it when made; we found it existing before us, and shall leave it to exist for ever after us; all we do is to make use of it, knowing that you and everybody else, having the same power as we have, would do the same as we do.[66]

The Melians' final argument was that the Spartans, who were Dorians like themselves, would not allow their kinfolk to be destroyed and would come to their aid. The Athenians rejected this argument as well. The Athenians knew that the Spartans were not irrational. They could accurately evaluate the risks and the rewards, and they were not likely to leave their home on the Peloponnese and send a fleet of ships across the sea to fight against an Athenian armada.

The Athenian's arguments might seem irrational to a modern reader who might think that it would be to Athens' advantage to leave Melos as a neutral state. It would be better to recognize Melos' neutrality and not antagonize potential allies rather than to pursue a policy that would compel an infinite expansion of Athens' empire. Athens' arguments must have been even more shocking to his readers in the ancient world because they opposed every common belief and practice. The Athenians at Melos advocated a stark materialistic calculation of strengths, and weaknesses, which rejected all ideas of justice, of right and wrong, of the gods and prophecies, of friendship based on blood and ancestry, and even of hope itself.

The Melians, perhaps not surprisingly, rejected all of these arguments and refused to submit, and the Athenians began their siege of the city. Within months, as the Athenians predicted, the Melians were forced to surrender, and the Athenians put to death all the men of the polis and sold the women and children as slaves, and then sent out five hundred Athenians to colonize the island.

The fate of the Melians shocked most of the Hellenic world and inspired Euripides the following year, in 415, to write *The Trojan Women*, describing the horrors of war, in what some people have called the world's first anti-war drama.

NOTES

1. Kurt A. Raaflaub, "Warfare and Athenian Society," in *The Cambridge Companion to the Age of Pericles*, ed. Loren J. Samons II (Cambridge: Cambridge University Press, 2007), 96–124, "200 men on a trireme, includes rowers, officers, and *epibatai*, hoplites who fought on

deck. A trireme cost one talent to build and one talent to pay crew for one month" (98–99). Equals six thousand drachmas, drachma = average workman's day's pay.

2. Thucydides, 1.48–54.

3. The Athenians blamed the generals for offering too lenient terms to the inhabitants of the city, all of whom were expelled, and the city was subsequently colonized by Athenian citizens.

4. Thucydides, 1.69.4.

5. Thucydides, 1.75–1.76.

6. "The growth of the power of Athens, and the alarm which this inspired in Sparta, made war inevitable" (Thucydides, 1.23). "I consider the truest cause" of the war, "to be this: the Athenians were becoming powerful and inspired fear in the Spartans and so forced them into war" in Thucydides, *Thucydides: The War of the Peloponnesians and the Athenians* (*Cambridge Texts in the History of Political Thought*), ed. and trans. Jeremy Mynott (New York: Cambridge University Press, 2013), 1.23. "The Spartans . . . feared the growth of the power of the Athenians" (Thucydides, 1.88.1).

7. Key references to the "Athenian thesis" in Thucydides, 1.75–1.76, 3.37–3.40, 5.89, 6.85. A partial bibliography of works discussing the Athenian thesis (to 1998): Leo Strauss coined the term in *The City and Man* (Charlottesville: University of Virginia Press, 1964), 183. The Realist school of international relations claims that a nation is constrained by its relations vis-à-vis other states, dismisses humanitarian and political ideology from active role in inter-state relations. See Clifford Orwin, *The Humanity of Thucydides* (Princeton, NJ: Princeton University Press, 1994); Laurie M. Johnson, *Thucydides, Hobbes, and the Interpretation of Realism* (DeKalb: Northern Illinois University Press, 1993); Laurie M. Johnson Bagby, "The Use and Abuse of Thucydides in International Relations," *International Organization* 48, no. 1 (1994): 131–53, https://www.jstor.org/stable/2706917; Gregory Crane, Thucydides and the Ancient Simplicity: The Limits of Political Realism (Berkeley: University of California Press, 1998); Richard K. Ashley, "The Poverty of Neorealism," in *Neorealism and Its Critics*, ed. R. O. Keohane (New York: Columbia University Press, 1986), 255–300; James Der Derian, "A Reinterpretation of Realism: Genealogy, Semiology Dromology," in *International Theory: Critical Investigations*, ed. James Der Derian (New York: Macmillan, 1995), 363–96.

8. Thucydides, 1.144.2, 2.7.1, and 7.18.2. See Simon Hornblower, *Commentary on Thucydides* (New York: Oxford University Press, 1991–2008), vol. 1, 236ff.

9. Thucydides, 2.2–2.3, I have combined information from *The Landmark Thucydides: A Comprehensive Guide to the Peloponnesian War*, ed. Robert B. Strassler (New York: Free Press, 1996), based on Richard Crawley's translation (1874) and *Thucydides: The War of the Peloponnesians and the Athenians* (*Cambridge Texts in the History of Political Thought*), ed. and trans. Jeremy Mynott (New York: Cambridge University Press, 2013).

10. Thucydides, 2.65.7.

11. Thucydides, 1.144.

12. Thucydides, 2.65.

13. Thucydides, 2.65.

14. Nels M. Bailkey, ed., *Readings in Ancient History, Thought and Experience from Gilgamesh to St. Augustine*, 4th ed. (Lexington, MA: Cengage Learning, 1992), 195.

15. Bailkey, *Readings in Ancient History*, 196.

16. Bailkey, *Readings in Ancient History*, 197.

17. Thucydides, 3.104.

18. Diogenes Laertius, *Lives of the Eminent Philosophers*, ed. James Miller, trans. Pamela Mensch (Oxford: Oxford University Press, 2018), ix, 2.

19. Plutarch, *Plutarch: The Rise and Fall of Athens: Nine Greek Lives*, trans. Ian Scott-Kilvert. (London: Penguin, 1960), 214.

20. Thucydides, 5.16.

21. Thucydides, 4.42–45.

22. See the discussion of the Battle of Arginusae, below.

23. Thucydides, 3.36.

24. Plutarch. *The Rise and Fall of Athens*, 217.

25. Thucydides, 3.16.

26. Mytilenian debate, see Thucydides, 3.37–3.49.
27. Thucydides, 3.37.
28. Thucydides, 3.38.
29. Thucydides, 3.38.
30. Thucydides, 3.42.2.
31. Thucydides, 3.38.
32. Thucydides, 3.42.
33. Thucydides, 3.44.
34. Thucydides, 3.81.5.
35. Thucydides, 3.82.2. *Thucydides*, trans. Benjamin Jowett, 2nd ed. (Oxford: Clarendon Press, 1900), says "rough master." *Thucydides*, ed. Mynott, says "violent master." Others say "harsh teacher."
36. Thucydides, 3.82.
37. Thucydides, 3.98.
38. Thucydides, 3.107ff.
39. Summer 425 BCE.
40. Thucydides, 4.17.
41. Thucydides, 4.22.
42. Thucydides, 4.21–4.22 (425 BCE).
43. Later, Spartans made a proclamation offering freedom to those helots who claimed to have most distinguished themselves against their enemies. Knowing that those helots who claimed the distinction were the most high-spirited and most likely to rebel, the Spartans "soon afterwards did away with them" (Thucydides, 4.80).
44. Thucydides, 4.27.
45. Thucydides, 4.27–4.28.
46. A Trojan shield taken at Pylos is now on display at the Stoa of Attalos, Museum of the Ancient Agora, in Athens.
47. Thucydides, 4.40.
48. Thucydides, 4.65 (424 BCE).
49. 431 BCE, Thucydides, 2.25.
50. 424 BCE, Thucydides, 4.66–4.74.
51. Acanthus, 4.84–4.87.
52. Military histories of the battle include Victor Davis Hanson, *Ripples of Battle: How Wars of the Past Still Determine How We Fight, How We Live, and How We Think* (New York: Anchor Books, 2004), chap. 3; and Donald Kagan, *The Archidamian War* (Ithaca, NY: Cornell University Press, 1974), 281–304.
53. Plato, *Symposium*, 220d–221c, in Plato, *Lysis; Symposium; Gorgias*, trans. W. R. M. Lamb (Cambridge, MA: Harvard University Press, 1983), vol. 3 of 12.
54. Thucydides, 5.2ff.
55. Thucydides, 5.6–5.11 (422 BCE).
56. The Spartans had an unusual system of two hereditary kings, one of which would lead their forces in battle, while the other stayed in Sparta, thus ensuring that Sparta would almost never be without a regent. The real power in Sparta, however, was held by the oligarchic council, the Gerousia, the council of elders.
57. Thucydides, 5.16.
58. Pleistonax's returned to Sparta in 428 BCE.
59. Thucydides judgement of Alcibiades character evolved over the course of his narrative. Much of what follows is taken from Plutarch.
60. 447 BCE.
61. Thucydides, 5.48.
62. Thucydides, 5.64, 5.74.
63. Thucydides 5.65.
64. Thucydides, 5.66.
65. Thucydides, 5.89. See Hesiod: "Here is how the hawk addressed the dapple-throat nightingale as he carried her high in the clouds, grasping her in his claws; impaled on the curved talons, she was weeping piteously, but he addressed her sternly: 'Goodness, why are

you screaming? You are in the power of one much superior, and you will go whichever way I take you, singer though you are. I will make you my dinner if I like, or let you go. He is a fool who seeks to compete against the stronger: he both loses the struggle and suffers injury on top of insult'" (*Hesiod: Theogony* and *Works and Days*, trans. and intro. M. L. West [New York: Oxford University Press, 1988], 42–43).

66. Thucydides, 5.105.

Chapter Three

The Sicilian Campaign

SICILY

A great collision of the continents of Africa and Eurasia millions of years ago. A tremendous gurgling in the sea. Steam and then molten rock broke the surface of the waters forming the largest island in the Mediterranean. On a map, Sicily looks like a football at the end of the boot of Italy. Since ancient times, its location, moderate climate, and fertile fields have attracted people from all around the Mediterranean and beyond. Before the beginning of the iron age about three thousand years ago, wandering tribes from areas around the Mediterranean now inhabited by the modern nations of Spain, Turkey, and Italy settled on the island. The Sicels, Sicani, and Elymians, in, respectively, the east, middle, and west of the island greeted the Phoenician seamen who arrived around 1000 BCE and established trading posts on the northwestern coast, connecting the island with trading routes that from the Near East to the Atlantic Ocean. Mycenaean merchants from the kingdoms of Achilles, Agamemnon, and Menelaus visited the island, bringing word of it to the blind poet Homer. By the middle of the eighth century, during the great era of Hellenic expansion, Greek settlers arrived and established great cities that rivaled those on the mainland in size, population, and prosperity. After the Greeks, Sicily was dominated by the Carthaginians, Romans, Ostrogoths, Byzantines, Muslims, Normans, Spaniards, and French. Finally, in the nineteenth century, Sicily was absorbed by its neighbor Italy.

Sicily's ancient economy, based on fishing and the cultivation of wheat, olives, and grapes, has been augmented in modern times by manufacturing, industry, and tourism. Visitors from around the world visit Sicily's luxurious hotels and shops, play on its beaches, and visit its numerous historical sites. Sicily has seven World Heritage Sites identified by United Nations Educational, Scientific and Cultural Organization (UNESCO), including the Norman palace and castle in Palermo, baroque churches in Noto, Greek and Roman theaters in Taormina and Syracuse, the Roman mosaics at the Villa Romana del Casale, and Mount Etna, the largest active volcano in Europe. The most spectacular historical sites in Sicily, however, arguably, are the numerous Greek temples at Agrigento and Selunite. These are some of the largest and best-preserved classical Greek temples anywhere in the world. They stand today as silent witnesses to the great contests of empires in the ancient world.

When visiting Sicily, if you can see past the tourists and all the accretions of the modern world, you can imagine the lost mythological world of Homer and Hesiod. Coming to the island from the Italian mainland by ferry, you can see the rocks and swirling waters that the ancient Greeks associated with the sea monsters, the Scylla and Charybdis. Here, according to Odysseus' account,

> Scylla pounced down suddenly upon us and snatched up my six best men. I was looking at once after both ship and men, and in a moment I saw their hands and feet ever so high above me, struggling in the air as Scylla was carrying them off, and I heard them call out my name in one last despairing cry. . . . Scylla [placed] these panting creatures on her rock and munch[ed] them up at the mouth of her den, while they screamed and stretched out their hands to me in their mortal agony. This was the most sickening sight that I saw throughout all my voyages.[1]

At Mount Etna, you can imagine, Hephaestus, the Greek god of craftsmen and blacksmiths, working at his forge beneath the volcano. A local guide on the island might point out to you the actual spot where Hades abducted Persephone and brought her down to the underworld. Another might show you where King Minos was murdered after pursing Daedalus to Sicily when Daedalus famously escaped from his prison on Crete, on wings made from feathers and wax.[2]

Thucydides, and later the Sicilian historian, Diodorus Siculus, give us our first glimpses of Sicily's history without such mythological stories.[3] They tell us that the first Greek colony on Sicily was Naxos on the eastern coast of Sicily. This was the first port on the island where a ship coming from Greece would find harbor. Naxos was founded around 734 BCE by an Athenian named Thoucles who led a party of settlers from Chalcis on Euboea, a polis fifty miles north of Athens. The following year, a Corinthian named Arcias founded the colony of Syracuse. In the next few years, both settlements expanded and established new colonies. Naxos established Ionian-speaking colonies across the north and east coasts of Sicily, while Syracuse expanded its influence over Dorian-speaking colonies along the southern coast.

The first thing one notices when visiting Syracuse is the beauty of its wide harbor. For Arcias, the most notable thing was probably the protection it offered ships from both storms at sea and from possible enemies.

The north end of the harbor is closed by the island of Ortygia, the commercial, political, and ceremonial center of Syracuse. The freshwater fountain of Arethusa on Ortygia made the island a natural fortress able to withstand the longest siege. Today the shops, restaurants, and homes on the narrow streets of Ortygia probably look much like they may have looked in the classical era. The most significant differences are that one of Ortygia's major temples is now a picturesque archaeological ruin in the middle of a high-end shopping area, and the columns of another Greek temple are embedded in the walls of a baroque eighteenth-century cathedral.

Across a narrow channel from Ortygia is the outer city. This area, which is now a commercial district in the modern city, in the ancient era contained houses, shops, an amphitheater, an agora, and an imposing statue of Apollo Temenites. Beyond that, to the south and west were marshes, and to the north was an extensive network of deep quarries—the source of stones for the city's temples and other buildings. And beyond that was the great plateau, Epipoli (literally on or above the city), which would play a major role in the Athenian attempt to take Syracuse.

TYRANNY OF GELON

Syracuse, like most Greek city-states (*poleis*) in the seventh and sixth centuries, was ruled by a succession of tyrants. Scholars see this age of tyrants as a transitional phase from the closed societies, dominated by local aristocratic landowners, to the later broader-based political systems, either oligarchic or democratic or a combination of both, which arose at the beginning of the fifth century. The tyrants were essential in organizing societies during in a period of rapid economic and urban growth and prepared the way for more democratic systems by eliminating their rival aristocratic families.[4]

The most famous tyrant of Syracuse was Gelon. His career began as a commander of the cavalry in the Sicilian city of Gela. When the tyrant of Gela died, Gelon assumed his position, and when the people of Syracuse rebelled against their aristocrats, Gelon crushed the revolt and took power for himself. From this position, he launched a succession of raids which brought most of eastern Sicily under his control.

Gelon moved the wealthiest citizens in all the territories that he conquered into Syracuse. At the same time, he forced all the common people and the indigenous Sicel population to work as slaves in the fields and orchards, growing wheat and olives. These crops were exported to Italy and the Peloponnese making Sicily renown as the granary of the Mediterranean. Gelon and his brother, Hiero, who succeeded him, expanded the port at Syracuse to facilitate this trade, and also built temples and a theater that attracted more people to the city.[5]

Gelon and Hiero made Syracuse a major cultural center as well. The tyrants supported the cults of the major Greek gods and made offerings to the Delphic oracle. They won chariot races in the Olympics. They welcomed poets, dramatists, and philosophers into the city, and their accomplishments were celebrated in plays by Aeschylus and poems by Pindar. Soon, Syracuse was the premier city in the western Greek world, rivaling the size and power of Athens.[6]

All of Greece recognized the power of Gelon in Syracuse. When Xerxes, the Persian emperor, invaded Greece in 480, Athens and Sparta sent a delegation to Syracuse pleading with Gelon for his help in defending Greece from the barbarians.[7] Gelon agreed and promised to send two hundred *triremes* and twenty thousand *hoplites* to defend Greece, but only if he was given command of all the Greek forces. The Athenians and the Spartans rejected this offer, and Gelon offered as an alternative only that he would command of all the land forces. The Spartans, who were the supreme Greek force on land, quickly refused the offer. Gelon then offered to command only the naval forces, and the Athenians, the dominant Greek force on the sea, refused. The disappointed emissaries left, having accomplished nothing.

Either by plan or by coincidence at the same time that Xerxes invaded Greece, the Carthaginian king, Hamilcar, invaded Sicily. For five hundred years the Carthaginians were the greatest commercial and naval power in the western Mediterranean. According to Diodorus, as Xerxes led his army and navy toward mainland Greece, Hamilcar brought three thousand ships with three hundred thousand men from north Africa to Sicily. Gelon faced him with an army of perhaps only fifty thousand men and surprisingly defeated him at the Battle of Himera. Hamilcar and most of his men died in the battle. Diodorus' story of a Sicilian victory over the Carthaginians at the Battle of Himera was generally thought to be a legend, but it was confirmed in 2008 when workmen, building a railroad line near the site of the ancient battle, found mass graves containing the skeletal remains of more than ten thousand men and thirty horses along with weapons and armor. Ancient sources equated Gelon's victory over Hamilcar at Himera with Themistocles' victory over Xerxes at Salamis, believing that they both happened on the same day. Together the two victories were said to have saved Greek civilization, from Persia to the east, and from Carthage to the west.

Diodorus claims that despite his harsh rule, the people of Syracuse loved Gelon. They praised him for his wise and fair rule, and credited him with bringing order, prosperity, and fame to the city. After the Battle of Himera, Gelon distributed the spoils of battle, including many enslaved Carthaginian captives, equally among his allies. This windfall financed the building of magnificent temples throughout Sicily, and especially in Agrigento, where their ruins today attract thousands of visitors each year. Diodorus notes that "Gelon after the battle received greater approbation every year at the hands of the Syracusans, grew old in the kingship, and died in the esteem of his people."[8]

Gelon's brother Hiero, who succeeded him, followed many of Gelon's policies, and continued to expand Syracuse's power and fame. Hiero consolidated Syracuse's power over Naxos and Catana by moving their Ionian populations to Leontini and replacing them with friendly Dorians, and he led Greek forces against the Etruscans in southern Italy, saving them from Etruscan rule. He was also a patron of artists and writers, including the dramatist, Aeschylus and the poet Pindar, who wrote an ode praising him.

Hiero, as well, followed the typical Greek pattern of tyrannies that collapsed after their popular founders died. Hiero was described by Diodorus as "avaricious and violent,"[9] and he was hated by the people of Syracuse. When Hiero died, he was succeeded by a third brother, Thrasybulus, who was even more disliked. He was "a violent man and murderous by nature," and his rule ended when the people of Syracuse rose up against him and established a democracy.[10]

SYRACUSE'S DEMOCRACY

The Syracusan democracy, like that of the Athenians, vested all power in the Assembly, but, unlike Athens, there was no upper council that set the agenda. In Syracuse, as in Athens before Cleisthenes, daily business was generally handled by a committee of *archons*. (Times when there were no archons were called anarchies). The Syracusans in their Assembly voted for their archons, who were chosen only from the wealthiest families. This differed from the Athenian system in which, after the reforms of Cleisthenes, archons were selected by lot from the body of all citizens. The Syracusans also adopted a form of ostracism similar to that in Athens. They called their system *petalism* because instead of using broken shards of pottery (*ostracons*) they used the leaves (petals) of olive trees. Syracuse eventually abandoned this practice, however, when they found that it discouraged too many prominent people from participating in civic affairs.

The rise of democracy in Syracuse, after many years of living under a tyrant, did not lead to social stability. The mercenary army of the tyrants was not disbanded after the tyrants left, and conflict between them and the common people of the city raged for many years. In addition, persistent social inequality (as in most Greek poleis) split a popular faction (the *demos*) and the elite (the *oligarchs*).

Shortly after the rise of democracy in Syracuse, a popular leader, named Tyndarides, emerged and challenged the power of the oligarchs. Tyndarides, who Diodorus described as "a rash fellow, full of effrontery," was accused by the oligarchs in the city of trying to gain supreme power and was seized and killed along with many of his supporters. According to Diodorus, "this sort of thing happened time and again."[11]

The end of the rule by tyrants, also opened an opportunity for many Sicel slaves, who had fought alongside many Syracusans in the opening days of the democracy, to restore the original population in Catana. One Sicel slave, named Ducetius, used his leveraged his leadership in that battle to lead some Sicels to create their own short-lived state. At first, he had the support of many Syracusans, but they turned against him as his power increased and he led his army of followers to create a large state in the interior of Sicily, which became a haven for runaway slaves. Syracuse and Acragas soon became alarmed by Ducetius' growing power and led a combined force against the Sicel state. Ducetius' forces won an initial engagement but were ultimately defeated in a second engagement in 450. Ducetius was captured in the battle and brought to Syracuse, but he was able to escape from his captors and he fled to an altar and claimed sanctuary. The Assembly in Syracuse debated whether they should seize him in the sanctuary and kill him but eventually voted to banish Ducetius forever from Sicily. Ducetius soon afterward, however, returned to Sicily and set up another colony of Sicels and Greeks, which for a brief time dominated much of the northeast of the island. His state fell apart, however, after he died from an illness in 440.[12]

Another consequence of the fall of the tyrants is that it left the shaky democracy to try to reconcile the conflicting interests of its mixed population of old and new citizens and of the mercenaries and the elites from Syracuse's conquered cities. These factions kept the law courts busy deciding among the competing claims between the previous and more recent occupants of houses and land. As a result, many Syracusans became skilled in arguing cases before the law courts and the Assembly. Their skills in oratory and rhetoric shaped an emerging class of teachers and philosophers known as *sophists*, many of whom found their way to Athens, where they nourished the early roots of the western philosophical tradition.[13]

In addition to all of this, the end of the tyrants' rule in Syracuse had significant consequences for the whole of Sicily and beyond. It created a period of unstable relations among all the major states in Sicily, which were closely watched by the Greeks on the mainland, and especially by many Athenians who saw it as an opening to some promising opportunities.

EARLY EXPEDITIONS TO SICILY

The great expedition to Sicily of 415 through 413, which is a focus of this book, was actually Athens' third attempt to subdue the island.[14] The first came about in 427 when Syracuse attacked its neighbor, the city of Leontini, which lay about twenty miles to the north. Many of the Leontini population were the poorer people of Naxos who spoke the Ionian dialect, and who had been transported there by the tyrant Hiero. As Ionians, they were the natural allies of Athens. When they were attacked, therefore, the Leontini appointed a delegation led by the sophist, Gorgias, to go to Athens to ask for help. His mission was successful in two ways. The Athenians agreed to come to the aid of Leontini, and Gorgias decided to stay in Athens after his mission where he taught, spreading the ideas and techniques of the sophists to the Athenians.[15]

The ties of culture and of language were important in Athens' decision to come to the aid of the Leontini. Moreover, the Athenians had reasons other than just tribal or ethic loyalty for supporting the Leontini. Probably more important was Athens' observation that Sicily was a natural competitor in the rivalry among Greek states. Its timber was essential to ship building in the western Mediterranean, and its wheat was an essential part of the diet of the populations of Italy and the Peloponnese.

With these considerations in mind, the Athenian Assembly decided to answer the appeal of the Leontini, and they appointed two generals, Laches and Charoeades, to go to Sicily with twenty ships to support the Leontini. We know almost nothing about Charoeades, who died soon after arriving in Sicily. We know more about Laches, however. As mentioned above, after the death of Cleon in 421, Laches worked with Nicias to establish a truce with Sparta which led to the Peace of Nicias.[16]

When Laches and Charoeades arrived at Sicily, they decided to divide their forces. Laches sailed south and quickly ran into an enemy force, losing a ship in the engagement. Charoeades, meanwhile, sailed north, where he also met an enemy force. Charoeades was not as fortunate as Laches, however, in the battle he received a wound that shortly proved fatal.

Laches, now as the sole commander of the Athenian forces, ran up success after success. His first act was to turn north to the south Italian city of Rhegium, which was a long-time ally of Athens. There he was able to add get reinforcements and add ten more ships to his fleet.[17]

From his base at Rhegium, Laches made raids on the Aeolian islands and overran "with great slaughter" the Syracusan fortifications at Mylae on the northern coast of Sicily. Marching with the captured soldiers from Mylae, he proceeded to Messana, on the northernmost tip of Sicily, which surrendered without a fight.[18] Laches thus controlled the critical straits of Messana, through which grain and timber passed on the way to the Peloponnese.

Laches secured the loyalty of his Rhegian allies by fighting with them against their enemies in the neighboring Italian polis of Locri, during which he captured five Locrian ships. Laches also formed alliances with many Sicel slaves who revolted against their Syracusan masters. With this force of Sicel slaves, Laches attacked the Sicel city of Inessa, which was being held by a Syracusan force.[19] Although this attack was unsuccessful, the Sicel forces were valuable allies of Laches in successive fighting on the island.

As it happened, while Laches was fighting in Sicily, the annual election of generals took place in Athens, and, despite Laches' success in taking Messana and building alliances with Rhegium and with Sicel slaves, the Assembly decided to remove Laches from command. To take his place, the Assembly sent out three new generals, Pythodorus, Sophocles (not the great playwright), and Eurymedon, along with another forty ships. The Assembly had perhaps not heard of Laches' victories but they had heard that the Syracusans were busy building their own navy. The Assembly decided to send this second great armada, as Thucydides says, to give their ships' crews exercise. Laches learned that he had been removed from command when he returned to Rhegium and found Pythodorus waiting for him with news of his dismissal. This was the first in a series of decisions by the Athenian Assembly that would, step by step, lead their attempt to control Sicily to disaster.

To this point, the city of Syracuse had mostly been on the defense, but with the removal of Laches and with their new fleet of ships, they now moved to the offense. The Syracusans responded to the removal of Laches by quickly orchestrating a revolt in Messana that allowed them to regain the critical control of the straits. Coming to the aid of Locri, the Syracusans took back a fort previously overrun by Laches and engaged the combined forces of Athens and Rhegium in a battle at sea, which only ended when nightfall forced both sides to withdraw. Fighting between the Syracusans and their Locrian allies and Athens and Rhegians continued over the next few days in a series of bloody conflicts for control of the straits of Messana, and then spread from there to the neighboring polis of Naxos. In these battles, the Athenians were aided by the Sicels who had been befriended by Laches, who attacked by land, while Athenians attacked by sea. Nevertheless, by the end of 425, the military situation in Sicily was a virtual stalemate.

Throughout this time, while the Syracusans fought the Athenians, a general state of war existed among most of the other Greek states in Sicily. These conflicts generally pitted the Dorians against the Ionians (see maps 1 and 2). Two Greek states in Sicily, however, attempted to remain neutral. The Dorian cities of Camarina and Gela, on the southern coast of Sicily, had been untouched by most of the fighting, and in the summer of 424, they invited the other states to join them at an assembly in Gela to discuss a general truce among all of the Greek states in Sicily.

At the Assembly, the Syracusan general, Hermocrates, spoke. Thucydides called him "the most influential man" in Syracuse, and in fact, his long shadow would fall over much of Syracuse's history over the next two decades.[20] Very early, Hermocrates recognized that Athens represented a threat not only to Syracuse but also to all of Sicily, and he realized that Athens' greatest advantage in a struggle over the island was Sicilian disunity. Hermocrates warned the delegates from the cities of Sicily that they were all in danger if the Athenians were victorious and he pleaded with them to put aside their differences and establish peace among themselves. The rivalry between Ionians and Dorians, he said, should be put aside, claiming "we are neighbors, live in the same country, are girt by the same sea, and go by the name of Sicilians."[21] His speech won over the Assembly, and the cities, including even those who were the Ionian allies of Athens, agreed on a treaty of peace.

Confronted now with a unified Sicily, the Athenian generals in Sicily realized that their mission was a failure, and they sailed for home.

Back in Athens, many people were not happy with this turn of events. Rumors spread that the Athenian generals had been bribed by the Syracusans to leave the island. Coincidentally, it happened that news of the failure of the Athenian mission in Sicily reached Athens shortly after the capture of the Spartans on Sphacteria, and many Athenians expected that the Sicilian mission should have been equally successful. The Athenians felt that their success in Sphacteria was a sign that they were invincible, and they would not be satisfied now with anything other than more great victories. As a result, they blamed their generals for their failure to conquer Sicily. Eurymedon was fortunate in getting off with a heavy fine, while Pythodorus and Sophocles were banished from Athens.

Thus ended Athens' first attempt to subdue Sicily.

A second attempt, in 422, was similarly fruitless. In the years following the conference at Gela and the departure of the Athenians, the cities of Sicily once again began to fight among themselves. In Leontini, a popular party had grown in influence and considered a plan to redistribute the land, taking it from the aristocrats and dividing it among the common people. When the aristocrats heard this, they reacted swiftly. Calling on Syracuse for help, they drove the commoners from the city, "tore down its buildings and walls, and moved to Syracuse where they became citizens." Despite the destruction of the city, the Leontini aristocrats, with the help of Syracuse, continued an ongoing war against the dispersed Leontini population.[22]

Athens saw these events as further evidence of Syracuse's growing power and, at the same time, they saw these events as a new opportunity. Consequently, they sent the Athenian general, Phaeax, to Sicily to seek a coalition of Sicilian states against Syracuse in defense of the Leontini people. Phaeax succeeded in reaching agreements with the Dorian cities of Camarina and

Acragas, but Gela refused to join. Recognizing that without Gela, the mission was a failure, Phaeax returned to Athens. This ended the Athenians' second mission in Sicily.

THE FIRST YEAR OF THE EXPEDITION

The Beginning of the Great Expedition to Sicily

A few years later (in 416/415), envoys from Sicily again appeared in Athens asking for help. This time they were from Egesta (modern-day Segesta) in northwestern Sicily. The Egestans were Elymoi, one of the three major indigenous groups in Sicily. According to legend, they escaped from Troy as it fell to the Greeks and sailed from there to Sicily. They had been at war for many years with its much wealthier Greek neighbor, Selinus (modern-day Selinunte). (A sense of their comparative wealth perhaps can be seen today in the one temple that still stands in Segesta and the five remains of temples in Selinunte.)

The Egestans claimed that they had supported Laches when he led his expedition to Sicily, and that they could not sustain themselves against Selinus and its ally Syracuse. The Egestans in Athens warned that if Athens did not come to their aid, all of Sicily might come under Syracuse's control, and a united Sicily would inevitably become ally with Sparta, tipping the balance of power against Athens.

If this did not convince the Athenians, the Egestans, despite their poverty, promised that they would pay for an Athenian expedition to come to Sicily. The Athenians were skeptical, but finally decided to send representatives to Egesta to assess the situation and to find out if Egesta was really wealthy enough to support an Athenian campaign in Sicily.

When the Athenian envoys came to Sicily, they came to the Elymian city of Eryx, on Sicily's western coast. In Eryx, they saw the temple of Aphrodite, and they saw its rich collection of silver bowls, wine-ladles, and censers. The Athenian envoys and their ships' crews were entertained at sumptuous banquets where food and wine were served in gold and silver cups. When the envoys returned to Athens, they brought with them sixty talents of silver (enough to pay for sixty ships operating for one month[23]) and stories of the Egestans' enormous wealth. Only much later, the Athenians learned that the Egestans had scoured the countryside, borrowing their valuable cups from near-by Phoenician and Greek settlements, and that the great wealth of the Egestans was largely a mirage.[24]

Back in Athens, the envoys gave their report to the Assembly, which quickly voted to approve an expedition to aid the Egestans and to restore Leontini, and, ambiguously, "to order all other matters in Sicily as they should deem best for the interests of Athens."[25] The Assembly chose three generals to lead this expedition, Nicias, Alcibiades, and Lamachus.

The surprising choice of these men to lead the expedition was based on the idea that the cautious Nicias and the bold Alcibiades would be balanced by the less-distinguished Lamachus, who would act as a mediator between the two more eminent generals. Lamachus was well known as an aggressive general, eager to take risks, but because he came from a poor family, he would always defer to Nicias and Alcibiades.

Shortly after this Assembly, a second meeting was called to discuss preparations for the expedition. Nicias was the most prominent leader in Athens at this time, but the younger Alcibiades, despite the failure of the Mantinea campaign, was a powerful rival. The contest between these two men and their followers would have significant consequences. In this second meeting of the Assembly, Nicias tried to convince the Athenians to reverse their decision to send an expedition to Sicily. There could be no real benefit to Athens, Nicias argued, in supporting the "barbarian" Egestans. He warned that aiding the Egestans was merely a pretext on the part of some Athenians to expand Athenian involvement in all of Sicily. The island was too far for Athens to send and supply a military force, and if Athens were successful in controlling part or all of Sicily, Athens would not be able to maintain its power in the distant land. In addition, the peace treaty with Sparta, which he had negotiated, was fragile, and any action might lead Sparta to repudiate it. If they did, then Athens would have to fight a war on two fronts—one in Greece and one in Sicily.

Although Nicias did not name Alcibiades directly, he criticized him sharply. Nicias denounced "any man here [who is] overjoyed at being chosen to command . . . especially if he is still too young to command."[26] The reference to Alcibiades was unmistakable. Alcibiades was about twenty years younger than Nicias. In 415, Alcibiades was about thirty-five—the youngest an Athenian could be elected as a general. In addition, Nicias accused the younger man of excessive pride and ambition. He claimed that Alcibiades hoped to profit from a command that would enable him to pay for his lavish lifestyle, and particularly to pay off debts that he owed for maintaining his horses. Nicias closed by asking the Athenians to vote a second time and to reject this "mad dream of conquest. Let the Sicilians resolve their own problems, they are no concern of Athens."

Alcibiades now rose to speak. He did not deny the charges against him of pride, ambition, or of having an extravagant lifestyle. These characteristics, he claimed, brought fame not only to himself and to his ancestors, but also to the city. His victories in the chariot races at the Olympic games brought credit to all of Athens. His wealth and position might be envied by some of his fellow Athenians, but to foreigners, they were signs of Athens' strength. He argued that his putting together a coalition against Sparta, even though it led to its defeat at Mantinea, showed his strong leadership and he claimed, as well, that the battle had weakened Sparta.

Alcibiades, furthermore, conceded that he was young, but claimed that his youth, combined with Nicias' experience, would bring success to their venture. Young and old must unite and bring together "levity, sobriety, and deliberate judgment."[27] With words such as these, Alcibiades showed that he had learned the lessons of the sophists of making the lesser arguments appear the stronger, turning negatives into positives, and criticisms into cause for praise.

Alcibiades then turned to pleading in favor of the Athenian expedition to Sicily. He claimed that the Sicilians were a "mob, and a "motley rabble" with no stable governments and no sense of patriotism. They were in constant conflict with each other, and that each faction could, therefore, be played off against the other and be defeated one by one, and in these conflicts, Athens could depend on the native Sicels as allies. Furthermore, there was no need to fear that Sparta might intervene. Sparta would be deterred from involvement in Sicily for the same reason that Nicias was—the difficulty of supplying an army at such a distance from Greece.

An Athenian campaign in Sicily, furthermore, would demonstrate Athens' power, and intimidate its enemies in the Peloponnese. Athens, Alcibiades said, could not choose to rest and could not accept the status quo. "We cannot fix the exact point at which our empire shall stop; we have reached a position in which we must not be content with retaining but must scheme to extend it, for, if we cease to rule others, we are in danger of being ruled ourselves."[28] Each new struggle, each fresh experience, would make Athens stronger. Action, not inaction, Alcibiades said, defined the character of Athens.

Nicias, realizing that Alcibiades' words had won over the Assembly and that the Assembly continued to support an invasion of Sicily, now reversed his argument. He proposed sending an even larger force than Alcibiades or anyone had yet considered, hoping that the Athenians would see that the costs of a war would be too high and that the Assembly would reverse its decision. It would be shameful, he said, if Athens sent out a force that might later require reinforcements or have to leave Sicily without a victory. The Assembly, therefore, should send out a massive force of soldiers, archers, and slingers, along with a cavalry and horses. Athens must maintain its superiority at sea with an imposing fleet of ships. It must ensure a supply of wheat and barley, along with bakers to feed its soldiers. In addition, the Athenians should bring as much money as possible to win over allies and to purchase supplies. Nicias advised that the expedition should become the masters of the field on the first day. The Athenians should leave nothing to chance and avoid the whims of fate.

Nicias hoped his words would make the Athenians rethink their rash decision to go to war. The effect of his speech made the populace, who were inspired by this vision of a great and invincible army, even more determined than before to send an army to Sicily. Nicias' speech had made the endeavor seem like a great adventure. Young men, who had no memory of the war before the Peace of Nicias, were excited by the dreams of glory, valor, and of military conquest. Older men believed that an army such as described by Nicias would be successful. The poor people of Athens, meanwhile, saw opportunities for wages as soldiers. And those who thought that an expedition to Sicily was folly were afraid that they would appear unpatriotic if they spoke, so they kept quiet. The tide to war was irresistible.

Nicias' strategy of persuading the populace through reverse psychology was a failure. Without knowing it, although Thucydides writing after the fact probably did, Nicias' speech was a catalog of all the errors that would lead to Athens' failure in Sicily.

As he had years earlier, before the expedition to Sphacteria, Nicias offered to resign his command and to let someone else take his place. This time, no one came forward.

Now, the Assembly asked Nicias specifically what was needed for the war. Nicias made a list. Athens would need to send out one hundred triremes and 5,000 hoplites in addition to archers, slingers, and supply ships. In explicably, Nicias failed to include horses. Perhaps, he thought they would take up too much room on the Athenian warships and could be purchased in Sicily. It proved, however, to be a critical omission. The Athenian Assembly at once agreed to Nicias' recommendations, and preparations began. Muster rolls were drawn up and posted in the agora, and messengers were sent out to Athens' allies to prepare for the expedition.[29]

The Destruction of the Hermes and the Defaming the Mysteries

As Athens was preparing for war, a striking event occurred in the city. At night, all the stone statues of the god Hermes, which guarded the homes and temples of the Athenians, were mutilated. These statues were typically stone posts with a tapered square base, some of which stood as tall as a man. On the top was the bearded face of the god, and at a distance below was an erect phallus.

The god Hermes, like all the Greek gods, took many forms. Most notably, he was the messenger of the gods, a mediator between the physical world of human beings and the metaphysical world of the gods. Standing between two realms, he was also a god of boundaries. As such, he marked the boundaries between homes and temples, and between public and private space. At the meeting place between worlds, Hermes' image with an erect phallus, appear-

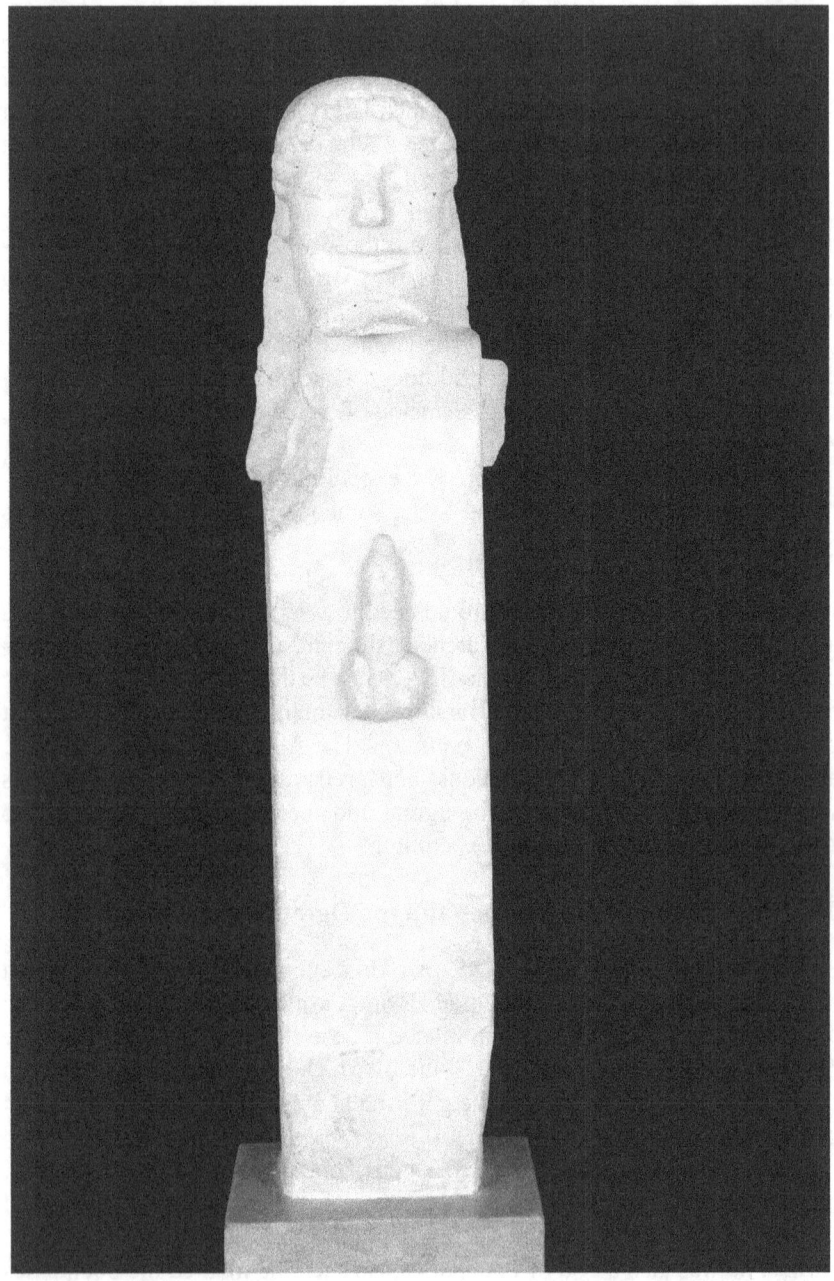

Figure 3.1.   Archaic Marble Herm from Siphnos c. 520 BCE. *(Courtesy of the Hellenic Ministry of Culture and Sports/Hellenic Organization of Cultural Resources Management and Development)*

ing on statues, vase painting, and other art, defined a boundary between tumultuous human desires and the immortal order of the gods.[30]

Soon after the discovery that the Hermai had been mutilated, an Athenian named Pythonicus came forward and charged that certain individuals had met at a private party where they ridiculed the Eleusinian mysteries. These mysteries were some of the oldest and most sacred rituals that had been celebrated in Greece since before the time of Homer.

These events, the mutilation of the Hermai and the defamation of the mysteries, were very serious matters. They represented a fracture in the sacred and the social order that initiated a turbulent period in Athens in which panic, fear, and distrust reigned throughout the city. A maelstrom of accusations, rumors, and lies swept through the city. Before it was over, dozens of people were condemned to death, and many fled the city. The consequences of these events would ricochet for many years to come.

One of the great legacies of ancient Athens to the modern world is the idea that human beings can use reason to understand the world without the intermediaries of supernatural beings and forces. The Eleusinian mysteries remind us, though, that the Greeks did not embrace the rationalism that would be a hallmark of the Western world. Their lives were dominated by the inscrutable cycles of life and death that were common to all agricultural societies.

For the Greeks, these cycles were embodied in the mythological figures of the two goddesses, Demeter and Persephone. In the myth, Demeter's daughter, Persephone was picking flowers in a meadow with some of her divine friends when Persephone became separated from the others. When she picked a narcissus, a flower associated with Hades, the god of the underworld, the ground suddenly opened up, and Hades burst forth riding in a golden chariot and kidnapped the terrified young god. Hades brought Persephone to his dark kingdom and made her his queen. This caused her mother, Demeter, in grief over her lost child, to leave Olympus, the home of the gods, and to search the world for her daughter.

In the earliest known version of the myth,[31] Demeter wandered over the earth and ultimately arrived at Eleusis, where she sat down near the Maiden's Well, and took on human form as an old woman. One day, the daughters of the king of Eleusis came to the well to fetch water, where they met Demeter, who told them that she had escaped from Cretan pirates who intended to sell her into slavery. This story and her dignified appearance won the sympathy of the girls, who brought her to their home and employed her as the nursemaid of their brother, Demophon.

Demeter, having lost her immortal daughter, now began to mold the infant Demophon into an immortal god. She denied him milk and food; she breathed on him with her divine breath; she rubbed him with ambrosia; and at night she placed him in a fire to burn off his mortal aspect. Every day, he grew more and more like a god.

Demophon's mother, however, one night spied on Demeter, and seeing her son burning in the fire, cried out in horror. Demeter suddenly, in a frenzy, threw the child to the ground. His chance at divine immortality ended.

Revealing herself now in her true form as the goddess, Demeter, she commanded that a temple and altar be built for her and gave specific instruction for rituals that must be performed and never divulged to others. There, in her temple, she sat grieving for her daughter and seething with anger at the stupidity of humans, she commanded that the earth would not be fertile. No seed would germinate. Oxen would pull their plows through the barren earth. This caused a great famine that brought all humans to near extinction when Zeus intervened. The great god recognized that if the humans perished, the gods would not receive their sacrifices, and sent his messenger, Hermes, down to the underworld to persuade Hades to release Persephone. Hades reluctantly agreed, but before he released Persephone, he cunningly fed her a pomegranate seed. The pomegranate with its many seeds was rich in mythological meaning to the Greeks, and consuming any food in the underworld, according to the Fates, prohibited anyone from leaving.

This taste of food prohibited Persephone from an eternal return to her mother and committed Persephone to spend part of every year in the underworld, while allowing her to spend the remaining part of the year among the gods. The joyful reunion of Demeter and her daughter ended the great famine and established the cycles growth and decay and life and death.

This myth was ritually reenacted in the autumn every year as men, women, and even slaves participated in the various stages of the story. The rituals began with several days of fasting, prayers, and sacrifices in Athens. Then in the morning, the participants left in a procession from the city gates along the sacred way to Eleusis. A priest carried a wooden statue likely representing the god Dionysus, the god associated with wine, drunkenness, and spiritual awakening. When the celebrants arrived at Eleusis later that day, they rejoiced with dancing and festivities. Here at Eleusis, they could see the original well where Demeter met the daughters of the king of Eleusis, and they could see the entrance to a cavern, cleft in the rock of the acropolis, containing a small temple, which was said to be the entrance to the underworld itself. The following day they fasted, consuming nothing except a special potion of water, barley, and mint, the drink that Demeter consumed while in human form in Eleusis, and which some say may have had psychotropic powers.[32]

On the final day, they entered the Telesterion, a large temple, which was built on the site of an ancient Mycenaean-era temple, and which had already been built and rebuilt multiple times in the ancient era.

During the years of the Periclean Age, the Telesterion was one of the largest buildings in the Greek world. In the front, a columned portico led to a cavernous room approximately two hundred feet square, with eight levels of seating carved out of the rock of the hillside. The building could hold an estimated three thousand people. In its center was the Anaktoron, or sacred chamber, which only the high priest could enter and which held the sacred objects of the cult. From this space, the priest and priestesses conducted the ritual ceremonies, the details of which were and have remained a mystery ever since. Revealing what was said or done during the ritual, was punishable by death. Probably these rites were a reenactment of the Demeter/Persephone myth, climaxing with the return from the dead and the reunion of the mother and daughter.

The significance of the ritual and the myth have been endlessly interpreted and hotly debated. Scholars have noted their similarities to other myths of the Earth Mothers of Neolithic cultures, and of Middle Eastern gods such as Adonis and Osiris, who die and are reborn, and their associations with seasonal agricultural cycles.[33] Beyond this, they remain, as their name indicates, mysteries. It is certain, however, that these ceremonies had a profound impact on the participants, many of whom experienced a sudden emotional and spiritual awakening. A door to a new understanding was opened to them. Similar religious experiences are common to most, perhaps all, cultures. In the specifically Eleusinian experience, they were associated with a release from the fear of death and a sense that the underworld held no torments for them. For those who experienced these mysteries, it marked an important event in their lives. As initiates in the cult, they gained a special status that transcended all divisions of class, gender, or ethnicity.

THE SEARCH FOR THE CONSPIRATORS

The mutilation of the Hermai and the defaming of the Eleusinian mysteries caused a great commotion in Athens. Some saw these events as a bad omen for the expedition to Sicily. Perhaps they were merely the acts of "young men in a drunken frolic."[34] Perhaps, however, they were part of a larger conspiracy to prevent the fleet from sailing on the Sicilian expedition, or even as part of a plot to overthrow the democracy.

Very quickly, eyes turned toward Alcibiades. Following the defeat in Mantinea, and his argument with Nicias and the Assembly over the Sicilian campaign, he had many enemies in Athens. In addition, his lavish lifestyle and arrogance marked him as someone with little regard for traditional morality. Pythonicus charged him explicitly before the Assembly and questioned his leadership of the Sicilian campaign declaring: "Countrymen, you are sending forth this mighty host in all its array upon a perilous enterprise.

Yet your commander, Alcibiades, has been holding celebrations of the Mysteries in a private house, and others with him; I will prove it."[35]

Judging from the number of reports that surfaced in the following days, performing the mysteries in a private house, either in serious devotion or as frivolous entertainment, was probably a common occurrence. Either way, it was likely to reveal the mysteries to the uninitiated and was, therefore, prohibited by law on pain of death.

A commission was immediately established and given extraordinary powers[36] to establish the truth in both the matters of the Hermes and of the Eleusinian mysteries and any other acts of suspected impiety. The commission, working in close collaboration with the Council, offered amnesty and a reward of one thousand drachmas, soon raised to ten thousand drachmas, to anyone with information.[37] The commission and the Council consisted of some of the most notable citizens of Athens. We can wonder how impartial the commissioners were because three of them were later accused of involvement in the crimes that they were investigating.[38]

Witnesses quickly came forward. Pythonicus, himself brought a slave named Andromachus to testify. Andromachus said that he saw Alcibiades and nine others perform the mysteries and that a flute player and several other slaves were also witnesses.

Another witness who came forward was a *metic* named Teucris. He probably offered the most accurate source of information since he implicated himself in the illicit performance of the mysteries.[39] He had fled Athens soon after the beginnings of these events but was persuaded, probably not very politely, to return to testify. He revealed the names of twenty-nine others who he said were guilty of crimes. Eleven of them had defamed the mysteries, and eighteen more were involved with the mutilation of the Hermes. One of those who he accused in the affair of the mysteries was the Athenian Diognetus, who was one of the commissioners.

A third witness was Agariste, the wife of the Athenian Alcmaeonides.[40] She claimed that Alcibiades and two others had performed the mysteries in the house of Charides. A fourth accuser, a slave, named Lydus, named four more. One of them was Leogoras, whose son, Andocides, according to Thucydides was "thought to be the most guilty of all."[41] Leogoras admitted that he had indeed attended a performance of the mysteries, but claimed in his defense that he was asleep with his cloak over his head during the night's entertainments.

The sounds of horses' hoofs thundered throughout the city as those who were accused quickly scattered. Others, who learned too late that they were on someone's list, were apprehended and summarily executed. By this time, the city was in a complete panic. Whenever a flag was raised signaling a new meeting of the Council, the agora emptied as people fled the marketplace, afraid that a new round of accusations and arrests was about to come.[42]

As bad as the situation in Athens was, things were about to get much worse.

What had begun as an inquiry into the mutilation of the Hermes, expanded into a general pursuit for evidence of any kind of impiety. The investigation was pursued most avidly, according to Thucydides, by the enemies of Alcibiades, who magnified every rumor, hoping to discredit him, and to claim the leadership of the popular faction.

At this point, the hunt for evil-doers took a new turn as a man named Diocleides came forward with a story so detailed and so incredible that it was instantly believed. He had, he said, awakened early on the night of the destruction of the Hermes. He had business at the silver mines at Laurium some twenty miles distant, where he needed to collect the wages of his slave who worked in the mines. When Diocleides passed the theater of Dionysus, at the foot of the Acropolis, he could see clearly by the light of a full moon, about three hundred men, in groups of five and ten and twenty. Not certain what was going on, he crouched behind the pedestal of a statue and watched for a while before continuing his journey to Laurium. He returned to Athens the next day to find the city all in a fury over the destruction of the Hermes. Putting two and two together, he conceived a plan to benefit himself from the situation. He went to the house of one of the conspirators, a man named Euphemus, and offered his silence for a price. Diocleides said that Euphemus and three others agreed to this bargain and offered him two talents of silver (substantially more than the tent housand drachmas offered by the city).

Euphemus and his fellow conspirators, however, failed to deliver the promised two talents, and Diocleides brought his accusations to the Council and named a total of forty-two alleged conspirators. Two of them, Mantitheus and Apsephion (like the already mentioned, Diognetus) were members of the Council itself. These two, hearing their names, hurried to take sanctuary on a sacred hearth, and appealed to the Council to be tried in a court of law. The Council agreed to release the two on receipt of a bond—probably not money, as we would expect, but individuals who would stand in for the two should they not appear for the trial. As soon the bonds were approved and Mantitheus and Apsephion were freed, they mounted their horses and made off for the border.

The Council was now in complete uproar. One of the Council members offered the radical proposal that the ancient law prohibiting the torture of Athenian citizens be revoked, and that all those who Diocleides implicated should be arrested before nightfall and be racked on the wheel. Upon hearing this proposal, Thucydides noted, "the Council broke into shouts of approval."[43]

The Council, in addition, declared martial law. All Athenian citizens were "to proceed under arms" to places of internment in the agora, and at the Piraeus (the harbor), and inside the Long Walls, which connected Athens with the Piraeus. The chief magistrates of the city meanwhile, gathered for protection on the Acropolis, and in the meeting place of the Council, and in the temple of Demeter and Persephone.[44]

All those who had been named and who had failed to leave the city were quickly imprisoned and as "darkness fell, and the gates were shut. Mothers, sisters, wives, and children had gathered. Nothing was to be heard save the cries and moans of grief-stricken wretches bewailing the calamity which had overtaken them."[45]

Many Athenians feared that the city was in real danger from an aristocratic plot, and some believed that aristocrats in the city planned to open the city gates in the middle of the night and allow Spartan force to enter. These fears were realistic. The Pisistratids had been removed and Cleisthenes had come to power with the help of a Spartan army in 510. Later on, in 411 and in 404, members of the Council would be involved in attempted coups and would appeal to Sparta for help.

A few days after this, when things had calmed down a bit, Diocleides was hailed as the savior of the city. A garland was placed on his head, and he was taken by ox cart to a feast in the Council chambers.[46]

What we know of all these events comes chiefly from one of the men accused by Diocleides. Andocides, the man who Thucydides said, was "thought to be the most guilty"[47] was able to avoid a death penalty but was expelled from Athens. Several years later, Andocides returned to the city and during a trial on an unrelated matter, he gave his side of the story. His narration of events was almost as unbelievable as that of his accuser, Diocleides. Not surprisingly, Andocides claimed his innocence. In his testimony in court, Andocides admitted that he was part of a social club (a *hetaireia*) that was responsible for destroying the Hermes. He had argued with other members of the club, however, against vandalizing the Hermes, and on the night in question, he was in bed as a result of a fall from his horse, which broke his collarbone and fractured his skull. To confirm his testimony, he offered to let his slave be tortured under examination.

When Andocides was brought to prison to stand trial, after the destruction of the Hermes, according to his testimony, at first he planned to say nothing. His family members who had also been accused, convinced him to plead for clemency and tell the Council what he knew. Posed with betraying either his friends or his family, Andocides decided to save himself and his family from a certain death and named the members of his social club who he believed were the culprits. His list of the guilty parties, however, included only those who had already fled or been executed.

The Council, after hearing Andocides' story, now belatedly recalled that there was no full moon the night of the Hermes' mutilation. Suspicion now turned toward Diocleides, who was summoned before the Council, where he admitted that he had lied and was promptly executed. Now that the affair was apparently resolved, Andocides and Pythonicus, the original accuser, both applied for the rewards which had been offered by the Council. The Council, however, denied them rewards, granting instead ten thousand drachmas to the slave, Andromachus, and one thousand drachmas to the metic, Teucris.

This seems to have satisfied most of the people in Athens, and those who had earlier fled the city were welcomed back. The consequences of these events, however, lingered for years, and many questions were never answered (and are still the source of academic arguments). Almost all of our information comes from two sources; Thucydides, who in this instance seems less than forthcoming about what he might have known, and Andocides, who was clearly a self-interested party. Despite the apparent resolution of the charges and the return to Athens of some semblance of tranquility, the cloud of lies and counter-lies still hangs over these events and obscures whatever the truth might have been.

Throughout all of these events, Alcibiades, the principal target of many of the accusations, denied any involvement, and asked that he be tried at once, saying that, if he were found guilty, he should be put to death immediately. His many enemies in Athens realized that if Alcibiades were put on trial, he would likely win over the support of the people, and, with the backing of the army, he would be acquitted. His enemies, therefore, held back. Meanwhile, they plotted and waited for their opportunity.

The Fleet Sails

As these events occurred, preparations for the expedition to Sicily continued, and about mid-summer, the fleet was ready to sail. At dawn on the appointed day, nearly all the populace of Athens and the surrounding countryside came down to the Piraeus to see their friends and loved ones off. This was the largest and most expensive force any Greek city had ever sent out. It surpassed in size and magnificence the campaigns of Pericles, and, it was said, even the legendary expedition to Troy. Sixty triremes and forty supply ships, all of them lavishly decorated, waited in the harbor. As the soldiers gathered, each soldier compared his arms and equipment with those of others. The festive mood seemed more like a celebration of the city's power and wealth than a preparation for war.

When everything was ready, a trumpet signaled silence. Every man and woman in the crowd now confronted their mixed emotions of hope and fear, saying goodbye to their friends and loved ones for the last time, or until they returned home in victory. The seriousness of the undertaking now struck them with a force more powerfully than when they had voted for it in the Assembly.

A herald led the amassed population in prayer. A hymn was sung. Libations were mixed in ceremonial vessels. And the ships, at last, moved out to sea. At first they followed each other in a single column, but once outside the harbor, they raced each other down the coast to Aegina. From there, they sailed around the Peloponnese into the Ionian Sea to Corcyra, where they joined the many supply ships that had already gathered.[48]

The Athenian fleet with their allies by now numbered 130 triremes, plus an equal number of men-of-war and troopships. One ship carried forty horses—not nearly enough for what lay ahead. The ships carried over five thousand Athenian hoplites, along with several hundred Argive allies, mercenaries from Mantinea, and some lightly-armed infantry, archers, and slingers.

Several dozen supply ships followed the fleet carrying cooks and grain for baking bread, and carpenters and masons for building fortifications, plus an untold number of ships carrying merchants who planned to trade with the soldiers for their daily wants.[49] We know as well that the fleet included numerous of slaves and women who provided a variety of services for the soldiers, but Thucydides says virtually nothing about them.

In Syracuse

Meanwhile, news of the coming expedition gradually filtered into Syracuse. At first, no one could believe it. Soon, however, the Assembly was called to discuss the reports, and Hermocrates once again came forward. A dozen years earlier, at the conference at Gela, Hermocrates had been able to unite the Sicilians when they were threatened by the Athenians led by Laches and his armada. Once more, he appealed for resistance to Athens. He told the Assembly at Syracuse that the reports that the Athenians were coming were true. Furthermore, he declared that the Athenians were coming not just to aid the Egestans in their conflict with Selinus, nor to restore Leontini. These were just pretexts, Hermocrates warned, to Athens' primary goal, which was the subjugation of all of Sicily.

Hermocrates urged Syracuse to begin preparations for the Athenian invasion. The Athenian armada, he said, posed a threat to every Greek polis on the island. Syracuse, therefore, should ask for help from all the poleis in Sicily, and from their Dorian kinsmen in Corinth and Sparta, and even from their frequent enemies in Carthage.

Hermocrates warned of the great dangers that confronted Syracuse, but he was optimistic that Syracuse could, if they acted swiftly, prevent a catastrophe. He said that the Athenian fleet would be traveling a long distance across the Ionian Sea between Greece and Sicily. The Athenians, he said, would necessarily be spread out, and a fleet of Sicilian ships could attack the dispersed detachments of Athenian ships. Hermocrates told the Assembly that he had received word that Nicias, the principal Athenian commander, had initially rejected the command and he would not be eager to fight. If the Syracusans were courageous and acted now, they could avoid a disaster.

After this speech, many in Syracuse were still not convinced. Some made jokes ridiculing Hermocrates for stirring up fear. The most vocal critic of Hermocrates was Athenagoras, the reputed "leader of the people" at Syracuse. Athenagoras dismissed Hermocrates' warnings. The Athenians, he said, were too smart to attempt such a grandiose expedition, especially not while they were still engaged in a conflict with Sparta in Greece. Athenagoras accused Hermocrates of manufacturing a threat so that he could take over the government and end the Syracusan democracy. Athenagoras claimed that Hermocrates believed that only aristocrats were wise enough to make decisions and were fit to rule. Hermocrates, Athenagoras said, wanted the common people to fight and suffer from all the hazards of war, while the rich enjoyed all the benefits and profits of war.[50] As events would soon prove, Athenagoras, while perhaps an astute social critic, had a very poor understanding of the Athenian threat.

One of the Syracusan generals now came forward trying to find common ground. He urged the Syracusans to be united and not to fight among themselves. If the reports of an Athenian invasion were wrong, he said that there was nevertheless no harm in making preparations. Syracuse, he said, should in any event build their defenses and acquire arms and horses just in case. The Assembly in Syracuse agreed with these words and slowly began to prepare.

Meanwhile, the Athenians, who had gathered at Corcyra, sent out three ships in advance of the main fleet to meet with their allies at Egesta. The rest of the ships followed a few days later across the Ionian gulf to Tarentum, inside the heel of Italy. From there, they followed the coast south planning to trade with their Italian allies for provisions. None of the cities of Italy, however, wanted to commit to helping the Athenians, and they shut their city gates and closed their markets. Even the polis of Rhegium, which had always been friendly to Athens, now claimed neutrality. When the Rhegians forbade the Athenians to enter the city, the Athenians, nevertheless, set up a camp outside the city walls and waited for word from the three ships which had been sent out earlier to Egesta.

By this time, Syracuse had definite reports that the Athenian force was on its way and finally began to make preparations in earnest. They set up garrisons around the city, sent merchants around the country to purchase arms and horses, and appealed to the native Sicels for aid.

The three ships sent to Egesta now returned with only thirty talents—only a fraction of what they had promised. The Athenians were coming to realize that they had been deceived by the Egestans who were too poor to support the Athenian expedition. Alcibiades, Lamachus, and the soldiers were disheartened by this turn of events. Only Nicias, apparently, was not surprised by this—the first of many calamitous events, which he had foretold.[51]

Now, the three Athenian generals conferred and began to make serious plans. Each one advocated a different strategy, and each one angrily insisted that his plan was the best. Nicias proposed sailing straight to Egesta and Selinus, the original reason for Athenian involvement. At Egesta, the Athenians would demand more of the money that they had been promised for the expedition. The Athenians would then use either diplomacy or force to settle the conflict between the Egestans and the Seluniti. They would then sail around the coast of Sicily to make a display of Athenian power, and having achieved their original mission, they would return home.

Alcibiades' plan was more ambitious but was also cautious. He proposed sending heralds to all the Greek cities in Sicily, excepting Syracuse and Selinus, to secure allies and acquire military aid and provisions. Alcibiades proposed concentrating on Messana, at the northern tip of Sicily, since it controlled the trade and communication between Sicily and Italy. The Athenians could use Messana as a base to attack Syracuse and Selinus. At the same time, the Athenians would encourage the Sicels to revolt.

Lamachus' plan was simple but more aggressive than either Nicias' or Alcibiades'. He advised sailing straight to Syracuse and attacking the city while the Syracusans were still unprepared They would hit the enemy while the Athenian troops were fresh and well-provisioned, striking panic in the enemy. They would take the city, and then force alliances with the rest of the Greek cities on Sicily.

Perhaps any one of these plans would have been successful if consistently followed. Unforeseeable events, however, have a way of disrupting the best of plans.

In the debate between the generals over the best course of action, Nicias' words were no match for Alcibiades' powerful personality, and the junior officer, Lamachus threw his support to Alcibiades' plan. Nicias then had no choice but to give in to the arguments of his fellow generals.

Alcibiades thereupon sailed with some ships to Messana. Alcibiades would later gain a reputation for his unerring military strategies, but this time his efforts to win over the Messanians failed.

The Athenians now decided to send a fleet down the eastern coast of Sicily past Naxos and Catana to Syracuse. At Syracuse, the Athenians ships made an elaborate display of their powers, sailing in single file into the Great Harbor while heralds called out to citizens in the city that the Athenians planned to restore Leontini. The Athenians observed the Syracusan defenses and sailed to back to Catana, having accomplished little other than to inspire the Syracusans to move more energetically to prepare for war.

At Catana, a strong pro-Syracusan party prohibited the Athenians from entering the city, but the people in the city allowed Alcibiades to address their Assembly. While Alcibiades was speaking to the enrapt Assembly, some Athenian soldiers broke through a poorly constructed city gate and entered the marketplace. Seeing the Athenian soldiers in the city, the pro-Syracusan party, fearing for their lives, fled the city. In their absence, the Catanan Assembly voted to ally with the Athenians, and invited them to move their base from Rhegium and to establish their camp at Catana.

The Recall of Alcibiades

While these events were happening in Sicily, in Athens the witch hunt for those responsible for the destruction of the Herms and the profaning of the mysteries was at its peak, and with Alcibiades out of the city, his enemies now saw their chance. In Alcibiades' absence, they spread stories implicating Alcibiades in these crimes. His enemies soon convinced the Athenians to order Alcibiades' return to Athens, where, without the protection of his army, he would be tried, and almost certainly convicted and executed. The Assembly sent out envoys in the trireme Salaminia, which along with its sister ship, the Paralus, were the official ships of the Athenian state. These were the fastest ships in the Aegean. Their crews were highly trained and highly paid and were responsible for carrying out the most important official missions of the Athenian polis.

The envoys on the Salaminia were directed not to arrest Alcibiades. His arrest would throw the army in Sicily into an uproar, and Mantinea and the Argive allies of Athens, who only came on the Sicilian expedition out of loyalty to Alcibiades, would likely defect from the army. The envoys were instructed instead to request Alcibiades return with them to stand trial.

Alcibiades agreed to the envoys' request, saying that he would return with them to Athens following the Salaminia in his own ship. Alcibiades understood, however, that the outcome of a trial in Athens was already predetermined. An Athenian jury would quickly condemn him and sentence him to death. Before the two ships left Italian waters, therefore, Alcibiades slipped away from the envoys.

Several weeks later, Alcibiades surprisingly appeared in Sparta, where he offered his services to the Spartan state. Alcibiades brought with him complete knowledge of Athens' strategy as well as his own formidable talents as a general. When the Athenian Assembly learned that Alcibiades had joined their enemy, they sentenced him to death in absentia.[52]

First Engagement

With Alcibiades gone, Nicias was now the senior commander of the Athenian forces, and Lamachus followed his decision to follow a cautious plan.

The first order of business was to visit Egesta to collect more funds to support their campaign.

On their way along the north coast of Sicily, the Athenians attacked Hycara, a fishing village near present-day Carini, where they quickly overcame all resistance and enslaved all the inhabitants. At Egesta, the Athenians were disappointed when the impoverished Egestans provided only another thirty talents. The Athenians' disappointment faded, however, when they sold the slaves they had captured at Hycara for 120 talents.

(Among those taken captive was a seven-year-old girl named Lais. She was bought by a Corinthian who brought her to Greece where she became a famous *hetaera* and had many lovers. She was noted for her extraordinary beauty and especially for her breasts, which attracted artists from all of Greece to paint her figure. It was said that the orator, Demosthenes, offered one thousand drachmas for a night with her, but when she saw him, she raised the price to ten thousand drachmas. She gave her favors for free, however, to Diogenes, the Cynic Philosopher. Lais met her end in a common Greek fashion. Great beauty, as well as great accomplishments, were not always rewarded in ancient Greece, and Lais was stoned to death by women in Thessaly who were jealous of her beauty.[53])

Nicias and Lamachus now returned to their base at Catana and discussed what to do next, meanwhile in Syracuse, many people were eager to confront the Athenians. Sensing that the Athenians were reluctant to fight, the Syracusans grew bolder and urged their generals to move against the Athenians at Catana. The generals, in response, sent their cavalry out to the Athenian encampment. The Athenians who lacked cavalry of their own could only watch from the city wall as the Syracusan horsemen rode around the Athenian camp and shouted insults, calling out to the Athenians asking whether they had come to Sicily to settle or to fight.

Nicias and Lamachus soon agreed on a clever plan. They sent a man who was a native of Catana to Syracuse, where he said claimed that many people in Catana were friends of Syracuse and were willing to betray the Athenians. The Athenians, he said, slept inside the city walls, but they kept all their arms in the camp outside the city. If the Syracusans attacked the Athenians at daybreak on a certain day, men inside of Catana would shut the city gates preventing the soldiers from getting their arms. The Syracusans could then destroy the Athenian camp and burn the Athenian ships in the port.

Syracuse's generals needed no convincing. During the night, they marched their army toward Catana, forty miles distant. The Athenians, knowing the Syracusans were coming, loaded their troops onto their ships and sailed down the coast to Syracuse. The Syracusan army reached the outskirts of Catana when they learned that the Athenians had left the city and were moving on Syracuse. They immediately turned around and marched back to Syracuse, where they found the Athenians firmly entrenched in a hastily built fort by the Great Harbor south of the city.

The next day both sides prepared for battle. The Athenians formed their traditional *phalanxes*, eight men deep. In their rear, they formed a hollow square of soldiers, also eight men deep, to protect their supplies and their camp followers, and ready to assist the front line if necessary.

The Hoplites

Every Athenian soldier had been in preparation for this moment, and for the possibility of his death in battle, for virtually all of his life.

We often forget that ancient Athens, which gave us the first written histories and the foundations of Western democracy, philosophy, and art, was essentially a warrior society. The citizen-farmer of Athens was also a hoplite warrior instilled with a warrior ethic and motivated by the twin desires to gain honor and to avoid shame. His character was often defined on the battlefield, and his greatest flaw was not, as often thought, *hybris* (excessive pride), but rather cowardice. The story of the mother who told her son to return from battle "with his shield or on it"—that is with his corpse carried home atop his shield—was familiar to all ancient Greeks.

The common soldier in Athens was proud of his rights as a citizen of a democracy, and this gave him reason to fight. With his own money, he

Figure 3.2. Hoplite Phalanx, detail from the Chigi Vase. Attributed to the Hirschfeld Workshop, c. 750–735 BCE. *(Alamy Stock Photo)*

bought the arms with which he went to war—his shield, spear, sword, chest plate, greaves, and helmet. These arms and armor were a symbol of his rights and privileges as a citizen of Athens.

Nevertheless, Athenian democracy did not foster individualism, and it is difficult to escape Thucydides' frequently expressed sentiment that the common citizens of Athens were driven by a herd mentality. Under arms, this was a good thing and was essential to a cohesive, disciplined fighting force.

No army in history, perhaps, had this fusing of individual will and group function more than the Greek hoplite phalanx. Facing the enemy, men stood in a tight-knit formation; each man pressed close to the man next to him, shoulder to shoulder. Each man held his round shield on his left arm, protecting his left side and the right side of the man standing beside him. If any soldier was a weak link in this human chain—if he became terrified and broke rank—the whole phalanx could collapse. A lost battle in the ancient world commonly meant the destruction of the city, the slaughter of the men, the rape of the women, and the selling into slavery of all the women and children. The safety of the polis thus depended on each man subordinating his individual will to the welfare of the community.

The cohesion of the hoplite phalanx was often reinforced by the homosexual ties of older men and their adolescent lovers, with whom they who sometimes fought side by side. The older man was a mentor to the younger, teaching him, among other things, skills essential in battle, and the mutual affection of the lovers and their desire for each other's respect were further inducements to bravery. (On vase paintings, the pairing of bearded men with his unbearded young lover is a common theme [see fig. 1.1].)

The social cohesion of the polis was defined, as well, by its spaces and buildings. Ancient Athens had very few private spaces. Virtually every act was performed in full view. Even the most elemental of bodily functions were carried out in public. Archaeologists have excavated numerous communal latrines in ancient cities. These were generally long stone slabs with dozens of holes for the ejection of human waste. The Cynic philosopher Diogenes, it is said, in his attempt to live in accord with nature, urinated, defecated, and masturbated in public. These acts probably drew much less attention from his contemporaries than they would to us today.

The Greek idea of bodily functions and of the body generally differed dramatically from that of the modern world. There was no modern "mind/body problem" in the ancient world before Plato. There was no inner essence of a person's "real nature" that was separate from his physical body. The classical Greek ideal, which found expression in the numerous statues of Greek athletes, was a harmony of body and of mind, and a union of the external and of the internal.[54] His character was defined by his actions and by his relations with other people. Character was, thus, not an internal unchanging quality but was only revealed over time, and a good death was the final defining event of a good life.

To the Athenian, death was a constant presence. On his farm, he butchered goats, sheep, and pigs for food. To predict future events or to understand present ones, he cut open the chests of birds and inspected their internal organs.

Greek history, literature, drama, and religion almost all have as a central theme the Greeks' encounter with death. The first great epic, *The Iliad*, is a virtual encyclopedia of the ways that men die in battle. Virtually every page depicts the slaughter of men. These deaths were not abstractions. Homer gives us the names, often with a short biography, of each of the victims, and he frequently gives very precise descriptions of the anatomical details of their deaths. A couple of examples:

> Meriones caught him quickly, running him down hard and speared him low in the right buttock—the point pounding under the pelvis, jabbed and pierced the bladder—he dropped to his knees, screaming, death swirling round him.[55]

> As Tros grasped his knees, desperate, begging, Achilles slit open his liver, the liver spurted loose, gushing with dark blood, drenched his lap and the night swirled down his eyes as his life breath slipped away.[56]

According to a well-known story told by Herodotus, death was not only inevitable but to be welcomed. He tells the story of the meeting of Solon, the wisest man in the world with Croesus, the wealthiest man in the world. Croesus asked Solon: who was the happiest man he had ever seen? Croesus clearly expected Solon to reply that it was he, Croesus, who was the happiest man. Solon, however, replied that the happiest man was an Athenian named Tellus. Croesus was astonished by this response and asked why Tellus was the happiest of men? Solon replied that Tellus came from an eminent city, he had good and noble children, he died a glorious death in battle, and he was commemorated by his countrymen with the honor of a public funeral.[57] Upon further questioning by Croesus, Solon listed several others who had died well, and concluded, "Call no man happy until he is dead."[58]

Death did not hold out the hope of an afterlife of eternal bliss for the Greeks, as it did for the Egyptians and Persians.[59] When Odysseus visited the underworld, he saw the zombie-like inhabitants of the darkness who lacked all of the characteristics of willful, living beings. There they flew wildly around aimlessly, screeching in the dark.[60] The soul of the dead Achilles, temporarily given speech, declares he would rather be the slave of a poor farmer than rule in the kingdom of the dead.[61]

The Greek underworld, it seems, was more like a Christian purgatory than a hell. It had no eternal torment, no burning fire. It was mostly the negation of all the characteristics common to life. The idea of not living in the physical world was beyond the imagination of most Greeks.

The physical world of the Greeks blended in gradual degrees into a spiritual realm of gods and spirits. The Greeks did not imagine a transcendent idealized world of divine ethical beings. The world of the gods was very much like their own. Zeus and his large family lived in a world of the senses, experiencing loves and hates, adventures and disappointments, just as their human counterparts. The ideal beings had only one great advantage over humans. They were immortal.

For the Greeks, the end of life and the passage from this world to another, as in almost every society, was a significant event, which required the performance of certain rituals. The earliest Greek vase paintings of the Archaic Era illustrate some of their ancient burial customs—the preparation of the body, and of women wailing and tearing their hair.

Many of these customs continued into the classical era, when they were described by Thucydides in the passage immediately preceding Pericles' funeral oration.[62] He described how the bodies of the war dead were cremated and their bones brought to Athens where they were laid out in a tent where friends and relatives could bring offerings. The bones were then placed in

Figure 3.3. Image of Prothesis (laying out of the dead) and a chariot race. From a terra cotta funerary plaque c. 520 BCE. *(Courtesy of the Metropolitan Museum of Art New York)*

cypress coffins—ten of them, one for each tribe, plus another empty coffin representing those whose bodies could not be recovered. These were transported in carts to "the most beautiful suburb in the city" (probably the ceramicus, just northwest of the agora)—where, after much wailing by the women, and after an address by an important figure, they were laid in the ground.

It was very important, therefore, to retrieve the body of a fallen warrior. The *Iliad* recounts the fierce struggle to rescue the body of Patroclus so that he could be given the proper funeral rites. In both the *Iliad* and *The Odyssey*, spirits of the dead (Patroclus in the *Iliad* and Elpinor in the *Odyssey*) plead to have their bodies recovered and buried with the appropriate rituals. Greek literature and drama provide numerous other examples of the importance of these rites. In Sophocles' play, for example, Antigone's passionate attempt to properly bury her brother, Polynices, results in her death and the deaths of two others.

If these rituals were not observed, the spirits of the deceased would fail to be accepted in Hades and would wander in a nether land and might bring misfortune to those who inhabit the physical world.[63]

It was perhaps thoughts of these things which passed through the minds of the hoplites as they lined for battle.

The First Engagement Continued

Across the field from the Athenians stood the Syracusan army formed sixteen deep. The Syracusan soldiers were mostly conscripts who had been quickly enlisted in a mass levy of the inhabitants of the town and countryside and had little training, but they were supported by a cavalry of 1,200 men and horses. Each side as well had a number of light infantry. These men generally could not afford the armor of a hoplite. They had only rocks, slings, and arrows for weapons, and had little organization and less discipline.

On both sides, the generals exhorted the soldiers with short speeches, and soothsayers made the appropriate sacrifices and delivered their prophecies. Before the sides met, the light infantry of each army ran toward each other and made wild charges and then retreated, to make counter-charges, and again retreat. The hoplites in their ranks probably saw little of this through the narrow slits in their helmets, and with their bronze armor weighing up to seventy pounds, were incapable at any rate of engaging them.

Trumpets sounded and the Athenians began to move forward singing their *paean*. Some of the Syracusan hoplites had not expected the Athenians to advance so soon and had gone into the town. As both forces moved forward, the Syracusans quickly returned to the field and found their places in line.

Whatever brought each of the individual soldiers to the field beside the Great Harbor before the city of Syracuse, at this moment, was now forgotten.

The two sides joined. Long spears jabbed into the wall of the opposing soldiers. For a long time, both sides held fast. Metal met flesh, cries and grunts rang out. Soon storm clouds rolled overhead. It began to rain, and the noise of the battle was accompanied by claps of thunder and flashes of lighting.

As the storm in the sky mirrored the struggle on the ground, the Argives on the right of the Athenian line began to push back the Syracusan left, which then broke, each man running to save himself. Seeing this, the Athenians pushed forward, running after them until they were stopped by the Syracusan cavalry.

The victory belonged to the Athenians. The Athenians had held the field, losing only fifty men, while the Syracusan dead numbered 260. The Athenians stripped these dead men of their armor and piled it up as a trophy. That night the Athenians built a funeral pyre of their fifty dead and watched as the flames reached up to the dark sky. The next day, the Syracusans sent a herald and received permission to collect the bodies of their dead comrades.

The Athenians now had the opportunity to march directly on the city of Syracuse. Nicias, however, inexplicably moved his troops from the field before Syracuse to winter camps at Naxos and Catana. Of the long list of mistakes that the Athenians made in the preparation and the execution of the war in Sicily (any one of which may have seemed reasonable at the time), this decision was perhaps the most fatal to Athens' hopes of conquering the island. The apparent reason not to immediately attack the city was the Athenians' lack of sufficient cavalry. The Syracusan cavalry, which had stopped the Athenian advance in the initial battle, would continue to prevent their assault on the city. Modern historians find this explanation quizzical. Nicias, in his initial argument against an invasion of Sicily, had specifically mentioned the need for a large cavalry force, but Nicias had subsequently failed to list cavalry in his recommendations for the composition of the Athenian force. Historians, today generally agree with Lamachus' original plan (and later, that of Demosthenes') that an immediate attack on Syracuse would succeed. However rational the decision to encamp for the winter might have been, critics of Nicias remember his early opposition to the expedition, and his legendary caution, and blame him for the decision to abandon the field of battle, arguing that the first and best opportunity for success in Sicily was lost.

When fighting would resume in the spring, the Athenians would need additional supplies. They would need money, horses, and grain, along with masons and carpenters to build fortifications for a siege of the city. Nicias, therefore, sent messengers to Athens and to their allies in Sicily requesting these items. Nicias, perhaps, could have easily financed his spring offensive by raiding the treasures of the temple of Olympian Zeus, the now-ruined columns of which still overlook Sicily's Great Harbor. The pious Nicias, however, believed that this would be a sacrilege, and decided to leave the temple and its riches undisturbed.[64]

The great optimism that prevailed at the beginning of the campaign, by now, had given way to the grim recognition that the campaign in Sicily would not be over soon.

Syracuse Prepares for War

In Syracuse, the glum mood following the Athenian victory changed to joy when the inhabitants of the city saw the Athenians depart. In the days that followed, Hermocrates spoke to the Assembly. He was not discouraged by the Syracusans' defeat. It was not caused by the soldier's lack of courage, but by their lack of organization. The Syracusan soldiers had little experience of war. They were an army of artisans who fought against one of the most experienced armies in Greece. Hermocrates urged the Syracusans to use the winter to prepare for the Athenians' return. They must get arms and compel all citizens to train for the upcoming battles. In addition, he said that the army was hampered by having too many generals. Syracuse had fifteen generals, all of whom shouted conflicting orders in battle, causing confusion among the troops. Hermocrates argued that the Syracusans should have only three generals, each with full powers of command. It would then be easy to see who was responsible for the army's success or failure.

The Syracusan Assembly approved of all that Hermocrates proposed and appointed him to be one of the generals along with two others, Heraclides and Sicanus. The Assembly also sent envoys to Corinth and Sparta to ask for assistance, and they ordered work crews to extend the city walls around the northern suburbs of the city and to build forts at critical outlying sites.

Meanwhile, the Athenians were not idle. Hearing that a faction in Messana would betray the city to the Athenians, the Athenian fleet sailed to Messana and waited for their allies inside the city to open the gates. What the Athenians did not know was that Alcibiades, after he was relieved of his command, had alerted some Messanans that they were about to be betrayed and they had killed the would-be conspirators. The Athenians waited thirteen days in bad weather and short of food before they abandoned Messana and returned to their winter camps at Naxos and Catana.

The Debate at Camarina

Over the winter, both sides sent messengers throughout Sicily seeking allies. As it happened, the Syracusan and the Athenian envoys arrived on the same day at the city of Camarina on the south coast of the island. The Camarinians had earlier formed alliances with both Athens (during the visit of Laches, 427

BCE), and with Syracuse, and the Athenian and the Syracusan envoys now urged the Camarinian Assembly to choose between them.

Hermocrates, who was the envoy from Syracuse, argued before the Assembly that the Athenians were false friends to the Camarinians. The Athenians' goal in Sicily, Hermocrates said, was not, as the Athenians claimed, to aid Egesta and Leontini. They wanted to conquer the whole island and to extend their empire. Hermocrates repeated many of the arguments for Sicilian unity that he had made years ago in Gela. An alliance with Syracuse, now, he said, might be the only chance for Camarina to remain independent. In addition, he appealed for unity based on the common ethnicity of Syracusans and Camarinians who were related to the free Dorians of the Peloponnese and were the eternal enemies of the Ionian allies of Athens.[65]

The Athenians' envoy, named Euphemus, made an argument that was the mirror of the argument of Hermocrates. He claimed that the Syracusans' motives were not benevolent. Syracuse intended to rule over Camarina and the whole of Sicily. When the Athenians left, Euphemus said, Syracuse would become their master. He denied that the Athenians had any intention of subjugating the Sicilians. The Athenians could not dominate Sicily because the distance between them was too great. The nearby Syracusans, however, were a greater threat. He reminded the Camarinians that the Athenians had come by invitation to aid those who were oppressed in Sicily.[66]

According to Thucydides, Euphemus further claimed that the Athenians were justified in having an empire. (If he had actually made this argument, it probably would not have strengthened the Athenian's plea for an alliance.) Euphemus claimed that the Athenians had earned their empire by taking the leadership of the Greeks by defeating the Persians. He claimed that the Athenians did not rely on any theoretical "fine professions of having a right to rule."[67] The Athenians had been forced to defend themselves, first against the Persians, and then against the more numerous Peloponnesian Dorians. Having gained their supremacy, Athens was now driven by their interest in maintaining their situation and their fear of being replaced by another power.

Athens acted, Euphemus declared (repeating common themes of the "Athenian thesis"), not out of any moral right, but out of expediency. "For a tyrant and imperial city nothing is unreasonable if expedient . . . friendship or enmity is everywhere an affair of time and circumstance. . . . In Hellas, we treat our allies as we find them useful."[68]

The Camarinian Assembly, after they heard the arguments of Hermocrates and Euphemus, tried to find a middle way. They had long-standing ties to the Athenians, but their fear of their neighbor, Syracuse, was stronger than their affections for Athens. They decided, therefore, to offer modest support to the Syracusans, but "as sparingly as possible."[69]

Alcibiades in Sparta

Meanwhile, that winter, Alcibiades, on the run from Athens, made his way to Sparta, where he pledged his support to Athens' enemy. The Spartans were obviously skeptical of Alcibiades' sudden conversion. Alcibiades, after all, had been the leader of the war-hawks in Athens and had fought against the Spartans at Mantinea just a year earlier.

In a speech to the Spartan Assembly, Alcibiades tried to convince the Spartans that his new affection for the Spartan cause was sincere.[70] He began by claiming that his family had long been *proxenoi* to the Spartans. The proxenoi were citizens of one polis who were recognized as the semi-official friends of another polis. Alcibiades admitted that this link between his family and the Spartans had been weakened, but Alcibiades claimed that he had tried to restore it by befriending the Spartans who had been captured at Pylos.[71]

He said that while he was in Athens, it was necessary to conform to the popular opinion, but that he had tried to moderate the "licentious temper of the times" (glossing over the fact that he had been the most active in encouraging it).

Alcibiades claimed that he had always taken the side of the people in Athens and that the people were always opposed to arbitrary power. This argument was tailored to the Spartans, who claimed to be fighting to free the Greeks from Athenian enslavement. Despite being a leader of the popular party, he further proclaimed that democracy was "a patent absurdity."

> As for democracy, the men of sense among us knew what it was, and I perhaps as well as any, as I have the more cause to complain of it; but there is nothing new to be said of a patent absurdity.[72]

Alcibiades then revealed what he said were the real reasons for the Athenians' invasion of Sicily, and which he, as their author, knew better than anyone. He outlined the plan in which the Athenians would first take Sicily, then Italy, and then Carthage. Then they would bring all their forces to bear against the Peloponnese. With money and grain from their conquered territories, and with plenty of timber from Italy to build more ships, and with barbarian mercenaries from Iberia, they would blockade the peninsula and besiege its cities. These things they believed they could easily accomplish and a victorious Athens would then rule over all of the Greeks.

This threat being real, Sparta must act by sending aid to Syracuse, the first domino in the Athenian plan. Sparta must send troops and an able commander to Syracuse. In addition, Sparta must more actively engage the Athenians on their homeland. Instead of merely launching annual summertime raids in Attica, they must fortify the village of Decelea, which sat about a dozen miles from the outskirts of Athens. This village from ancient times had a special relationship with Sparta dating back to the Trojan War when the Decelians did some favor for a Spartan king.[73]

The occupation of a Spartan garrison in Decelea, would strike the Athenians with fear. At the same time, the Spartans at Decelea would cut off Athens' communication with their allies by land and prevent the importation of silver from their mines in Laurium.

Alcibiades said that even though he now wished to join Athens' enemy, he still loved Athens. He did not reject Athens, but Athens rejected him. His enemy was not Sparta, but those who drove him out of Athens. He declared that as one who truly loved Athens; he would do whatever he could to reclaim his city. In conclusion, he said that if he had previously done harm to Sparta as an enemy, he could do a great deal more for Sparta as a friend.

Incredibly, Alcibiades won over the Spartans, who quickly agreed to follow his advice. Most importantly, the Spartans decided to send an army to permanently occupy Decelea. From that point on, Athens fought a war on two fronts, one at home and one in Sicily. The Spartans decided, as well, to send a general to Syracuse. The Spartans, however, were probably still not completely convinced that aiding Sicily was in their interest. They sent, therefore, a man named Gylippus, who was not a true Spartan but a *mothax*, a man of inferior status since his mother was a helot slave. If Gylippus were to fail, it would be of little significance.

According to Plutarch and other sources, Alcibiades, the Athenian aristocratic playboy, now adopted the lifestyle of a Spartan hoplite. In Athens, he had enjoyed all the luxuries of an Athenian aristocrat—the finest food and drink, the softest bed, the fastest horses. Now, he grew his hair long and took cold baths. He ate coarse bread and the Spartan's famously foul-tasting black broth. Alcibiades did not, however, altogether adopt an ascetic lifestyle. A rumor circulated that he had an affair with Timaea, the wife of the Spartan king, Agis II, and that Alcibiades was the real father of Agis' son and heir, Leotychides. Agis, hearing these rumors, sent orders to kill Alcibiades, who was warned by friends and fled from Sparta.

Alcibiades then made his way to Persia, where for a while, he was welcomed by the king's satrap, Tissaphernes. Alcibiades, in his new position as an advisor to the satrap, continued to play a game of intrigue. His short life would continue on an erratic path, driven by a mixture of circumstances and overweening ambition. He would return to Athens in 411 in triumph and would again be forced into exile, where he met his death at the hands of assassins at the age of forty-six years. (More will be said of him in a later chapter.)

THE SECOND YEAR OF THE EXPEDITION

Spring of 414 BCE

In the spring of 414, the fighting resumed in Sicily, and over the next few months, both sides saw opportunities appear and vanish. Doors would open and then suddenly be slammed shut. Great hopes alternated with even greater despair.

Over the winter, Nicias and Lamachus had received reinforcements from Athens, including thirty archers, 250 horsemen with their equipment, and 300 talents of silver for the Athenians to buy horses and supplies on the island.

Meanwhile, both sides had finally recognized that the key to an Athenian victory was Epipoli, the great plateau rising above steep rocky walls, which overlooked the city from the north. In Syracuse, early one morning just at daybreak, Hermocrates and his newly appointed generals called a muster in the meadow near the Anapus River, south of the city. They selected a special force of six hundred hoplites led by Diomilus to guard Euryelus, the single access route on the western edge of Epipoli.

No sooner had they done this when they noticed an Athenian force moving toward Euryelus. The Athenians had landed a fleet in the small harbor north of Epipoli, out of sight of the Syracusans, and had raced up to take the pass. Diomilus and his troops responded quickly, running as fast as they could over the nearly three miles toward the Athenians' position. As they ran, some soldiers ran faster than others and their ranks broke apart so that when they met the Athenians, their force was in complete disorder. The Athenians slaughtered three hundred of the elite Syracusan troops, including their commander Diomilus. His command had lasted less than half a day.

Battle of the Walls Begins

The Athenians were now the masters of Epipoli, where they quickly constructed a garrison at Labdalum, in the west near Euryelus, and a fort, called the Circle, in the center of the plateau.[74]

The day after they secured their position on Epipoli, the Athenians placed an army before the city walls, offering battle to the Syracusans, but the Syracusans did not come out. Over the next few days, as the Athenians fortified their positions, the Syracusans watched from atop the city walls. Finally, they decided to fight. The Syracusan army filed out from the city gates, and the two armies began to form their lines in the field before the city. The inexperienced Syracusan troops were in complete disorder, however, and were unable to form an organized line of battle, and their generals reluctantly led the army back into the city.

By now, both sides were beginning to realize that the struggle for control of Syracuse would be a long one. No single battle would win the war. The Athenians would have to besiege the city, encircling it with walls, cutting off its access to its allies and to food and provisions. Victory would be won, not with spears and swords, but with shovels and axes. The Athenians had prepared for this possibility from the beginning. The first wave of Athenians to Sicily included carpenters and masons, and, over the winter, more arrived. The Athenians had already collected bricks and iron for the walls.[75] Now they gathered stones and timber as well and began to build a wall across Epipoli from the Circle fort, north to the sea. At the same time, they dug up and destroyed the underground pipes that brought drinking water into the city.

The Syracusans also began to build walls. They had already extended their city walls to include the suburbs to the north of the city. Now Hermocrates, seeing the progress of the Athenian walls to the north, determined to build a counter-wall to intersect the anticipated extension of the Athenian wall south of the Circle fort.

Work began the morning after the Syracusans had left the field of battle. The Athenians worked on their walls to the north, while the Syracusans worked on their walls to the south. The Syracusans cut down the sacred olive trees which stood in their way and built wooden towers to observe the area. Neither side, for a while, attempted to impede the other. They each focused their energies on building their walls, wanting to avoid a battle until their work was done. The Syracusans, however, soon began to feel confident in their progress and began to relax their guard. The Athenians meanwhile had been watching the Syracusans carefully. They noticed that the Syracusans commonly took a break at mid-day, some going to their tents, some even going back to the city. The Athenians seized this opportunity and attacked. Three hundred specially-selected Athenian hoplites, along with some lightly-armed troops, made a rush for the unfinished southern fortifications and overran the guard. They quickly demolished the Syracusans' wall, taking away much of the material to build their own wall.

Soon thereafter, as the Athenians continued to fortify Epipoli, the Syracusans began another wall. This one was further south of the first one, across a marshy area. Along its course, they dug a ditch. This wall and ditch, they hoped, would cross any wall that the Athenians might build to cut off the city from that direction.

In response, the Athenians again attacked. At night, the Athenians ripped the doors off nearby houses and laid them across the marsh, and crossing over these, before the sun rose, the Athenians had taken command of the second Syracusan wall.

The Death of Lamachus

The Syracusans who had been guarding this wall, scattered. Some ran to the city, others to the river. The elite unit of three hundred Athenians chased after the Syracusans as they ran toward the river, but the Syracusan cavalry, led by a general named Calicrates, attacked the three hundred Athenians. Lamachus, seeing this, brought a small force forward to protect his troops. Crossing a ditch, he and his men became separated from the main body of the Athenian army. Calicrates, now finding Lamachus isolated, called out and challenged him to single combat, and Lamachus accepted. As the men engaged each other, Calicrates struck Lamachus and drew the first blood, but the injured Lamachus struck back, his blade meeting its mark as both men fell to the ground with fatal wounds.[76]

Nicias, the Athenian general, who since the beginning had been the least eager for war, was now the sole leader of the Athenian expedition.

The Syracusans, believing that the tide of the battle had turned with the death of Lamachus, now regrouped. Some of those who had earlier fled to the city saw that Epipoli was lightly defended and came out from the city to attack the small Athenian force on the plateau. They quickly overran the outworks of the Athenians and moved toward the Circle fort. Nicias, with few troops to protect the fort, ordered his slaves to set fire to the timber and siege weapons around the cliffs. This succeeded in preventing the Syracusans from overtaking the Circle until more Athenian troops could arrive. This action probably saved the entire Athenian expedition from an immediate defeat.

Nicias organized this make-shift defense while he was lying on a sickbed showing the first signs of an illness that would incapacitate him during much of the remainder of the expedition. Although, Nicias, throughout his career as a general, had avoided battle, his actions in defense of the Circle show that he was capable of quick and decisive action when necessary.

Shortly after this, the Athenian fleet, which had remained at the Little Harbor north of Syracuse, now sailed around the island of Ortygia and entered the Great Harbor, and the whole Syracusan army retreated into the city.

Athenian Hopes and Syracusan Despair

The middle of the summer of 414, despite the death of Lamachus, was a high point in Athens' hopes for victory in Sicily. Most historians believe that the Athenians had squandered an opportunity to take the city the previous year. Now, with the arrival of the fleet in the harbor and after crushing two attempts by the Syracusans to build counter-walls to block the Athenian walls, and the failure of the Syracusans to take Epipoli, the Athenians' confidence swelled. Many Sicels now joined the Athenian army, and fresh provisions soon arrived from friendly cities in Italy.

The Athenians now began to build two closely parallel walls south of the Circle fort, which would cut Syracuse off completely from the mainland. Inside this double wall, the Athenian troops could safely defend themselves from Syracuse's army on the one side, and from Syracuse's allies on the other.

The Syracusans were soon convinced that they could not stop the Athenians from completely encircling them. Inside the city, there was talk of surrender. Secret messages were sent between Nicias and Syracusans in the city discussing the terms of capitulation.

Throughout the city, rumors and suspicions spread. Many people blamed Hermocrates and his generals for their desperate situation. In response, the Assembly deposed them and replaced them with new generals: the relatively undistinguished Heraclides, Eucles, and Telias. Meanwhile, word of the Athenians' imminent victory spread throughout Sicily and Italy.

During this time, the Spartan commander, Gyllipus, who had been hurrying to Sicily with a Corinthian fleet, learned of the Athenian successes and heard that the Athenian walls were complete. This actually was not true. The Athenians, sensing victory, had slowed down their work building walls. The southern double wall still had a gap near the Great Harbor, and other places were weak. The north wall, as well, was incomplete. Stones for its construction still lay scattered on the ground waiting to be lifted into place. Not knowing this, Gylippus abandoned hope of saving Syracuse, and turned his ships toward Italy, afraid that the Athenians would strike there next.

Gylippus Arrives

A short time later, when Gylippus finally learned the truth of the situation in Syracuse, he resumed sailing toward Sicily. Deciding against a direct attack on the Athenian position at Syracuse, Gylippus sailed in a single ship through the straits of Messana, narrowly evading four Athenian ships which were looking out for him and made his way to the Dorian city of Himera on the north coast of the island. At Himera, he convinced the city to support him with arms and supplies. Fortuitously, as well, a king of the Sicels named Archonidas, formerly an Athenian ally, had recently died, and his forces now came over to Gylippus. Rounding out this army were a number of Geloans and Selinuntines who rallied to Gylippus. With this force of about two thousand men and a hundred cavalry, Gylippus marched overland toward Syracuse.

At the same time, the Corinthian fleet sailed toward Syracuse. The first ship to reach the city was commanded by Gongylus, who happened to arrive just as the Syracusan Assembly was debating the terms of a surrender to the

Athenians. Gongylus told the Syracusans that the Corinthian fleet was coming and that Gylippus, the Spartan commander, was marching with his army toward Syracuse. Hearing this, the Syracusans regained their hopes and sent out their army to meet him. According to Plutarch, when the two forces met, the Syracusans flocked around Gylippus, "like birds around an owl."[77] The combined forces marched toward the city and passed through Euryelus to the heights of Epipoli. There they drew up in battle formation. The Athenians, caught by surprise, quickly overcame their confusion and formed their own lines.

As the two armies faced each other on Epipoli, Gylippus sent a herald to the Athenians, offering a truce if the Athenians would leave the island within five days' time. Nicias contemptuously sent the herald back without an answer. Then Athenian soldiers, meanwhile, jeered at the herald, calling out that they were not afraid of a Spartan cloak and staff—the symbols of a Spartan general. They reminded the herald of the Spartans who had been captured at Sphacteria. They, the Athenians said, were "all bigger men and had longer hair than Gylippus."[78]

The two armies now prepared for battle, but Gylippus, seeing that the Syracusan troops were disorganized and could not line up, moved his forces back. Nicias did not move. After a while, Gylippus led his army off the field and made camp in the suburbs of the city. The next day, Gylippus again brought his army out to face the Athenians. Again, neither side moved. While the armies stood watching each other, however, Gylippus sent a force behind the Athenian lines and attacked the Athenian garrison at Labdalum, killing all who guarded it and capturing a large amount of the Athenian supplies.

The Syracusans, newly energized by Gylippus' arrival, now began a third wall in the north, their previous efforts to build the two walls in the south having failed. The new wall ran up the rock face of Epipoli at a right angle toward the still unfinished Athenian wall. Meanwhile, Gylippus found a weak spot in the southern Athenian wall and led a night-time attack on it. The Athenians, who had camped outside of their walls, quickly responded and drove Gylippus' forces away, and in the morning reinforced the wall and set a stronger guard to protect it.[79]

Despite this fleeting victory, Nicias, now saw that the possibility of encircling the Syracusans by land was increasingly remote. Turning his attention to the sea, Nicias divided his forces, sending part of them to Plemmyrium, the rocky promontory that overlooked the mouth of the Great Harbor on the south. He fortified three sites there, mooring his supply ships and his triremes, and moving there what was left of his supplies after the capture of Labdalum. Here, Nicias thought, the Athenians would be able to have access to the sea in case of virtually any eventuality.

Plemmyrium, where a luxurious five-star hotel stands today, had few comforts for the Athenians. There was no fresh water and no firewood on the rocky cliffs, and the Athenian soldiers who left camp to forage the countryside for water and wood were constantly attacked by the fast-moving Syracusan cavalry.

Meanwhile, the Syracusans continued to build their counter-wall across Epipoli using stones that the Athenians had previously set aside for their own wall.

For days the stand-off between the two armies facing each other on Epipoli continued until at last, Gylippus attacked. When the armies closed in on each other, the front lines soon became too close for the use of the Hoplites' long spears, and the soldiers drew their swords and fought hand to hand. This benefited the Athenians since the armies were so close to each other and to the walls of the city that the Syracusan cavalry had no room to maneuver. The Athenians took advantage of the opportunity and soundly defeated Gylippus and his inexperienced Syracusan army. When the fighting stopped, the Athenians stripped the armor of the enemy dead and set up a trophy, and the Syracusans sent out their herald to call a truce and collect their dead.[80]

After this, Gylippus called the Syracusan army together. He said that he was responsible for the defeat by forming the army too close to the walls. He appealed to the Syracusans to remain steadfast, reminding them of the ties that bound the Syracusans and the Spartans together. It would be inglorious, he claimed, for Dorians to be defeated by Ionians and the "motley rabble" who now besieged their city.

At the first opportunity after this, Gylippus again led his army out for battle, this time leaving room between the armies and their walls. This time, the Syracusan cavalry decisively pushed back the Athenian left flank and then pushed deep into the Athenian line.

Both sides had realized by now that the outcome of the war depended on the walls that the Athenians and the Syracusans were building, and that were now nearly touching each other. That night the Syracusans, having the field to themselves, continued their wall past the Athenian wall. In the morning, as the soldiers on both sides awoke, the significance of this was clear to all. The Athenians might win every new battle from this point on, but without being able to encircle the city, their siege of Syracuse would ultimately fail.

Soon thereafter, the remaining twelve ships of the Corinthian fleet sailed into the Great Harbor. The tide of battle had irreversibly turned.

Over the next few weeks, the Syracusans consolidated their position. Their army continued to build the wall cutting across Epipoli, while Gylippus raised new troops in the interior of the island where cities that had heretofore remained neutral now recognized Syracuse's growing strength and came to its side. Syracuse itself, meanwhile, began a new experiment—building their own triremes and training their own crews as they prepared to fight against the greatest naval power of the Hellenic world.

Nicias' Letter

Nicias, for his part, decided to avoid any new conflicts, and as the summer gave way to autumn, he wrote an extraordinary letter to the Assembly in Athens. Usually, he would communicate with Athens by a messenger who would recite the words which he had memorized. This time, however, not trusting a messenger to deliver his meaning accurately and with the right emphasis, Nicias communicated with a written text.

Thucydides gives us the text in full. Nicias began by recounting the expedition's early victories in Sicily, but then very candidly he described the numerous setbacks that the campaign had suffered. The Syracusan cavalry had put the Athenians on the defensive, and the Athenians could not risk attacking the Syracusans because their first priority was protecting their walls. The arrival of Gylippus, with his joint force of troops from the Peloponnese and from Sicily had dramatically changed the situation, and the Athenians currently were avoiding any contact with the enemy. At the same time, the Syracusans had successfully built a wall intersecting the Athenian wall, preventing the Athenians from building their wall around the city. The consequence of all this was that the former besiegers were now the besieged.

As Nicias watched the newly formed Syracusan navy daily practicing their maneuvers in the harbor, he saw that Gylippus would soon be able to launch a simultaneous attack on the Athenians by land and by sea. Every day, the skill of the Syracusan navy improved, and the numbers of their soldiers increased. At the same time, the Athenian fleet, which had been at sea for over a year guarding their supply lines, was no longer in peak condition. The crews were worn out, and being constantly at sea, the ships' wooden hulls were beginning to rot. All the while, the Syracusan cavalry were hunting down and killing the Athenians who left their forts to scavenge for food and water, and the slaves and the foreign mercenaries who were with the campaign, seeing the dangers, were running off into the countryside. Nicias recognized, as well, that if his supply line by sea from the Italian cities were cut off, the Athenians would be starved into submission without a battle being fought.

Moreover, Nicias wrote that his biggest problem was that every day the demoralization and the discord in his forces increased. In an unnecessary aside, he noted that "your Athenian temperament is a hard one to control."

Nicias was aware that the Athenians would not be happy with this report. The Athenians, he knew, liked only good news. "It is your nature [he said] to love to be told the best side of things." Nicias believed, however, that a clear understanding of the facts was necessary. He knew that the Athenians would blame him if they heard more bad news, but he believed it was less risky if he told the truth.

The Athenian army in Sicily, Nicias continued, had not failed in its original mission, but the situation has changed. All of Sicily was now united against them, and Nicias expected a fresh army would soon arrive from Sparta. After this long catalog of difficulties, Nicias concluded his letter by presenting the Athenians with some difficult decisions. He said that Athens must either recall the entire force, or send out another army, as large as the first, and with significant funds. In either event, they must send a replacement for Nicias himself. He had developed a disease of his kidneys, which incapacitated him from command.

Whatever the Athenians decided, Nicias said, they must act quickly.[81]

That winter, the Athenian Assembly deliberated on how to respond to Nicias' letter. In hindsight, more than two thousand years later, it seems like the most logical decision would have been for Athens to withdraw its troops from its clearly untenable situation. Athens, however, was unable to admit defeat, and out of either misplaced optimism or narrow-minded intransigence, they decided to send out a new force as large as the first.

Even more difficult to understand, perhaps, is the Assembly's decision to refuse to accept Nicias' resignation from command of the Athenian forces. Instead, they appointed two junior officers who were already in Sicily to share command with Nicias—two individuals of little distinction named Menander and Euthydemus. More importantly, they decided to send out two new generals from Athens to join him.

The new generals were Demosthenes and Eurymedon. Demosthenes was one of the most able, if unheralded, generals in Athens. We have already seen how his plans led to the capture of the Spartan troops on Sphacteria (although Cleon received the credit). His departure from Athens, however, was delayed until the spring while he organized a new Athenian army for its expedition to Sicily. Eurymedon, who had previously served in Sicily, and was fined by the Assembly for the failure of the mission of 427–426 BCE, on the other hand, was sent off immediately with ten ships and 120 talents of silver, and with the word that more reinforcements were on the way.

THE THIRD YEAR OF THE EXPEDITION

Spring 413 BCE

The increasingly desperate turn of events in Sicily coincided with a heating up of the war in Greece. While the Syracusans had gained the advantage in Sicily over the summer and fall of 414, Sparta had initiated a new phase of the war in Greece by invading Argos on the strategic northern neck of the Peloponnese, a gateway to Attica. Athens responded by sending thirty ships to Argos. They quickly captured the city and used it as a base of operations with which to launch further raids in the Peloponnese. As a result, Sparta believed that a fragile balance of forces now existed between themselves and Athens and they requested arbitration of the conflict as required by the Peace of Nicias of 421. Up until now, both sides had carefully kept to the strict wording of the Peace of Nicias, even during the battles at Mantinea and the fighting in Sicily. The Athenians were not ready to negotiate, however, and refused the Spartan request. With Athens' refusal to arbitrate, any pretense of peace was abandoned.

Up until this time, the Spartans believed that their own refusal of arbitration of the Plataean conflict in 431 gave them the blame for starting the war. This, they believed, laid a burden of guilt upon them, which, according to their rigid piety, they believed was the cause of the capture of their soldiers on Sphacteria and all of their other misfortunes. Now that the Athenians had refused arbitration, the burden of the moral responsibility for the war lay on Athens.[82] The Spartans could now fight, free of any guilt, believing that they were in the right and that the Athenians, who had broken their sacred oaths, were in the wrong. This belief in the rightness of their cause, along with the good news from Sicily, newly energized the Spartans.

In the spring of 413, the Spartans now put Alcibiades' plans in place. Instead of sending troops on brief raids into Attica each summer, the Spartans sent a permanent force to occupy Decelea. From this base, the Spartans devastated the countryside around Athens. They destroyed the Athenians' crops in the fields and killed their sheep and other livestock. The Spartan occupation, in addition, cut off Athens' access to the north, stopping their supply of grain from Euboea. All the food for the city of Athens now had to come by sea.

Day and night, guards on Athens' city walls stood on the lookout for further threats from the Spartans, while the Athenian cavalry exhausted itself attempting to protect the countryside. Meanwhile, the costs of the war and the rise of inflation forced Athens to revise the payment of tribute from its allies, replacing it with a tax of five percent on all imports or exports by sea. Twenty thousand slaves, many of them skilled artisans, meanwhile, recognized that Athens' situation was desperate and fled the city. For Athens' citizens, the city had become a jail.

Athens, with an enemy before its gates and another army in Sicily, was now fighting two wars at once.

One consequence of Athens' financial crisis was that Athens was unable to pay a band of Thracian mercenaries who arrived too late to sail to Sicily with Demosthenes. On their way back to Thrace, empty-handed, disappointed, and angry, they attacked the undefended town of Mycalessus and its local school for boys. The Thracians burst into the town at daybreak, destroying homes and sacking the temples. They senselessly slaughtered everyone they saw, young and old, men and women, even the farm animals. Many of the children in the town ran into the school, followed by the Thracian barbarians who killed them all.

Syracuse Goes on the Offensive: The First Battle in the Great Harbor

Throughout the Spring and Summer of 413, new armies from Greece and from the Sicilian cities moved toward Syracuse, some to attack, and some to defend the city.[83] Eurymedon, with his small force, arrived, while Demosthenes gathered new troops and supplies for a major invasion. At the same time, troops from Corinth and Sparta as well as many from the cities in Sicily, journeyed to help the Syracusans.

Meanwhile, Gylippus and Hermocrates prepared their new plans. They would challenge the Athenians at sea. This seemed preposterous to many Syracusans who thought that it was suicide to fight a naval war against the Athenians—the masters of the Aegean and the Mediterranean. Gylippus and Hermocrates, however, argued that the sheer audacity of the plan would perplex the Athenians and give the inexperienced Syracusan seamen an advantage over their more skilled enemy. The Syracusans could then attack the Athenian forts at Plemmyrium simultaneously on two fronts—by land and by sea.

Gylippus and Hermocrates ultimately succeeded in persuading the Syracusans to launch thirty-five ships one night from their base in the Great Harbor and forty-five more from the Little Harbor to the north. The plan was to link these two forces together, while at the same time, Syracusan hoplites would attack the Athenian forts on Plemmyrium.

The Athenians, seeing the Syracusan ships on the move, quickly sent out twenty ships to fight the Syracusan ships in the Great Harbor and another thirty-five against the Syracusan ships which had come from the Little Harbor and were now gathered at the mouth of the Great Harbor.

In the light of the early morning, the ships engaged each other, and for some time, neither side was able to gain the advantage. Many of the Athenian soldiers at Plemmyrium decided to watch the battle between the ships in the Great Harbor and went down to the beaches. Gylippus now seized this opportunity and attacked the poorly defended Athenian forts, taking them easily, and killing all of the Athenians who had failed to escape. By now, the Syracusan ships seemed to be winning the battles in both the Great Harbor and at its mouth. As the inexperienced Syracusan fleet sailed into the Great Harbor, however, in their excitement, they lost all order and ran afoul of each other. The Athenians then turned on them. They attacked the disorganized Syracusan ships, sinking eleven of them and killing most of their crew.

At the end of the day, the Athenians set up a trophy for their victory in the Great Harbor, but it was hollow victory. The Syracusans, at the same time, set up trophies for their victories at Plemmyrium, They had captured much of the Athenians store of food and supplies, including even those of the merchants who sailed with the Athenian fleet. Worse: the Athenians, in order to make their ships as light and maneuverable as possible, as they usually did, had put the triremes' sails and equipment on shore before the battle. These also were now lost to the Syracusans and with them the Athenians' ability to sail home. On top of all this, Syracusan ships now controlled of the mouth of the Great Harbor. The Athenians would have to fight their way through the Syracusan fleet to either escape from Syracuse or to bring in supplies.

In the days following this first battle at sea between the Athenians and the Syracusans, both sides fortified their positions around the Great Harbor. The Syracusans drove piles in the water to protect their fleet in the harbor. In response, the Athenians fitted out their largest supply ship with armor and with wooden towers and used this as a virtual floating island from which they sent out smaller boats. The crews of these boats tied ropes to the piles placed by the Syracusans and used winches to pull them up. Some of the piles were placed underwater to rip through the hulls of any Athenian ships running against them. Athenian swimmers dived under the water and cut these down. All the while, both sides hurled rocks and taunts at each other, as they each set and destroyed new piles.

The Athenian soldiers, who were now dispossessed from Plemmyrium and scattered around the marshy plain before Syracuse, wondered how things could get any worse, and yet they soon would.

The Second Battle in the Great Harbor

After the capture of Plemmyrium, Syracuse again dispatched envoys throughout Sicily to ask for aid.[84] Many of the Greek cities that had waited all this time to see which way the fighting went, now came to Syracuse's aid, sending ships, and hoplites with full panoplies of armor, along with javelin-throwers, archers, cavalry, and horses. Nicias' allies among the native Sicel tribes made raids on some of these in the mountain passes as they made their way toward the coast, but their small victories did little to reduce the tide of forces flowing into Syracuse. Meanwhile, Nicias continued to avoid any further battles and hoped that Demosthenes and his fleet would soon arrive.

Meanwhile, back in Greece, a sea battle near the city of Naupactus would give Gylippus and the Syracusans the key to their final victory over the Athenians in the Great Harbor.

Naupactus was an Athenian naval base near the mouth of the Gulf of Corinth, which had been settled by helots who had revolted against Sparta. From this strategic location, the Athenians could watch every movement of Corinthian ships. When a Corinthians fleet attacked the Athenians at Naupactus, the result of the battle was inconclusive, but both sides with specious logic claimed victory since neither had been defeated, and both sides set up trophies.

The significance of this battle did not rest on its ambiguous conclusion, but on the Corinthians' new tactics. Before the battle, the Corinthians had reinforced the bronze prows of their ships with cross timbers, and when they met the Athenian ships, they rammed them head-on and disabled seven of the Athenian ships. Despite the inconclusive outcome, the Corinthians at Naupactus had rewritten the rules of trireme warfare.

The Athenian navy was the greatest in the Greek world because their triremes were lighter and faster than their opponents and because their crews were specially trained to respond quickly and with precision to the commands of their experienced captains. The most common strategy of the Athenians at sea was to separate their forces in battle and to outflank their enemies, driving with great speed into the hulls of their enemies. The Corinthians, who had strengthened the prows of their ships at Naupactus, however, drove straight into the Athenian ships, striking them prow against prow. Although not decisive at Naupactus, the Corinthians brought this new tactic to Syracuse, where they hoped that their brute force might defeat the Athenians' superior skills.

Gylippus and Hermocrates learned of these developments about the same time that they heard that Demosthenes and his fleet was coming to Sicily, and they acted quickly. In preparation for an Athenian attack, they adapted their ships in imitation of the Corinthians. They shortened their prows to make them stronger and reinforced them with stout timbers bracing them at angles to the ships' hulls. Beyond the sight of the Athenians, in the Little Harbor to the north, the Syracusans practiced their new tactics with their reinforced prows.

When these preparations were complete, the Syracusans attacked the Athenians again by land and by sea. The land forces attacked from two directions. Gylippus led a force of hoplites out from the city, while another force of hoplites, cavalry and light infantry came down from the temple of Olympian Zeus in the west. The Athenians reacted swiftly to all three threats. They defended their walls and sent out seventy-five Athenian ships to meet about eighty Syracusan ships in the harbor. The fighting on all fronts raged for several hours, but neither side gained the advantage either on land or at sea, and both retired for the day.

The following day, the Syracusans did not come out for battle, and the Athenians repaired their crippled triremes and formed a stockade around their ships with piles in the water. At the same time, Nicias moved the larger merchant ships to the outer boundaries to protect the triremes for the next round of fighting that he knew was coming.

Early the next morning, the Syracusans attacked again, and once again, neither side was able to push through the enemy's lines. Around midday, the

Syracusan ships unexpectedly backwatered and withdrew from the battle. At the behest of a Corinthian commander, the merchants of the city had set up a market on the shore to sell food to the crews of the Syracusan ships. The Athenians, seeing the enemy retreat, thought that they had won a victory, and returned to shore where they leisurely began their own mid-day meal, believing that their fighting was done for the day. The Syracusans, however, quickly ate their meal, and returned to their ships and formed their lines across the harbor. The Athenians with empty stomachs returned to their boats and set out into the harbor.

For a short time, both lines of ships faced each other without moving, until the Athenians, hungry and tired of waiting, manned their oars and with a great cheer set out against the Syracusan ships. The Syracusans had waited until now to exercise their new tactic. Turning their vessels facing the Athenians, they rowed as fast as they could, ramming the Athenian ships, prow to prow. At the same time, smaller Syracusan vessels carrying javelin-throwers approached under the oars of the Athenian ships and hurled their weapons at the Athenians. The Athenians soon recognized they were beaten and retreated into their newly strengthened stockade on the shore. In the engagement, the Syracusans had sunk seven Athenian ships and crippled several others, killing or capturing their crews, and only lost two ships of their own. As usual, the Syracusans celebrated by setting up trophies to mark their victories. They now controlled the Great Harbor and looked forward to their victory over the Athenians on land as well.

Demosthenes Arrives

The elation of the Syracusans, however, was short-lived. Soon after these events, they looked out over their sea walls toward the hazy line where blue water meets blue sky and saw a massive fleet of ships sailing toward them. Demosthenes had set out early in the spring of 413 and now arrived in the middle of the summer with seventy-three ships and five thousand hoplites, accompanied by javelin-throwers, slingers, archers, and their equipment.[85]

Although Thucydides tells us that Demosthenes proceeded "without delay" and "as quickly as possible,"[86] the long voyage suggests that Demosthenes had read Nicias' letter closely. He realized that the situation in Sicily was desperate, perhaps beyond saving, and his behavior suggests that he was in no hurry to get to Sicily. After leaving Athens, he sailed around the Peloponnese, raiding settlements along the southern tip of the great peninsula, and built a garrison for escaping helots (which was abandoned the following year).

Along the way, he met Eurymedon, who came now from Syracuse, bringing news that Plemmyrium had been taken. The two commanders continued along the coast to the islands of Zacynthus and Cephallenia, off the west coast of Greece, and on to the towns of Alyzia, and Anactorum, where he recruited light infantry troops. At Corcyra, Demosthenes and Eurymedon sent some of their forces to reinforce those that had fought at Naupactus. From there, they sailed across the Ionian Gulf, arriving on the inside of the arch of the Italian boot, all the while gathering men and arms. Off the coast of Italy, they stopped at the Choerades Isles on the heel of Italy and at Metapontum in the arch. Arriving next at Thurii, they found the citizens there friendly to the Athenians, formed an alliance with them, and recruited some into his growing army. Here, he held a muster of all his land troops, making sure that none "had been left behind." From Thurii, they sailed south, touching on all the cities along the way, except for Syracuse's ally, Locri, until they reached Petra on the southern toe of Italy, from which they set sail and finally arrived at Syracuse in mid-summer.

Demosthenes' fleet, by this time, was nearly as large as the first expedition that had set out the previous year. In addition to the ships, soldiers, and crew, plus the light infantry and ships that he gathered en route, he brought a large sum of money along with siege machines and other armaments. Once again, the expectation of victory and the fear of defeat moved from one army to the other. The Athenians' despair vanished, and the Syracusan hopes disappeared.

"Armies Clash by Night"[87]

Demosthenes did not need much time to assess the situation. He, and most historians ever since, believed that Nicias had missed a great opportunity by not attacking immediately upon his first arrival in Sicily. Demosthenes disregarded the difficulties posed by the Athenians' lack of cavalry when they first arrived on the island, believing that a quick attack on the walls of Syracuse, while the Syracusans were unprepared and before they had appealed to Sparta for help, could have brought an early victory.

Demosthenes now acted on this idea. He would wager all on a single battle. The Athenians would either triumph over the Syracusans, or, if they were defeated, they would leave Sicily before they wasted more lives and treasure. After testing the Syracusan defenses, he decided to attack Epipoli at night. He realized that an attack by day was impractical since the Syracusans, from their high point, could see the Athenians coming. Nicias was perhaps not convinced that the plan would succeed but gave his approval.

On a night when the moon was nearly full, Demosthenes, with Eurymedon and Menander, led the attack, while Nicias, still ill, stayed behind. The Athenians optimistically carried five days rations and brought with them a contingent of masons and carpenters, intending to hold their positions on Epipoli long enough to dismantle the Syracusan fortifications and to quickly construct new ones of their own.

During the guard's first watch, the Athenian troops poured through the lightly guarded pass of Euryelus. They quickly overwhelmed the lightly defended garrison, killing a few of its defenders. Most of the guards, however, escaped and sounded a general alarm awakening the Syracusan army, who quickly formed a haphazard line of battle. The Athenians advanced quickly through this first line of Syracusan defenders, and a contingent of the Athenian forces made for the Syracusan cross wall and began to dismantle it. The Athenians, buoyed by their success to this point and inspired by the fever of battle, rushed forward, pursuing the fleeing enemy, and hoping to overtake them before they could regroup. In the process, however, they lost all discipline; some troops were way ahead and others far behind. The leading forces of the Athenians soon met a force of Boeotian allies of the Syracusans, who stood their ground against the onslaught and forced the Athenians back. These Athenians now retreated in disarray into the Athenians who were coming up behind them. In the moonlight, the soldiers could only see the dark forms of bodies moving in and out of shadows. The Athenians could not tell friend from foe and slaughtered all who came running toward them.

A great roar covered the field of battle as swords and shields clashed. Triumphant soldiers shouted and dying soldiers groaned. In the chaos, the Athenians called out the watchword to each other, which was soon heard by their enemies who used it in turn to spread more terror and confusion. Adding to the terror, from all sides the Athenians could hear the Dorian battle cry being sung both by their Spartan enemies and by their Dorian allies, the Argives and Corcyrians.

As the Athenian attack collapsed, many soldiers cast off their armor and their weapons and jumped from the cliffs of Epipoli to their deaths. Those who safely reached the plain below wandered aimlessly through the night, unfamiliar with the territory, until the following morning when most of them were hunted down and killed by the Syracusan cavalry.

In the daylight, the Syracusans set up their trophies and allowed the Athenians to retrieve their dead. Once again, hope and despair, like phantoms, passed each other as they flew through the dawn's rosy mist.

The Decision to Leave Is Delayed

After the night battle on Epipoli, the Athenians' dreams of victory were replaced by an unshakable dread. Many of the soldiers had now been in Sicily for over a year. Many had been killed; others suffered from diseases (probably malaria from their encampment near the marsh south of the city). All of them wanted nothing more than to leave this benighted island and return home.

Seeing the dejection of the soldiers, at this point, the Athenian generals took the rare step of calling a council of war. We do not know how many junior officers and common soldiers might have taken part, but this extraordinary act suggests that the Athenian commanders no longer exercised absolute control of their forces and were forced to listen to the lower ranks. In the council, Demosthenes sided with the majority and cast his vote to leave. He argued that the troops in Sicily should return to Greece and help in the defense of Athens, which was (on Alcibiades' advice) now facing attacks from the Spartan forces at Decelea. Remaining in Sicily was a waste of resources, of men, and of money, since any chance of victory was gone.

Nicias, however, still had hope. He said that he had communicated with friends within Syracuse's city walls who told him that the citizens of Syracuse were as desperate as the Athenians. His informers said that they would soon open the city gates at night to let the Athenian army in.

Nicias said, as well, that the Syracusans had borrowed heavily to pay their navy and the mercenaries who helped defend the city, and that they would soon exhaust their funds. In addition, as long as the Athenian navy still dominated at sea, although it would be difficult, the Athenians would still be able to get provisions and maintain the siege.

In addition to these practical reasons, Nicias had personal reasons for staying in Sicily. He knew that the citizens of Athenians would never approve of a withdrawal from Sicily, not after two years of struggle, the number of lives lost, the great expense, and their extravagant hopes of success, and with nothing but dishonor to show for it. Nicias imagined that a clever speaker would rise up in the Assembly one day and heap criticisms on the leaders of the expedition. The soldiers who were now in the field and crying to return would claim that victory was almost within their grasp, but the generals had been bribed by the enemy to retreat. Nicias had good reason to fear a return to Athens. He knew how the Assembly treated unsuccessful generals. Pythodorus and Sophocles were lucky only to have been banished. Other Athenian generals were executed for far less failures that those in Sicily. Nicias decided that he would rather die an honorable death at the hands of the enemy than a dishonorable death at the hands of his own countrymen.

Demosthenes was still adamant that they should abandon the siege. At the very least, they should move "at once, quickly, and without delay"[88] to another location, either north to Thapsus or to Catana. The Athenian army could live off the land, plundering the enemy's fields, while their fleet could fight in the open sea. Eurymedon agreed with Demosthenes, but Nicias continued to insist on staying. As the generals and the soldiers continued to discuss and to argue among themselves, no decision was made, and the army did not move.

Meanwhile, Gylippus, who had been away recruiting more troops from the interior, returned to Syracuse, and fresh troops arrived from Sparta. Eventually, the Athenians, afraid that the Syracusans would soon attack, were convinced that they must leave, and even Nicias agreed to abandon the camp. The orders were sent throughout the camp with the utmost secrecy. A messenger was sent to Catana to tell them to stop sending any more provisions to the camp. All were to move quickly when the signal was given to board the ships and sail back to Athens.

Everything was ready, and the command to depart was just about to be given when, on August 27, 413 BCE, the moon passed behind the earth's shadow. The soothsayers, who Nicias had brought along on the expedition, were now consulted. What would be the gods' response to a lunar eclipse?

Thucydides, up to this point in his narrative, has said relatively little about divination, oracles, or prophecies, leading most historians to conclude that he was skeptical of the value of these customs. To the common people of the ancient world, however, these practices united them, their families, and their polis in a web of cosmic forces. Like many other elite Athenians, Thucydides seems to have moved into a different mental world. Influenced by the natural philosophers of Miletus and Ionia, and the rhetorical methods of the sophists, he turned to more rationalistic explanations of the nature of the world.

Nicias, however, Thucydides says, was "somewhat over-addicted to divination and that kind of thing."[89] Nicias' superstitious nature now had disastrous consequences. The soothsayers declared that the Athenians should not move for "thrice nine days"[90] (or as we would say twenty-seven days). The exhausted Athenian soldiers, emotionally distressed and alarmed by the eclipse, probably would not have moved in any case.

The Syracusans Attack

The Syracusans were eager to fight, but with time on their side, they prepared their offense for several days.[91] When they at last attacked the Athenian camp, a small force of Athenian hoplites and cavalry came out from the gates around their camp to meet them but were shortly beaten back, and both sides retired.

The next day, seventy-six Syracusan ships met an Athenian fleet of eighty-six ships outside the Great Harbor. For perhaps the first time in Athenian history, the classic naval maneuvers of the Athenians failed. The Athenians, through their training and through many battles at sea, had perfected the tactic of outflanking their enemies at sea, which was the key to the Athenian dominance on the water, and the basis of their control of their empire. On this day, the Syracusans dominated the center of the Athenian line. Under normal circumstances, this might have been an opportunity for the Athenians to separate their forces and attack the right and the left of the Syracusan fleet. Accordingly, Eurymedon on the right flank moved his ships off to encircle the enemy but soon ran out of room as his ships came too close to land. Here the Syracusans were able to trap him in a narrow inlet. They boarded his ship and killed him and his crew. The Syracusans then chased the rest of the Athenian fleet to shore, where Gylippus' army hunted down and killed many of their crew. The remainder of the crew were rescued by a force of Tyrrhenians who were allies of the Athenians. The Athenians set up a trophy for this "victory," but it was now clear that the Syracusans, who also (and more appropriately) set up a trophy, were the victors in this battle, and would likely prevail in future encounters.

The Athenians, by this time, recognized that their situation was desperate. There was now no possibility of reinforcements or of fresh provisions. They were encircled by their enemies on land, and they had lost control of the sea—their only lifeline to Athens and their distant allies. A dark cloud descended on the Athenian camp.

The Syracusans, on the other hand, were jubilant. Until this point, they had been fighting to save themselves. Now they had the taste of victory in their mouths. No longer on the defensive, they wanted to totally crush the invaders. None would escape. Succumbing to the same elation that the Athenians had felt at the beginning of the campaign, the Syracusans now dreamed of the glory that would soon be theirs. By destroying the Athenian army, Syracuse would take its place along with Sparta and Corinth as the liberators of Greece from the slavery of the Athenians.

From this point on, the end was quickly coming.

The Final Battle in the Great Harbor

The Syracusan navy practiced their skills at sea for days before the final battle in the Great Harbor. They had strengthened the prows of their ships in the Corinthian fashion and spread animal hides across their decks to prevent the Athenians from using grappling hooks to pull them close for battle. Following these preparations, they moved quickly to close off the Athenian escape route by anchoring and chaining together boats of every type from warships to merchant vessels across the mile-wide mouth of the Great Harbor.

The Athenians on the shore watched as the Syracusans moved into position. Beyond the swaying masts and the fluttering sails of the Syracusan ships, they could see the open sea and the road to home. Nicias and Demosthenes, whose authority was no longer absolute, called a meeting with the individual commanders of the hoplite forces where they decided to risk all in a charge against the massed Syracusan ships. The Athenians would force their way through the blockade and make their run to safety.

Every man capable of action boarded the waiting ships. This battle would be unlike any others that the Athenians had fought at sea. The great numbers of crew, hoplites, and light infantry weighed down the ships, slowing them down and making them difficult to react to the helmsmens' orders. The

Athenian ships, in addition, were hardly seaworthy. They had suffered damages from their many battles, and their hulls were rotting. In addition, and most critically, within the confines of the Great Harbor, the Athenians could not rely on their superior tactics, which required great expanses of open water.

On each side, the commanders spoke to their troops. Both Nicias to the Athenians and Gylippus to the Syracusans told their men what they probably already knew. A defeat or a victory in this battle would decide their fate. Everything was now at stake.

Before any battle, the generals on either side hope that they have made all the necessary preparations: they secured the necessary arms and supplies, developed their tactics and strategy, understood the geography and their troop positions, and those of the enemy. The last uncertain element of battle, however, is the morale and ardor of the men who wait for the call to battle. Nicias and Gylippus now reminded their soldiers of their duty and commended their strength and courage.

Gylippus understood what the Athenians were thinking. The Athenians, he said, were desperate. They had lost their sense of purpose and questioned their strength and their judgment. They would consequently fail to recognize and use the advantages that they still had. Their fears and their hopes, rather than their reason, would lead them to make mistakes. He reminded the Syracusans that the Athenians came to Sicily to enslave them and abuse their women and children. After months of battle, the Syracusans' passion was justified, and revenge, "the sweetest of all pleasures," was now within their grasp.

Nicias, for his part, spoke to his men and called out to his captains by name. He reminded them of their fathers and ancestors, of their wives and children, of their ancestral gods, and of the greatness of Athens. He spoke of freedom and of honor. He spoke all of the words that were typically said at great occasions, hoping that these traditional words might be useful, but knowing at some level that this was not enough. He thought, Thucydides, tells us, "as men are apt to think in great crises, that when all has been done, they have still something left to do, and when all has been said that they have not yet said enough."[92]

In normal times, the Great Harbor is a beautiful circle of blue water about two miles wide, which offers pleasure ships and commercial vessels safe harbor from the rough waters of the Aegean Sea. A strong swimmer could swim across the harbor's narrow opening in calm weather in an afternoon. On this day, 110 Athenian ships filled the harbor, and moved quickly toward the Syracusan blockade. Seventy-six Syracusan ships came out from their base in the harbor in pursuit.

When the Athenian ships met the barrier, they quickly overpowered the forces on the waiting ships, and began to break their chains and raise their anchors. Before they were able to break free, however, the Syracusan ships in the harbor, like swarming bees, came at the Athenians from all sides and forced them back.

In the small harbor, ships charged into each other in a confused choreography. One ship attacked another while being attacked by a third ship and colliding with a fourth. From each ship, the light infantry threw stones, shot arrows, and launched javelins, until the ships came close together, and the hoplites jumped from one ship to another, sometimes abandoning their own ships and commandeering another.

The crashing of ship against ship, the splintering of oars, the clashing of swords and spears, of shields and helmets, and the cries of the soldiers drowned out the commands of the helmsmen who gave orders to the rowers, now for defense, now for offense. The battered ribs of ships cracked, and water poured into the ships' hulls, drowning the rowers who were unable to get on deck above. Some were able to escape and swam away, only to be speared like fish by men from their boats.

From the walls of the city, Syracusan wives and children watched their husbands and fathers, as they met the enemy. Some of the older children launched small boats into the harbor and threw stones at the Athenians.

The two armies on the shore similarly watched with each soldier's emotions changing rapidly from one extreme to the other as the sea battle raged. With the outcome still uncertain, some, from where they stood, saw their side winning, while others a short distance away or looking in a different direction, saw their side losing. Their bodies swayed in unison as the battle went one way and then the next. They saw their friends on the water exulting in victory and saw their friends slain. They prayed to the gods, and they cried in sorrow. All in the same moment, some shouted in joy, others in grief; "We win!" "We lose!"

At last, after a long battle, the Syracusans, with joyful shouting, chased the Athenians to shore. Some of the Athenians on the shore ran to help the defeated crews, while others guarded the walls of their camps, but most thought only of how to save themselves.

As night fell, the Athenians were completely overcome. Unless something extraordinary happened, they had no hope of escape. With this great loss, the Athenians abandoned the usual actions of a defeated Greek army. They left their disabled ships where they were on land or at sea and left the bloodied bodies of their comrades floating in the harbor.

While the whole Athenian army gave in to despair, only Demosthenes still had hope and a plan. That night, he met with Nicias and argued that, at dawn the following day, the Athenians should try again to force their way through the barricade. The Syracusans would be celebrating their victory and would not expect another attempt. The Athenians, with all of their forces, would either succeed or fail in a great onrush against the Syracusan ships.

Both sides had lost about half their fleet in the day's fight, but Athens still had a numerical superiority with about sixty ships as opposed to Syracuse's fifty. Nicias agreed to this, but when they brought these plans before the crews, they found that the sailors had had enough. They were utterly demoralized, incapable of either thought or action, and refused to renew the struggle.

Nicias and Demosthenes both recognized that their position on the shore of the Great Harbor outside the city walls was untenable. If they stayed, they would be destroyed. The Athenians had only one last hope of escape. They must immediately set out into the interior of the island. By going west, away from the coast, they might join up with some friendly Sicels and then circle north to their allies in Catana.

Meanwhile, in the city, Hermocrates recognized that the Athenians would attempt to break out of their camp and urged the Syracusans to set up barricades that night on the main roads that the Athenians might take. The Syracusan troops, like the Athenians, however, were in no mood for more fighting. They were exhausted after the great sea battle and were celebrating with sacrifices to their Dorian hero, Heracles. The soldiers, their bellies full of wine and food, would not march out in the middle of the night.

Faced with this reality, Hermocrates devised another plan. Knowing that Nicias had informers in Syracuse, Hermocrates sent out horsemen to the Athenian camp who portrayed themselves as friends to the Athenians. The horsemen warned the Athenians that the Syracusans had indeed sent out soldiers to guard the roads and that the Athenians should wait until daybreak and prepare properly for their flight. The Athenians, believed this story to be true, and did as the night riders advised. The Athenians waited throughout the night. The next morning, they decided to wait another day to give the soldiers time to gather their possessions and prepare to leave. While the Athenians, thus, delayed, Gylippus and the Syracusans sent out horsemen and soldiers to block every avenue of escape.

The next day, the Athenians burned as many of their ships as they could, as the Syracusans, unimpeded, towed away the rest. The Athenian soldiers packed their possessions, leaving behind everything that was not essential. Since the army's provisions were exhausted, each soldier scavenged what little food he could find. They would have to carry this and all of their equipment themselves since the few slaves who had not fled into the countryside could not be trusted. On the third day after the great sea battle, the Athenians finally left their position on the shore of the Great Harbor and began their march into the interior.

Thucydides' description of the Athenians breaking camp at Syracuse is certainly one of the saddest passages in history. "In leaving the camp, there were things most grievous for every eye and heart to contemplate. The dead lay unburied, and each man as he recognized a friend among them shuddered with grief and horror."[93]

Even more distressing than leaving unburied the bodies of their fallen comrades, they left the sick and wounded who were incapable of traveling. As the soldiers filed into their irregular formations and began moving forward, the injured men called out to their tent-mates as they passed, begging them not to leave them behind. They wrapped their arms around them, and when they could no longer hold on, they stumbled forward "following as far as they could, and, when their bodily strength failed them, calling again and again upon heaven and shrieking aloud as they were left behind."[94] Every soldier in the army wept as they parted from their friends and marched into the interior where almost certain destruction waited.

The sounds of the trumpets, prayers, and paeans that filled the air when their decorated ships set out from Athens two years ago were long forgotten.

The Long March

The Athenian army, despite all of its losses, still comprised, according to Thucydides, forty thousand men, although scholars think this is number is exaggerated.[95] The retreating army was drawn up into two groups, with Nicias leading the forward group, followed by Demosthenes. Each band was formed in a hollow square, with the soldiers on the outside protecting the baggage carriers and camp followers within.

As they marched, Nicias walked among his men, speaking to them in groups. Men, he said, have survived worse dangers than this. He, himself, although weak and sick, still had hope. He had always been devoted to the gods and believed in justice and tried to do no harm to any man. The gods, he hoped, would now put this in the balance when considering the Athenians' fate. If they had ever offended any of the gods, they should now be satisfied that the Athenians have been punished enough. They should look on the Athenians with pity rather than anger. Nicias told his soldiers that he had sent men ahead to friendly Sicels who would soon come with food and provisions. He admitted that the army had no fortifications and no ships, but the army itself was a city wherever it was. A city was the spirit of the people, and "men make the city and not walls or ships without men in them."[96]

At the Anapus River, the Athenians were able to force their way through a Syracusan battalion, putting them to flight. Soon after this, the Athenians were ambushed in what would become a familiar pattern over the next few days. The Syracusan cavalry attacked them as their light infantry rushed at the Athenian ranks, threw their spears, and quickly retreated. The Syracusans held back their hoplites. There was no purpose in risking them against a defeated enemy.

After traveling about five miles, the Athenians set up camp for the night by the side of a hill. The following day, they were able to move only about two and a half miles to a small village, which they plundered for food and water. The Syracusans meanwhile went ahead of the Athenians and hastily built a wall across the Athenians' route. The Athenians broke their camp on the third day and reached a pass known as the Acraean Crag. There they were hemmed in by a steep hill on one side, a fast-moving river on the other side, and the Syracusan army behind their wall ahead of them. A battle lasted most of the day, as Syracusan cavalry and light infantry tried to break the Athenian ranks. Finally, the Athenians retreated to their previous night's camp.

Early the next day, the Athenians moved forward again, and again they tried to break through the Syracusan wall. The Syracusan position, however, was too strong, and the Athenians again fell back, only to find that the Syracusans had begun to build another wall blocking their retreat. The Athenians broke through the unfinished wall, but even the weather seemed to conspire against them, as rain and a thunderstorm now drenched the army.

Day five was much the same as the previous four. The Athenian army was surrounded by Syracusan light infantry who ran toward the Athenian lines, pelted the soldiers with missiles, and then retreated before the heavily-armored Athenian hoplites could follow.

That night, Nicias and Demosthenes devised a new plan. They ordered the soldiers to light as many campfires as possible in order to deceive the watching Syracusan army, and to set out that night, not to their original destination, north to Catana, but west toward the ocean and Gela and Camarina.

The plan began to unravel as soon as it started. The troops, demoralized, and short of sleep, food, and water, now experienced strange fears and fantasies as they moved by night through enemy territory. In the darkness, the two armies became separated. Nevertheless, marching throughout the night, they both reached the shore by dawn. From there, they took the Helorine road into the interior to the Cacyparis River. There, the Athenians forced their way past a wall and a stockade, which the Syracusans had hastily constructed, and continued to the Erineus River. These directions and locations are nearly impossible to follow today. Over two millennia, the names of roads and rivers have changed, some rivers have changed course, and others have silted up and no longer exist.

The Syracusans, led by Gylippus, had no difficulty tracing the route of the Athenian armies. By midday, the Syracusan cavalry caught up with Demosthenes' exhausted and disorganized troops. They encircled Demosthenes' men and herded them like sheep into a small clearing.

On another day, this place would have been a peaceful place for a traveler to stop and rest on the side of a road next to a wall and some olive trees. On this day, the Athenians were barraged from all sides as the Syracusan light infantry pelted them with rocks and any other objects they could find. The main body of the Syracusan army continued to hold back, there being no need to risk hand-to-hand fighting against a desperate and already beaten army.

Eventually, Gylippus sent word to the Athenians that any Sicilians who were in their army could go free. A few of them did. Subsequently, the Syracusans offered terms of surrender to the Athenians, promising them that their lives would be spared. Demosthenes' army, which now numbered about six thousand men, had no choice but to surrender and lay down their arms. Some of the men had carried a few coins with them through their long journey hoping to buy food along the way. They were forced to give this up, and they filled four over-turned shields with their coins. After this, Demosthenes' men were marched back to Syracuse.

Meanwhile, Nicias' army had hurried on and was about six miles ahead, anxious to get as much distance as possible between themselves and the pursuing Syracusans. They camped that night on high ground near the Erineus River. The following morning, the Syracusan forces caught up with Nicias and informed him that Demosthenes had surrendered and that Nicias should do so as well. Nicias at first did not believe this and asked for a truce while a horseman was sent out to find out if it were true. A rider set out and soon returned, with the news confirming Demosthenes' surrender. When Nicias got this news, he tried to negotiate the terms of a surrender with the Syracusans. To save the lives of his men, he promised that Athens would pay for the whole cost of the war. This would have been an enormous sum, which Nicias would guarantee by giving one Athenian hostage to the Syracusans for every talent that Athens owed. Gylippus and the Syracusans recognized the impracticality of the plan and rejected it outright. This ended the truce.

Once again, the light infantry attacked throwing missiles of every kind at the surrounded Athenian army. The barrage continued until nightfall when Nicias' army again set campfires and attempted to slip out of camp. The Syracusans this time quickly saw through the Athenians' plan and raised a battle cry. Seeing that their plan was discovered, most of the Athenians abandoned the attempt and settled down for the night. Three hundred men, however, forced their way through the Syracusan guards and made their escape, only to be rounded up the following day.

At daybreak, a week and a day since they began their retreat, Nicias moved his army out, hoping to reach the Assinarus River. If they succeeded, the Athenian troops believed they might yet be saved. Perhaps on the other side of the river, a curtain would lift, and the green hills and the rich plains on the other side would open before them, and their torment would end.

As they slowly moved forward, they were attacked again by the Syracusan cavalry and by the light forces throwing rocks and javelins. At last, Nicias' troops reached the Assinarus River. Exhausted, hungry, thirsty. Instead of relief, the Athenian army faced one final horrific scene. Thucydides' famous description of it is without parallel in historical writing.

> Once there they rushed in, and all order was at an end, each man wanting to cross first, and the attacks of the enemy making it difficult to cross at all; forced to huddle together, they fell against and trod down one another, some dying immediately upon the javelins, others getting entangled together and stumbling over the articles of baggage, without being able to rise again. Meanwhile the opposite bank, which was steep, was lined by the Syracusans, who showered missiles down upon the Athenians, most of them drinking greedily and heaped together in disorder in the hollow bed of the river. The Peloponnesians also came down and butchered them, especially those in the water, which was thus immediately spoiled, but which they went on drinking just the same, mud and all, bloody as it was, most even fighting to have it. At last, when many dead now lay piled one upon another in the stream, and part of the army had been destroyed at the river, and the few that escaped from thence cut off by the cavalry, Nicias surrendered himself to Gylippus.

Nicias pleaded with Gylippus to stop the slaughter of his troops, and to do what he wanted with him. Gylippus agreed and ordered an end to the carnage.

"Call No Man Happy"

Nicias had reason to hope that Gylippus might show him some mercy. Nicias considered himself a friend of Sparta. He had served as a leader of the peace party in Athens. He had helped the return of the Spartan prisoners captured at Pylos, and he was the principal author of the Peace of Nicias, ending the first ten years of the war between Athens and Sparta. Gylippus, on his part, was eager to accept Nicias' surrender and that of Demosthenes, hoping to march the two Athenian generals through the streets of Sparta. In Sparta, Nicias might find his life spared, but Demosthenes' fate was certain. He was one of the Athenians most hated by Sparta. An aggressive and cunning general, he was a friend of the helots, and the one most responsible for the Athenian victory at Pylos.

The Syracusans, however, had their own ideas. Unlike Gylippus, the Syracusans had no sympathy for either Nicias or Demosthenes. They had invaded their country, besieged their city, and caused the deaths of many of their fellow citizens. They deserved no leniency. They feared that Nicias might buy his freedom and his life with his great wealth. In addition, the men in Syracuse who may have secretly plotted with Nicias to betray the city were afraid that if Nicias lived and was tortured, he would reveal their names.

Nicias' and Demosthenes' fates were now clear. Their lives were ended far from home with swift strokes of a knife to their throats. One wonders if either of them thought at that moment of Herodotus' words, "call no man happy until he is dead."[97]

The remnant of the Athenians who had thus far survived were rounded up and marched back to Syracuse where they were imprisoned in the maze of quarries at the foot of the Epipoli. With no shelter from the sun during the day and suffering from the cold at night, with little food and water, many died from wounds received in battle or from disease. The piles of their rotting bodies filled the air with a foul stench.[98]

A handful of Athenian soldiers who had escaped from the Syracusans thus far and were wandering around the fields and woods of Sicily were soon captured by Syracusans soldiers who sold them as slaves to wealthy customers. A few of the Athenian prisoners who were imprisoned in the quarries, and who could recite lines from Euripides' plays, were also sold as slaves to act as tutors to the children of wealthy clients. Only a small fragment of the once-great Athenian army escaped the sufferings of these final days and found their way to Catana, and from there back to Athens.

A Russian proverb: "The road to war is wide, the path home narrow."

NOTES

1. Homer, *The Odyssey*, trans. Samuel Butler (London: A. C. Fifield, 1900), bk. 12.
2. The death of his son, Icarus, who disobeyed his father, and flew too close to the sun, which melted the wax holding his wings together, is frequently cited as an illustration of hybris, the pride that makes one think that they are like a god, and which will lead ultimately to one's ruin. Scholars more accurately describe hubris as "intentionally dishonoring behavior," taking pleasure in humiliating a victim. A good summary of recent interpretations of hubris is in *The Oxford Classical Dictionary*, 4th ed., ed. Simon Hornblower, Antony Spawforth, and Esther Eidinow (New York: Oxford University Press, 2012), 712.
3. In addition to Herodotus, Thucydides, and Diodorus Siculus as sources on Sicily's history, see Franco De Angelis, *Archaic and Classical Greek Sicily: A Social and Economic History* (New York: Oxford University Press, 2016); and Simon Hornblower, *The Greek World, 479–323 BC* (New York: Routledge, 1983).
4. John V. A. Fine, *The Ancient Greeks: A Critical History* (Cambridge, MA: Harvard University Press, 1983), 105–9, 131–34.
5. The columns of the temple of Athena, built by Gelon, are incorporated in the walls of the Cathedral of Syracuse on Ortygia. The amphitheater is preserved in the Archaeological Park.
6. Both cities had estimated populations of about 250,000 and controlled larger outlying populations of 100,000.
7. The term "barbarian" referred to anyone who did not speak Greek and whose utterances sounded like a meaningless "bar, bar, bar."
8. Diodorus Siculus, *The Library of History of Diodorus Siculus*, trans. C. H. Oldfather (Cambridge, MA: Loeb Classical Library, 1946), vol. 4, at bk. 11, 23 (hereafter cited as Diodorus). https://penelope.uchicago.edu/Thayer/E/Roman/Texts/Diodorus_Siculus/home.html (accessed March 26, 2018).
9. Diodorus, bk. 11, 67.
10. Diodorus, bk. 11, 67.
11. Diodorus, bk. 11, 86.
12. Diodorus, bk. 11, 76, 78, 88–92, 12.8, 29.

13. Robert W. Wallace, "Plato's Sophists, Intellectual History after 450, and Sokrates," in *The Cambridge Companion to the Age of Pericles*, ed. Loren G. Samons II (Cambridge: Cambridge University Press, 2007), 215–37.

14. On the Laches mission, see Brian Bosworth, "Athens' First Intervention in Sicily: Thucydides and the Sicilian Tradition," *Classical Quarterly* 42, no. 1 (1992): 46–55, https://jstor.org/stable/639143.

15. De Angelis, *Archaic and Classical Greek Sicily*: Leontini was a "collection basin" for Chalcidian Sicilians, 106. Catanians return home from Leontini (206). Leontini gained its independence following the Congress at Gela (424, 206). The aristocrats of Leontini, supported by Syracuse, returned to Leontini in conflict with democratic faction intent on land redistribution (422), Leontini again became a dependency of Syracuse (206–7).

16. The philosopher, Plato, was not an admirer of either Laches or Nicias. After the war was over, Plato named a Socratic dialogue after Laches, in which he and Nicias are foils for Socrates who demolishes their definitions of "courage."

17. Simon Hornblower, *Commentary on Thucydides* (New York: Oxford University Press, 1991–2008), vol. 1, 495. The chronology of these events is confusing. Thucydides' text with that of Diodorus and a fragment from an ancient history of Sicily do not help. See Bosworth, "Athens' First Intervention in Sicily."

18. The Latin spelling *Messana* is used here to distinguish it from the Peloponnesian Messena.

19. Thucydides 3.103.

20. Thucydides 4.58.

21. Thucydides, 4.64.

22. Thucydides, 5.4.

23. One talent = six thousand drachma. An unskilled worker in Athens in the fifth century might earn a drachma a day. See *The Landmark Thucydides: A Comprehensive Guide to the Peloponnesian War*, ed. Robert B. Strassler (New York: Free Press, 1996), Appendix J, 620–22.

24. Thucydides, 6.46.

25. Thucydides, 6.8.

26. Thucydides, 6.12.

27. Thucydides, 6.18

28. Thucydides, 6.18.

29. Thucydides, 6.26. See also Kurt A. Raaflaub, "Warfare and Athenian Society," in *The Cambridge Companion to the Age of Pericles*, ed. Loren J. Samons II (Cambridge: Cambridge University Press, 2007), 96–124, at 106.

30. Walter Burkert, *Greek Religion* (Cambridge MA: Harvard University Press, 1985), 156–59.

31. "Hymn 2: To Demeter," in *The Homeric Hymns*, trans. Michael Crudden (New York: OxfordUniversity Press, 2001), 4–22.

32. Brian C. Muraresku, *The Immortality Key: The Secret History of the Religion with No Name* (New York: St. Martin's Press, 2020).

33. Burkert, *Greek Religion*, 285–90; Carl A. P. Ruck and Danny Staples, *The World of Classical Myth: Gods and Goddesses, Heroines and Heroes* (Dunham, NC: Carolina Academic Press, 1994).

34. Thucydides, 6.28.

35. Andocides, *On the Mysteries, Minor Attic Orators in Two Volumes*. Volume 1. *Antiphon Andocide*, English trans. K. J. Maidment (Cambridge, MA: Harvard University Press; London: William Heinemann, 1968), http://www.perseus.tufts.edu/hopper/text?doc=Andoc.+1+1&redirect=true (accessed September 27, 2020).

36. Andocides, *On the Mysteries*, 1.15.

37. A drachma was considered a good days' pay for a skilled workman.

38. Mantitheus Apsephion, and Diognetus.

39. In addition, he correctly identified Meletus and Euphiletus.

40. It was her second marriage.

41. Thucydides, 6.60.

42. Andocides, *On the Mysteries*, 1.36.
43. Andocides, *On the Mysteries*, 1.43.
44. The Prytanies are the fifty members who were selected by lot from each of the ten tribes, who were the temporary executive officers of the Council, in the Prytaneum (the Tholos, a round, domed building in the agora, the meeting place for the Prytanies), and others in the temple of Demeter and Persephone.
45. Andocides, *On the Mysteries*, 1.48.
46. Andocides, *On the Mysteries*, 1.45n38.
47. Thucydides, 6.60.
48. Thucydides, 6.32 (415 BCE).
49. Thucydides, 6.44.
50. Thucydides, 6.39 (415 BCE). Athenagoras' speech in praise of democracy is the only time that Thucydides gives an argument that is critical of aristocracy. It is clear that the aristocratic Thucydides sees Athenagoras' argument as a foil to the better argument of Hermocrates.
51. Thucydides reports that the Athenians received thirty talents from the Egestans twice, once at 6:46 and once at 6:62. However, I think that there was only one transfer of the thirty talents, probably related at 6:62.
52. Thucydides, 6.61 (415 BCE).
53. *Dictionary of Greek and Roman Biography and Mythology*, ed. William Smith Sr. (Boston: Little, Brown, 1867), vol. 2, 712, available online at *The Making of America Books*, https://quod.lib.umich.edu/m/moa/ACL3129.0002.001/722?rgn=full+text;view=image;q1=lais (accessed April 23, 2020); Athenaeus, *Athenaeus: The Deipnosophists*, trans. C. D. Yonge (London: Henry G. Bohn, 1854), bk. 13, p 588, no. 54–55, http://www.attalus.org/old/athenaeus13b.html#c54 (accessed April 23, 2020).
54. H. D. F. Kitto, *The Greeks* (Baltimore, MD: Penguin, 1951), 173.
55. Homer, *The Iliad*, trans. Robert Fagles (New York, Penguin, 1990), bk. 5, 72–76.
56. Homer, *Iliad*, bk. 20: 529–33.
57. Herodotus, *The Landmark Herodotus: The Histories*, ed. Robert B. Strassler, trans. AndreaL. Purvis (New York: Anchor Books, 2009), 1.30 (hereafter cited Herodotus).
58. This is a very loose quote in Herodotus, 1.32. Aeschylus and Sophocles made similar statements.
59. The Elysian fields were reserved for only a select, virtuous few.
60. Homer, *Odyssey*, trans. Butler bk. 11, passim; 24, 7–9.
61. Homer, *The Odyssey*, trans. Robert Fagels (New York: Viking Penguin, 1996), 555–58.
62. Thucydides, 2.34.
63. Homer, *Iliad*, bk. 23, 81–91; Homer, *Odyssey*, trans. Fagles, bk. 11, 56–88.
64. Plutarch was especially critical of Nicias, as have been most subsequent historians, for his failure to move troops in the first year to take the temple of Olympian Zeus that was a short distance from the Great Harbor. Its horde of gold and silver might have helped finance Athenian operations in Sicily, but Nicias was afraid of committing a sacrilege. See Plutarch, *Plutarch: The Rise and Fall of Athens: Nine Greek Lives*, trans. Ian Scott-Kilvert (London: Penguin, 1960), 228.
65. Thucydides, 6.77.1 and 6.80.2.
66. Thucydides, 6.87.2.
67. Thucydides, 6.83.2.
68. Thucydides, 6.85.
69. Thucydides, 6.88.1.
70. Thucydides, 6.89–6.92.
71. See Thucydides, 5.43.2.
72. Thucydides, 6.89.6. Jeremy Mynott's translation reads, "as for democracy, anyone with any sense knew what that was like, and as its victim I had better reason than most to revile it. However, there is nothing new to be said about such an acknowledged folly." *Thucydides: The War of the Peloponnesians and the Athenians* (*Cambridge Texts in the History of Political Thought*), ed. and trans. Jeremy Mynott (New York: Cambridge University Press, 2013), 441.
73. Herodotus, 9.73.

74. The exact locations of the garrison at Labdalum and the Circle, which was probably not really a circle, as well as the exact locations of the fortifications and walls here and in what follows is the subject of much scholarly dispute. The numerous historical maps and descriptions vary considerably from each other.
75. Thucydides, 6.88.6.
76. The story of Lamachus' death is told by Plutarch. It was too good to leave out.
77. A vivid if ambiguous simile. See Plutarch, "Life of Nicias," in *Plutarch: The Rise and Fall of Athens*, 231.
78. Plutarch, "Life of Nicias," 231.
79. Thucydides, 7.4.
80. Thucydides, 7.5.
81. Thucydides, 7.15.
82. The word *paranomema*, translated as transgression, implies moral guilt. The Spartans had a greater attachment to the idea of morality, sacred oaths, and rights than Thucydides attributes to the Athenians, particularly as revealed at Melos.
83. First Sea Battle, in Thucydides, 7.21–7.25.
84. Second Sea Battle, in Thucydides, 7.36–7.41.
85. Thucydides, 7.42.
86. Thucydides, 7.26, trans. Crawley; and *Thucydides*, ed. Mynott.
87. Matthew Arnold, "Dover Beach, "And here we are as on a darkling plain / Swept with confused alarms of struggle and / Where ignorant armies clash by night," in *New Poems* (London, Macmillan, 1867), 112–14, lines 35–37, https://archive.org/details/new-poems00arnorich/page/112/mode/2up (accessed March 6, 2021).
88. Thucydides, 7.49.
89. Thucydides, 7.50.
90. Thucydides, 7.50.
91. Thucydides, 7.51 ff.
92. Thucydides, 7.69.2.
93. Thucydides, 7.75.
94. Thucydides, 7.75.
95. Thucydides, 7.74.
96. Thucydides, 7.77.
97. Herodotus, 1.32.
98. Of the forty thousand who began the inland journey from the great harbor, Thucydides estimated that seven thousand were captured by the Syracusans and sent to the quarries.

Chapter Four

The Aftermath

THE AFTERMATH OF ATHENS DEFEAT IN SICILY

Athens was stunned by the disaster in Sicily. When the great ship, the Paralus, arrived in Athens in the middle of the night with word of the destruction of the army, the news passed from one person to another, and the sound of wailing travelled from the Piraeus along the city walls, and no one slept that night.[1]

When day broke, panic and fear swept through the city. The Athenians believed that Sparta would soon attack, and with few defenses left, Athens' destruction seemed certain. In the weeks and months that followed, Athens' problems mounted. While a Spartan army occupied Decelea, a dozen miles from Athens' walls, the Peloponnesian fleet, now supported by Persian money, welcomed twenty more ships from Sicily led by Hermocrates, and more were expected from Persia. To add to these troubles, many of Athens' allies revolted, cutting off Athens' primary source of income and shrinking the ranks of its army. Athens' treasury, already critically depleted from eighteen years of war, was now nearly bankrupt. In this situation, a number of aristocrats saw an opportunity in 411 BCE to end the democracy and orchestrated a coup d'état, which put in place a short-lived government led by four hundred of their number.

Incredibly, Athens survived these calamities and fought on for another nine years before it was finally forced to surrender. The Athenians were fortunate in the first years after the disaster in Sicily that the Spartan forces in the Aegean Sea were led by one of the worst generals in Sparta's history. The Spartan general, Astyochus, in addition to being inept and corrupt, also shared the anomaly of many Spartans, and of Nicias, of avoiding fighting whenever possible. Thucydides commented on this Spartan trait saying that this "slowness and want of energy" of the Spartans proved that the Spartans were "the most convenient people in the world for the Athenians to be at war with."[2] In the case of Astyochus, his efforts to avoid fighting angered his soldiers, who were further angered when he refused to pay them. For these reasons, Astyochus' troops ultimately rose against him and would have killed him, if he had not taken refuge at an altar.

Alcibiades' Role

Alcibiades played an over-sized role in these final years of the Peloponnesian War. After the Athenian defeat in Sicily, Alcibiades continued to serve Sparta leading Athens' Chios and Miletus to revolt, and successfully negotiating an alliance between Sparta and Persia. After the rumor spread that Alcibiades had an affair and a child with the Spartan king's wife, Alcibiades was once again forced to flee and once again change his loyalty. This time he found a home in the court of Tissaphernes, the satrap of one of Persia's western provinces, and he soon became an influential advisor to the satrap. In this new position, Alcibiades recommended that Persia reduce its payments to the Spartan fleet and maintain a military balance between Sparta and Athens. The two competing *poleis* would thus wear each other down, and Persia would then be able to enter the Aegean Sea and dominate the war-weakened Greeks.

At the same time that he was advising the Persians how to conquer Greece, Alcibiades began secretly communicating with some of the oligarchs in Athens. He let them know that he was so influential and well liked among the Persians that he could bring them into an alliance with the Athenians against the Spartans. He would do this, however, only if the Athenians ended their democracy and set up a government ruled by the oligarchs.

Despite some skepticism of Alcibiades' motives, some of aristocrats in Athens were encouraged by these words and began a plot to take over the government. In preparation for the coup, popular leaders who were the enemies of Alcibiades, and "some other inconvenient people" were murdered. Following this, the conspirators with a band of 120 youths with daggers entered the Council chamber and ordered the members to disband. To show their good intentions, as the councilors left the chambers, each one was given his annual salary.

The conspirators then established a government led by four hundred of Athens' "best" citizens. Some of the moderate members of this new government, however, soon began to question the goals of the more extreme members, and the new government began to unravel when one of its more conservative members went to Sparta to negotiate a surrender. When he returned to Athens, a crowd of citizens slew him in the agora. Resistance to the oligarchs escalated when workers began to build a wall on the Piraeus, which many believed was to create a safe space for a Spartan army to disembark and enter the city. When citizens gathered at the building site, a riot broke out. The men who were building the wall joined the protest and began to tear down the work that they had started and called "all who wanted the People to govern" to join them.[3] The next day, they marched in a body to the city where they met with some of the moderate leaders of the government to settle their disagreements.

At this point, a Peloponnesian fleet appeared off the coast, making its way straight toward Athens. The discussion between the people and the moderate oligarchs quickly ended, as the two sides united to defend the city. Men from all walks of life ran to the Piraeus and boarded ships and set out, without training or plans, to confront the Spartans. The battle was a disaster for the Athenians who lost twenty-two ships, and whose crews were either killed or enslaved.

Athens was now undefended. The door to Sparta's victory in the Peloponnesian War was wide open. Instead of moving on Athens, however, the Peloponnesian force, in typical fashion, inexplicably sailed past Athens and sailed to Euboea, where they fomented a revolt from Athenian rule. The large island to Athens' north was a principal source of grain and cattle and was also a strategically important Athenian trading port. The defeat of the Athenian ships and their crew, as well as the loss of Euboea, were great disasters, but Athens, at least for the time being, was saved.

After these events, the government of the four hundred was now formally deposed, and a new government was formed. The extreme oligarchs were thoroughly discredited, and fled the city, joining the Spartan army at Decelea. The new government, however, was not a restoration of the radical democracy of Pericles. The *thetes* were completely disenfranchised, losing all their rights as citizens. This new government was a democracy dominated by the *hoplites*. Citizens would no longer be paid for serving on juries or other public offices. This had always been a goal of the conservatives who saw these payments as a system of public welfare. Thucydides was pleased by this, stating that at this time "the Athenians appear to have enjoyed the best government that they ever did, at least in my lifetime."[4]

One of the first acts of the new government was to recall Alcibiades. The citizens of Athens now saw Alcibiades as their savior. They forgot all his offenses and their own anger at him. They believed that he could bring Persia to their side in the war, bring them victory over Sparta, end civil strife, and restore Athens to its former glory.

When Alcibiades returned to Athens, the whole city crowded down to the Piraeus to greet him. Women, children, free and slave, all vied with each other to get close to him. Shouting praise and with tears of joy, they placed garlands on his head. At a meeting of the Assembly, a golden crown was placed on his head, and he was elected a general and given supreme powers.

The Assembly, in addition, voted to restore his property and revoked the curses that had been placed on him earlier. A large stone, which had been inscribed with curses on Alcibiades, was thrown into the sea. Shortly after this, Alcibiades led a procession to Eleusis under the protection of his army, partially erasing the memory from four years earlier, when he was accused of mocking the ceremony.

In the months after his return to Athens, Alcibiades led the Athenian navy in a string of victories over the Spartans. The most important of these was in the Sea of Marmara, between the Black Sea and the Aegean Sea, near the town of Cyzicus. There, Alcibiades destroyed a combined Spartan and Syracusan fleet, giving Athens, once again, control over the Hellespont, and recovering some of the allies who had revolted after Athens' defeat in Sicily.

Athens' confidence was restored by these events, and they now brought back many of the forms Periclean democracy. The franchise was restored to all citizens, including the thetes. Payment for jury duty and other public services was resumed. Small allotments were even granted to the neediest citizens who had suffered the most during the war. Work began again on the buildings and monuments on the Acropolis, which had halted the during the war.

The mood in Sparta was exactly the opposite. Sensing defeat, the Spartans sent an emissary to Athens seeking peace. As they had in the past, Athens once again rejected the Spartan's offer of peace.

It was at this time that Thucydides stopped writing his history. His text mysteriously ends in mid-sentence shortly after his description of the Battle of Cyzicus in 410. He continued to revise the portions of the text, however, for at least another six years. We know this because his history refers to events after the end of the Peloponnesian War in 404.[5] After 410, our best primary source is the history, *The Hellenica*, written by the Athenian general, Xenophon.

Throughout this time, Alcibiades' enemies in Athens were quietly waiting for an opportunity to again discredit him. The opportunity came when a subordinate of Alcibiades initiated an attack on a Spartan fleet, despite Alcibiades' specific orders not to. When the attack failed, Alcibiades was blamed. He was removed from his position as a general and he went into self-imposed exile in an area on the coast of the Hellespont.

Without Alcibiades, by 406, the Athenians were once again in a desperate situation. Persia had resumed funding the Spartan fleet, and many Athenian seamen were deserting the Athenian navy to join the Spartans who could now pay them more. The end of the war seemed imminent when the Athenians lost thirty ships in a battle with a Spartan fleet near Mytilene in Lesbos, and the remainder of the Athenian forces were trapped in the harbor at Mytilene by a much larger Spartan force.

In addition, the Spartans had finally found a smart and aggressive general named Lysander to command of their fleet. Like Gylippus, the Spartan general in Sicily, Lysander was a *mothax*, his mother was a helot, and he was not afraid to fight.

Athens responded to this crisis by removing the silver and gold from the temples and the statues on the acropolis, even including the colossal statue of Athena in the Parthenon, to finance a new navy. Every able-bodied man in the city, rich and poor alike, was enlisted to serve. Non-citizens were given citizenship, and slaves were given their freedom, to serve in hastily built ships. With a fresh armada of 150 ships, these inexperienced crews sailed against 120 Spartan ships at Arginusae, on the coast of present-day Turkey. This was perhaps the greatest number of ships that had engaged in a sea battle in the ancient world up to that time. In this battle, the Athenians were victorious, destroying much of the Spartan fleet and killing its commander, Callicratidas, who had temporarily replaced Lysander. The Spartans upon this defeat, sent heralds to Athens, as they had many times in the preceding years, suing for peace. And once again, the Athenians refused.

The joy in Athens following the victory was short-lived. News arrived in Athens that a sudden storm had prevented the commanders of the Athenian fleet from recovering the bodies of the dead and from rescuing some of their sailors who had been stranded on an island during the storm. The Athenian Assembly met to consider how to punish the eight generals who they held responsible. Two of these generals heard of the Assembly's deliberations while they were still out at sea, and in fear of the Assembly, did not return to Athens. The six others, which included Pericles' son, were tried, convicted, and executed. (By an odd coincidence, the presiding officer of the Assembly, a position that changed daily, was the philosopher, Socrates, who tried, without success to dissuade the Assembly from their harsh judgment.)

The execution of the Athenian generals following the battle at Arginusae was Athens' final great mistake of the Peloponnesian War. The following year, the Athenian navy, without its best generals, was soundly defeated by a Spartan fleet, commanded by Lysander, at Aegospotami in the Hellespont.

Ironically, the site of the final battle at Aegospotami was only a few miles from the castle, which Alcibiades had built as a retreat while in his final exile from Athens. There, Alcibiades saw that the Athenians had scattered their boats along the beach without a lookout and that each soldier roamed at will around the countryside. Alcibiades went to the generals and warned them of their vulnerability, but the generals ridiculed him, saying he was not a general anymore, and that they had no need of his advice. Soon thereafter, the Spartans attacked the unprepared Athenians, capturing two hundred Athenian triremes and killing three thousand of their crew.

The Spartan victory gave them control of the Hellespont and closed off the supply of grain to Athens from the Black Sea. After this, Athens' fall was inevitable. Athens, without a navy and without food, withstood a Spartan siege of the city for eight months until its starving citizens finally surrendered to the Spartans, ending the Peloponnesian War, in 403.

Alcibiades did not live to see Athens' final surrender. There are many stories of his death. With enemies in Athens, Sparta, and Persia, his fate was certain. According to Plutarch, agents of the Persian satrap, at the request of Sparta, set his house on fire, and slew Alcibiades as he fled the burning building.

The Spartans were uncharacteristically generous victors. Although urged by their allies to destroy Athens, kill all the men, and enslave the women and children, the Spartan demands were few. Probably they saw that Athens would be a valuable asset in the continuing wars among the Greek city-states. The Spartans, therefore, installed a short-lived oligarchic pro-Spartan government in Athens. In addition, the Spartans demanded that the city walls of Athens be torn down, and that the Athenian fleet be destroyed. The new government led by a clique known as the "Thirty Tyrants," lasted only a few months. A series of bloody proscriptions ran its course, and democratic government was eventually restored. Athens' political and military power, however, was at an end. Its dream of empire vanished.

Thucydides and the "Athenian Thesis"

Despite the critical role that Alcibiades played in the Sicilian campaign and the Peloponnesian War, the person who comes most vitally alive in Thucydides' narrative, to this reader, is Nicias.

While Alcibiades' dramatic career is driven by the single-minded motivation of ambition, Nicias' life, thoughts, and actions are fraught with contradictions and ironies. Throughout his life, he continually worked and failed to win popularity. He was a military general who was committed to avoiding battle. He was the leader of the peace party, who became the leader of the most daring campaign of the war. In Sicily, his decisions, most of which seemed reasonable at the time, pulled him step-by-step toward his and Athens' tragic end.

Thucydides gives us deeper insights into the character of Nicias than that of any other individual in his history. Several times he enters into Nicias' mind, telling us things that no one but Nicias could have known.[6] One of the most poignant examples of this occurs just before the final battle in the Great Harbor. Nicias addresses his troops using all the traditional words and "using arguments such as men would use at such a crisis, and which, with little alteration, are made to serve on all occasions alike." Nicias called on the gods, and the memories of ancestors, and the greatness of Athens, but "thinking as men are apt to think in great crises, that when all has been done they have still something left to do, and when all has been said that they have not yet said enough." Nicias in this moment of silent reflection concludes that all his words and preparations are insufficient. For a brief moment, Nicias seems to question all the things that held his life together—the gods, the ancestors, and Athens itself.[7]

Thucydides' intimate knowledge of Nicias leads him to his final words of praise for Nicias. Thucydides describes Nicias' death at the hands of the Syracusans and adds that he was "a man who of all the Hellenes in my time, least deserved such a fate, seeing that the whole course of his life had been regulated with strict attention to virtue."[8]

Modern scholars have not generally agreed with Thucydides' final assessment of Nicias. They criticize Nicias' desire for popularity and his desire to avoid conflict.[9] They criticize Nicias' refusal to leave Sicily, preferring an honorable death at the hands of the enemy, rather than censure from the Athenian citizens. This act put his own life and honor ahead of the lives of his soldiers whom he led.[10] Scholars generally agree, as well, with Demosthenes' criticism of Nicias' failure to take Syracuse in the first year of the occupation, and they fault his superstitious nature, which caused him to delay the final retreat from Syracuse.

In Nicias' defense, it should be noted that Nicias was prevented from taking Syracuse in the first year by his lack of cavalry.[11] On the charges that Nicias wanted to avoid conflict and sought an honorable death, these in other circumstances might be considered commendable.

In his judgment of Nicias, Thucydides looked not just at the tragic events of the Sicilian campaign, but at the whole course of Nicias' life. Before the Sicilian campaign, Nicias was a successful general.[12] Thucydides calls him "the most fortunate general of his time."[13] We must certainly praise Nicias for consistently opposing the reckless policies of Cleon and Alcibiades and recognize that Nicias was certainly correct in trying to dissuade the Athenians from invading Sicily.

Any evaluation of Nicias should also include perhaps his greatest accomplishment—the peace treaty with Sparta that was named after him, and which could have ended the Peloponnesian War. We could add to this list of virtues and accomplishments Nicias' devotion to the traditional religious values of the Athenians, and his lavish financing of the Pan-Hellenic cult on the island of Delos. In addition, Nicias, despite being incapacitated by an illness, was able to think quickly and devise a successful defense when the garrison on Epipoli was attacked.[14]

To understand Thucydides' praise for Nicias, it is worth noting that the two men had much in common. They had served together as Athenian generals from the beginning of the Peloponnesian War. Most importantly, they shared an aristocratic culture based on their ancestry and property. Thucydides had his gold mines in Thrace, and Nicias similarly had his silver mines in Laurium. Both men were also intimately familiar with the practice of the democratic Assembly of Athens of turning against its most brilliant aristocratic leaders. Thucydides and Nicias certainly were aware of the ostracisms of Cimon and Themistocles, and the banishment of Pythodorus and Sophocles following the first expedition to Sicily, and, of course, Thucydides' own exile. Neither would they have been surprised by the Assembly's decision, in 406, to condemn to death eight victorious generals (including a son of Pericles) for errors much less serious than their own.[15] Nicias was certainly being realistic when he imagined that he would be disgraced, banished, or executed if he returned to Athens without a victory in Sicily.

When we look at the culture of the Athenian aristocrats, it is sometimes jarring to note that the most conservative members of Athenian society were often great admirers of, and even often complicit with, Athens' greatest enemy, Sparta. Many conservatives in ancient Athens, and ever since, have been seduced by the attractions of ancient Sparta. They would prefer the quiet stability of oligarchy to the raucous tumult of democracy. Many Athenian aristocrats shared the vision of Aristides and Cimon of Athens and Sparta being "yoke fellows" in a unified Greek world, and many among the Athenian elite had long-standing ties of friendship with the Spartans. We have already seen how Pericles, Cimon, Alcibiades, and Nicias claimed a special status of friendship with the Spartans or the Spartan state. Some of these alliances were semi-formal arrangements in which a person was designated as a *proxenos*—a citizen of a foreign state who was a representative or friend of another state.

We are fortunate that Thucydides' own friendship with Sparta allowed him to write much of his history "behind enemy lines." This gave him the opportunity to describe the war from both sides of the conflict, which is largely responsible for his reputation for objectivity.

He is not at all objective, however, in describing the Athenian democracy, which he specifically blames for the debacle in Sicily. The Sicilian expedition, he said, ended in disaster because the soldiers were not supported by the Assembly. The expedition failed, he wrote, "through a fault in the senders [that is, the Assembly] in not taking the best measures afterward to assist those who had gone out." This failure came about because the successors of Pericles, while struggling for personal power, committed "the conduct of state affairs to the whims of the multitude."[16]

In placing the blame for Athens' failures on the members of the Assembly, Thucydides pays no respect to the people who were the foundation of the Athenian empire. These, of course, were the men who were the hoplites and thetes who filled the ranks of the army and the navy.

At every step, the expansion of Athens' economic and military power went hand in hand with the extension of political power to these men. The growing power of Athens under the Pisistratids and Cleisthenes was marked by the declining power of the old aristocrats and the extension of rights to the hoplite soldiers; and the expansion of the empire after the Persian War and under Pericles was dependent on the extension of rights to the thetes who manned the navy. Athens' empire and Athens' democracy were thus born together.

Thucydides, like other writers before and after him, pays almost no notice of the individual soldiers and seamen. Thucydides writes generally of the armies and navies of the Athenians or their enemies, but he has not a word to say of the individuals who comprised those forces. We know the names of the men who led these armies, but we do not know the name of a single individual who fought in the ranks.[17] Thucydides frequently refers to the common people who filled the armies' ranks as the "hoi polloi," literally "the many," in contrast to "the few."[18] This was not unusual. Texts written by wealthy conservatives like Thucydides commonly portrayed the common man only as part of a disorderly mob.[19]

The model for these ideas was set in *The Iliad*. In one passage, Homer describes Odysseus disciplining soldiers in the ranks. "When he caught some common soldier shouting out, he'd beat him with the scepter, dress him down: 'You fool—sit still! Obey the commands of others, your superiors—you, you deserter, rank coward. You count for nothing.'"[20]

Homer, in the text of the *Iliad* gives the name of only one common soldier. Thersites, Homer says, was the "ugliest man who ever came to Troy." He was "bandy-legged" with a club foot, humped shoulders, a caved-in chest, a pointed head topped by "clumps of scraggly wooly hair." Thersites, "full of obscenities, teeming with rant," criticized Agamemnon for keeping for himself all the captured loot, the most beautiful women, and the gold. Odysseus took offense at this and beat him while his fellow soldiers laughed at Thersites and called him a "babbling, foulmouthed fool."[21]

Throughout Thucydides' history, he follows this tradition when he describes the crucial blunders and miscalculations made by the people in the Athenian Assembly (rarely mentioning the Council, which set the Assembly's agenda). After these, he sometimes adds a dismissive statement like, "according to the way of the multitude."[22]

Thucydides' major departure from ancient tradition was his indifference to religion and his implicit rejection of the gods. Thucydides mocked Nicias' devotion to the gods, and his faith in oracles and prophecies. Nicias, Thucydides says, was "somewhat over-addicted to divination and that kind of thing."[23]

We can see in hindsight that Thucydides' exclusion of "that kind of thing" from his history was one of his greatest accomplishments. By writing a history without reference to transcendent spirits and demons, to gods and goddesses, Thucydides wrote the first apparently realistic history and paved the way for an understanding of the world in which man acted alone in the world as the author of his own destiny.

This momentous step, however, was not unproblematic. Without supernatural forces judging and directing human actions, individuals were constrained only by a set of natural laws, which, when Thucydides wrote, were still in the process of being formulated. It created one of the greatest moral questions: If there is no God, or are no gods, what is the basis of morality? The Western world has grappled with this question ever since.

For some contemporary political theorists, and particularly those who study international relations, the answer, at least in the political realm, has been found in the "Athenian thesis."[24] Governments should base their relations with other states on a *realpolitik* of the rational calculation of self-interest. They see in the "Athenian thesis" a universal law of international relations. According to the iron laws that govern the relations between states, issues of political ideology, and of humanity, have no rational role in determining states' actions. Power must be used or lost. In the twentieth century and beyond, the advisors to American Presidents have used this idea to justify America's involvement in the Vietnam War, the American invasion of Iraq in 2003, and the "America first" policies of the Trump administration.[25]

But did Thucydides himself believe in the "Athenian thesis"? Probably not.

There are four times that the Athenian thesis is most clearly expressed in Thucydides' text. The first occurs in the speech of the Athenian envoys in Sparta when the Corinthians were trying to persuade Sparta to join them in a war against Athens.[26] The second is in Cleon's speech during the debate on the fate of the Mytileneans.[27] The third is the speeches of the Athenian ambassadors in the Melian dialogue.[28] And the fourth is Euphemus' speech at Camarena.[29]

In these speeches, the Athenian thesis that the weak must submit to the strong is associated with a number of related ideas: the driving motives of human behavior are fear, honor, and interest; the Athenian empire is unjust, but that, nevertheless, Athens cannot give it up; and that expediency, and not questions of right or justice, is the only test of good policy. What all of these ideas have in common in each of these speeches is their justification for Athenian aggression and the expansion of its empire.

Throughout Thucydides' narrative, he implicitly rejects these ideas. Thucydides, of course, is famous for his impartiality. He often has characters give dueling speeches in favor of and against a course of action. He does not tell us which argument he agrees with and betrays no emotional attachment to one side or another. He treats Athenians and Spartans equally, apparently without bias in favor or against one polis or the other. This has allowed historians and philosophers unlimited opportunities to interpret Thucydides' ideas and to see him as a prophet of whatever ideas they espouse.

If we look at the individuals who Thucydides implicitly admires and those that Thucydides implicitly disparages, however, Thucydides' own ideas and biases become clear. Thucydides consistently praises men who favored moderate action and avoided needless conflict or aggression.

He praises Pericles' "correctness of . . . foresight" when he told the Athenians "to wait quietly . . . to attempt no new conquests, and to expose the city to no hazards during the war."[30] He implicitly sides with Diodotus when he argues against Cleon's policy of killing all the Mytileneans. He presumably sympathized, as well, with the Melians when the Athenians gave them no choice other than to submit or be destroyed. He likewise implicitly admired the humane policy of the Spartan general Brasidas who took Amphipolis without bloodshed. Thucydides' admiration for the pacific Nicias conforms to this pattern. Conversely, Thucydides implicitly disapproves of individuals who express some version of the Athenian thesis, especially Cleon and the Athenian generals at Melos.

The only idea associated with the Athenian thesis with which Thucydides may have agreed was the idea that expediency was more important than abstract questions of right and justice. This idea is commonly expressed by those who voiced some version of the thesis, but it is also expressed by Diodotus, who clearly speaks with Thucydides' voice when he argues against killing all the Mytileneans. In his debate with Cleon, Diododus agrees not to argue about right and justice but to base his argument solely on expediency.

But what is expedient? To Cleon and the Athenians at Melos, expediency necessitates killing all who are disloyal or will not submit. Diodotus and the Melians, however, argue that such brutality is counter-productive. Killing all the Mytileneans, Diodotus argues, would jeopardize Athens' relations with its allies and convince others to resist Athens more strenuously. Winning over allies who could be valuable assets through friendly acts rather than through violence is more likely to create lasting bonds. These arguments would be repeated by the Melians and would be effectively demonstrated by Brasidas in Thrace.

The Sicilian campaign can be seen as the great test of the Athenian thesis. The Athenians who believed that "the strong must do what they can and the weak must submit" led the Athenians to invade Sicily with tragic results—the deaths of thousands and ultimately to the end of the Athenian empire. Thucydides' history, like any great writing, can be interpreted in many ways. Thucydides may or may not have believed in what we call the Athenian thesis, but we should not be persuaded. The history of the Sicilian campaign shows where those ideas may lead.

Athenian Democracy and the Athenian Empire

Many students in high school or in college read Pericles' funeral speech and come away feeling a great admiration for ancient Athens and its democracy. We praise Athens as the birthplace of the world's first direct democracy. In the funeral speech, Pericles defined a democratic system of government that "favors the many instead of the few," and which promised "equal justice under the law,"[31] popular participation in government, and free speech.

It is ironic, however, that for most of the centuries since Thucydides wrote, the primary lesson from Thucydides was that democracies are always doomed to fail. The classical problem with democracy is: how can the rights of a minority be protected in a system where the majority rules? Or, as it is sometimes more pointedly stated: how can the property of the rich be protected from the greed of the poor? Democracy always contains the threat of the people "voting themselves a farm," or passing a tax on billionaires.

Even James Madison, the "father of the U.S. Constitution" and a reader of Thucydides, repeated the common perception of democracy when he wrote in 1787, that "democracies have ever been spectacles of turbulence and contention; have ever been found incompatible with personal security, or the rights of property; and have in general been as short in their lives, as they have been violent in their deaths."[32]

It has only been since the early years of the nineteenth century and the rise of romantic nationalism that the democracy of ancient Athens has become celebrated as the birthplace of the single best system of government.[33] The democratic system of ancient Athens, however, was not democratic by our standards today. As we have seen, only male citizens, and no women or the slaves who made up a large percentage of the population could participate in the Assembly. Neither could the large number of merchants and craftsmen who were foreigners, and who may have acted as a middle class, which bridged the gulf between the interests of the rich and the poor.

Also, sometimes overlooked in evaluating Athenian democracy were Athens' "allies"—the numerous states who joined the Delian League and subsequently became members of the Athenian empire. Although originally imagined as equals in the empire, they soon became subject states with no voice in the empire. Thucydides often describes these allies, following the political rhetoric of the Spartans, as "enslaved" by the Athenians. Athens frequently treated them harshly, and they had no say in the government of the empire. They were compelled to pay taxes and obey laws over which they had no say, and if they attempted to leave the alliance their efforts were countered with force. In many ways, however, they profited as allies of Athens. Their mostly democratic governments were protected by the Athenian fleet, and they benefited from a standardized currency, and protection from pirates in the Aegean Sea. Many people, as well, preferred to have democratic governments within the Athenian empire rather than have the "freedom" of being governed by local aristocrats, as is proven by their numerous revolts against oligarchic rule. Several centuries later, the Romans solved some of these problems by gradually extending levels of citizenship and rights to their conquered peoples. If Athens had followed such a practice, perhaps its empire would have been more stable.

When we factor in the lack of political power of the women, slaves, and metics in Athens, and the lack of representation of states within the Athenian empire in our estimation of Athenian democracy, we may conclude that one of its greatest faults might not have been too much democracy but too little.

The Athenian democracy was also plagued by the large social and economic gap among those few who had political power. Athens never completely eliminated the power of local feudal aristocrats, and the rising economic power of a middle class of metics was not matched by an equivalent rise in their political power. Endemic fears and resentments between the few and the many, thus, found no outlet, except when they were re-directed into foreign adventures by demagogues who believed in the idea that the strong must do what they can and the weak must submit.

The Ghost of Nicias

The death of Nicias on the island of Sicily, the destruction of the Athenian army in Sicily, and the fall of the Athenian empire, all had consequences that still reverberate over two thousand years later.

A quarter century after the tragic ending of the Sicilian campaign, Plato imagined Nicias and his friend Laches as participating in a conversation with Plato's mentor, Socrates. Plato in his Socratic dialogue, *The Laches*, uses the memories of the two peace-makers and their failed invasions of Sicily as backdrops to a discussion of the military education of the youth. In Plato's mini-drama, Nicias and Laches have just attended an exhibition of a man fighting in hoplite armor, and are invited to discuss the question with Socrates: should young men study the art of fighting in armor?[34]

Under questioning by Socrates, the discussion turns step-by-step from the question of the proper education of youth, to the nature of courage, to the nature of knowledge, to the perception of time, and, ultimately, to the nature of virtue. At each step, Socrates urges Nicias and Laches to seek deeper meanings beyond what is immediately apparent. The end goal is to discover the real, rather than the superficial, subject of discussion, which is increasingly abstract.

In this early Socratic dialogue, Plato gives a preview of a system of philosophy, which would transform the Western world. As elaborated in his more famous work, *The Republic*, Plato encourages his readers to look beyond their immediate experiences of the material world, which are in a constant state of change, and to see the eternal realities that lie beyond the ability of our physical senses to perceive them. In these works, Plato imagined a stark disjunction between the physical world and a realm of absolute ideas. In doing so, he broke with the traditional Greek celebration of the unity of body and mind.

Plato illustrated his ideas in *The Republic*, by asking us to imagine a man imprisoned in a cave, lit only by a fire that casts shadows on a wall. The man, who is accustomed to seeing nothing but shadows, assumes that the shadows are real things. Eventually, however, the man makes his way out of the cave and sees the world illuminated by the brilliant sun and he recognizes the true nature of things. In Plato's dialogues such as this, Socrates led his listeners to this greater understanding.

Not everyone in Athens, however, appreciated Socrates' attempt to educate them. In 399, Socrates was prosecuted by the Athenians on the charges of impiety and corrupting the youth. Not mentioned in the charges, but on everyone's mind, was the fact that Socrates was a friend and mentor to Alcibiades and to several members of the oligarchic coup which briefly overthrew the Athenian democracy after the Peloponnesian War. The Athenian Assembly, believing that Socrates and his ideas were the cause of all their troubles, found him guilty and condemned him to death.

All of the events of the preceding years—the increasing rejection of spiritual forces, the failure of democracy, the destruction of the Athenian empire, and the death of Socrates—inspired Plato to imagine an ideal, perfect, stable political system unlike the turbulent democracy which was the cause of all Athens' problems.

The contrast between the evils of the real world, which Plato saw all around him, and his vision of an idealized transcendent realm of Truth, Virtue, and Beauty is the principle subject of Plato's philosophy, and has been the foundation for virtually all of the Western world's great intellectual achievements ever since. It was the starting point for the philosophical system of Aristotle, it shaped the early theology of the Christian church, the intellectual blossoming of the Italian Renaissance, and the Scientific Revolution. It shaped the eighteenth-century Enlightenment, and it continues to shape the world that we live in today.

Thucydides and Plato wrote their great works at the beginning of a tradition that has survived in Western culture for over two thousand years. They represent a starting point for many of the questions for which we still seek answers. What is a just war? How can we act morally? How can we know truth? Their works mark the beginning of a Western tradition of thought, but they should not be considered as the final words.

They wrote at a time when modern ideas of benevolence, charity, and compassion were still incoherently formulated. The world today is a much more complex place than the ancient world of the Greek polis, and considerations of justice and humanity, along with wise considerations of expediency, hopefully, might lead us to write a new chapter in history with a different ending than that of the Sicilian campaign.

NOTES

1. Xenophon, *Hellenica*, ed. Carleton L. Brownson, vols. 1–2 (Cambridge, MA: Harvard University Press; London: William Heinemann, 1918–1921), bk. 2, chap. 2, 3 (2.2.3). http://www.perseus.tufts.edu/hopper/text?doc=Perseus%3Atext%3A1999.01.0206%3Abook%3D2%3Achapter%3D2%3Asection%3D3 (accessed March 11, 2021).
2. Thucydides, 8.96.5.
3. Thucydides, 8.92.11.
4. Thucydides, 8.97.2.
5. See Thucydides, 2.65, 2.100, 4.81, and 6.15.
6. Thucydides, 5.16.1, 6.19.2, 7.48.4, 7.69.2.
7. Thucydides, 7.69.2.
8. Thucydides, 7.86.
9. Thucydides, 5.16.1.
10. Thucydides, 7.48.2.
11. Which Nicias had previously warned about (Thucydides, 6.20.4, 6.21.1).
12. For example, Thucydides, 3.51, 4.129–4.130.
13. Thucydides, 5.16.
14. Thucydides, 6.102.2–3.
15. Following the sea battle at Arginusae, 406 BCE, Thucydides, 1.7.
16. Thucydides, 2.65.10–11.
17. The single possible exception is Athenagoras of Syracuse a demagogue in Syracuse whose speech in favor of democracy (unique in Thucydides) clearly does not represent Thucydides' opinion (Thucydides, 6.35–6.41).
18. Thucydides, 2.37.1.
19. It is ironic that the political legacies of the ancient world of democracy, equality, and free speech come almost entirely from the writings of conservatives like Thucydides, Plato, and Aristotle, who formed the arguments that are the basis of both conservative and liberal ideologies today.
20. Homer, *The Iliad*, trans. Robert Fagles (New York, Penguin, 1990), 2.229–2.233.
21. Homer, *Iliad*, 2.245–2.324.
22. Thucydides, 2.65, 4.28.3.
23. Thucydides, 7.50.4.
24. The Athenian thesis is most clearly stated at Thucydides, 1.75–1.76, 5.89, 6.18.3, 6.85.
25. See, for example, Lowell S. Gustafson, ed., *Thucydides' Theory of International Relations: A Lasting Possession* (Baton Rouge: Louisiana State University Press, 2000). For extensive confirmation of Thucydides influence on recent politics, one can access Google Scholar and the words "Thucydides" and "Bush," or "Trump." A good overview of Thucydides influence on U.S. foreign policy, with further citations, is John A. Bloxham, *Thucydides and US Foreign Policy Debates after the Cold War* (Boca Raton, FL: Dissertation.com, 2010). See also: Victor Davis Hanson, *Ripples of Battle: How Wars of the Past Still Determine How We Fight, How We Live, and How We Think* (New York: Anchor Books, 2004), 179; Nicholas Kristof, "Et Tu, George?" *New York Times*, January 23, 2007, https://www.nytimes.com/2007/01/23/opinion/23kristof.html?mcubz=3 (accessed June 21, 2017); Kori Schake, "The Summer of Misreading Thucydides," *Atlantic*, July 18, 2017, https://www.theatlantic.com/international/archive/2017/07/the-summer-of-misreading-thucydides/533859/ (accessed June 21, 2017); Michael Crowley, "Why the White House Is Reading Greek History," *Politico*, June 21, 2017, https://www.politico.com/magazine/story/2017/06/21/why-the-white-house-is-reading-greek-history-215287/ (accessed June 21, 2017); Pico Community, "Bush v. Thucydides: Staying the Course," *Daily Kos*, November 21, 2005, https://www.dailykos.com/stories/2005/11/21/166886/- (accessed June 21, 2017); James Jay Carafano, "Thucydides, Scahill and Dirty History," *Heritage Foundation*, June 14, 2013, https://www.heritage.org/asia/commentary/thucydides-scahill-and-dirty-history (accessed June 21, 2017); American Spectator, "Thinking about Iraq . . . and Thucydides," *American Spectator*(blog), November 15, 2013, https://spectator.org/56517_thinking-about-iraqand-thucydides/ (last accessed June 21, 2017); John Taylor, "Thucydides vs. Victor Davis Hanson," *Antiwar.com*, September 6, 2007, https://original.antiwar.com/

john-taylor/2007/09/06/thucydides-vs-victor-davis-hanson/ (accessed June 21, 2017); Gregory Crane, *Thucydides and the Ancient Simplicity: The Limits of Political Realism* (Berkeley: University of California Press, 1998), https://books.google.com/books?isbn=0520918746 (accessed June 21, 2017); Toivo Koivukoski and David Tabachnick, eds., *Confronting Tyranny: Ancient Lessons for Global Politics* (Lanham, MD: Rowman & Littlefield, 2005), https://books.google.com/books?isbn=074254401X (accessed June 21, 2017); Christopher Bruell, "Thucydides' View of Athenian Imperialism," *American Political Science Review* 68, no. 1 (1974): 11–17, https://doi.org/10.2307/1959737; and also quoted "The Trump team is obsessing over Thucydides, the ancient historian who wrote a seminal tract on war" (Crowley, "Why the White House").

26. Thucydides, 1.73–1.78.
27. Thucydides, 3.37–3.40.
28. Thucydides, 5.85–5.116.
29. Thucydides, 6.82–6.87.
30. Thucydides, 2.65.6–7.
31. Thucydides, 2.37.
32. James Madison, "Federalist #10-, The Federalist Papers, November 22, 1787," in *James Madison: Writings*, ed. Jack Rakove (New York: Library of America, 1999), 164.
33. In America, the problem of democracy was to some extent ameliorated by the multiplication of political units, and by the amelioration of class conflict by a strong (white) middle class that united the interests of richer and poorer Americans (and excluded Blacks).
34. Plato, *Laches, or Courage, A Dialogue: The Works of Plato*, trans. Benjamin Jowett (New York: Oxford University Press, 1920), 56, 61.

Bibliography

PRIMARY

Andocides. *On the Mysteries, Minor Attic Orators in Two Volumes.* Volume 1. *Antiphon Andocides.* English translation by K. J. Maidment. Cambridge, MA: Harvard University Press; London: William Heinemann, 1968. http://www.perseus.tufts.edu/hopper/text?doc=Andoc.+1+1&redirect=true (accessed September 27, 2020).

Aristotle. *Aristotle and Xenophon on Democracy and Oligarchy.* Translation, commentary, and introduction by J. M. Moore. Berkeley: University of California Press, 1975.

———. "The Athenian Constitution." In *Arisitole: The Politics and the Constitution of Athens, Aristotle,* edited by Stephen Everson, 209–64. New York: Cambridge University Press, 1996.

Athenaeus. *Athenaeus: The Deipnosophists.* Translated by C. D. Yonge. 3 vols. London: Henry G. Bohn, 1854. http://www.attalus.org/info/athenaeus.html (accessed March 11, 2021).

Diodorus Siculus. *The Library of History of Diodorus Siculus.* Volume 4. Translated by C. H. Oldfather. Cambridge, MA: Loeb Classical Library, 1946. https://penelope.uchicago.edu/Thayer/E/Roman/Texts/Diodorus_Siculus/home.html (accessed March 26, 2018).

Hegel, Georg Wilhelm Friedrich, and A.V. Miller, trans. *Hegel's Phenomenology of Spirit,* New York, Oxford University Press, 1977.

Hesiod. *Hesiod: Theogony* and *Works and Days.* Translation and Introduction by M. L. West. New York: Oxford University Press, 1988.

Homer. *The Homeric Hymns.* Translated by Michael Crudden. New York: Oxford University Press, 2001.

———. *Iliad.* Translated by Robert Fagles, New York, Penguin, 1990.

———. *The Odyssey.* Translated by Samuel Butler. London: A. C. Fifield, 1900.

———. *The Odyssey.* Translated by Robert Fagels. New York: Viking Penguin, 1996.

Laertius, Diogenes. *Lives of the Eminent Philosophers.* Edited by James Miller. Translated by Pamela Mensch. Oxford: Oxford University Press, 2018.

Plato. *Laches, or Courage, A Dialogue: The Works of Plato.* Translated by Benjamin Jowett. New York: Oxford University Press, 1920.

———. *Lysis; Symposium; Gorgias.* Volume 3 of 12. Translated by W. R. M. Lamb. Cambridge, MA: Harvard University Press, 1983.

Plutarch. *Plutarch: The Rise and Fall of Athens: Nine Greek Lives.* Translated by Ian Scott-Kilvert. London: Penguin, 1960.

Thucydides. [The History of the Peloponnesian War]. 8 books. c. 411 BCE.

———. *The Landmark Thucydides: A Comprehensive Guide to the Peloponnesian War*. Edited by Robert B. Strassler. Translation of 1874 by Richard Crawley. New York: Free Press, 1996.

———. *Thucydides*. Translated by Benjamin Jowett. 2nd ed. Oxford: Clarendon Press, 1900.

———. *Thucydides: The War of the Peloponnesians and the Athenians* (*Cambridge Texts in the History of Political Thought*). Edited and translated by Jeremy Mynott. New York: Cambridge University Press, 2013.

Xenophon. *Aristotle and Xenophon on Democracy and Oligarchy*. Translation, commentary, and introduction by J. M. Moore. Berkeley: University of California Press, 1975.

———. *Hellenica*. Edited by Carleton L. Brownson. Volumes 1–2. Cambridge, MA: Harvard University Press; London: William Heinemann, 1918–1921. http://www.perseus.tufts.edu/hopper/text?doc=Perseus:text:1999.01.0206 (accessed March 11, 2021).

SECONDARY

Aitken, James K., and Hillary F. Marlow, eds. *The City in the Hebrew Bible: Critical, Literary and Exegetical Approaches*. London: T&T Clark, 2018.

American Spectator. "Thinking about Iraq . . . and Thucydides."*American Spectator*(blog). November 15, 2013. https://spectator.org/56517_thinking-about-iraqand-thucydides/ (last accessed June 21, 2017).

Arnold, Matthew. "Dover Beach." In *New Poems*, 112–14. London, Macmillan, 1867. https://archive.org/details/newpoems00arnorich/page/112/mode/2up (accessed March 6, 2021).

Ashley, Richard K. "The Poverty of Neorealism." In *Neorealism and Its Critics*, edited by R. O. Keohane, 255–300. New York: Columbia University Press, 1986.

Bailkey, Nels M., ed. *Readings in Ancient History, Thought and Experience from Gilgamesh to St. Augustine*. 4th ed. Lexington, MA: Cengage Learning, 1992.

Bloxham, John A. *Thucydides and US Foreign Policy Debates after the Cold War*. Boca Raton, FL: Dissertation.com, 2010.

Bosworth, Brian. "Athens' First Intervention in Sicily: Thucydides and the Sicilian Tradition." *Classical Quarterly* 42, no. 1 (1992): 46–55. https://jstor.org/stable/639143.

Burkert, Walter. *Greek Religion*. Cambridge MA: Harvard University Press, 1985.

Carafano, James Jay. "Thucydides, Scahill and Dirty History." *Heritage Foundation*. June 14, 2013. https://www.heritage.org/asia/commentary/thucydides-scahill-and-dirty-history (accessed June 21, 2017).

Crane, Gregory. Thucydides and the Ancient Simplicity: The Limits of Political Realism. Berkeley: University of California Press, 1998. https://books.google.com/books?isbn=0520918746 (accessed June 21, 2017).

Crowley, Michael. "Why the White House Is Reading Greek History." *Politico*. June 21, 2017. https://www.politico.com/magazine/story/2017/06/21/why-the-white-house-is-reading-greek-history-215287/ (accessed June 21, 2017).

De Angelis, Franco. *Archaic and Classical Greek Sicily: A Social and Economic History*. New York: Oxford University Press, 2016.

Derian, James Der. "A Reinterpretation of Realism: Genealogy, Semiology Dromology." In *International Theory: Critical Investigations*, edited by James Der Derian, 363–96. New York: Macmillan, 1995.

De Ste. Croix, G. E. M. [Geoffrey Ernest Maurice]. *The Class Struggle in the Ancient Greek World: From the Archaic Age to the Arab Conquests*. Ithaca, NY: Cornell University Press, 1981.

———. *The Origins of the Peloponnesian War*. London, Duckworth, 1972.

Dictionary of Greek and Roman Biography and Mythology. Edited by William Smith Sr. 3 vols. Boston: Little, Brown, 1867. https://quod.lib.umich.edu/m/moa/acl3129.0002.001/5?q1=lais&view=image&size=100 (accessed March 11, 2021).

Fine, John V. A. *The Ancient Greeks: A Critical History*. Cambridge, MA: Harvard University Press, 1983.

Gomme, A. W., A. Andrewes, and K. J. Dover. *A Historical Commentary on Thucydides*. 5 vols. New York: Oxford University Press, 1945–1981.
Green, Peter. *Armada from Athens*. Garden City, NY: Doubleday, 1970.
Greenwood, Emily. *Thucydides and the Shaping of History*. London: Duckworth, 2006.
Gustafson, Lowell S., ed. *Thucydides' Theory of International Relations: A Lasting Possession*. Baton Rouge: Louisiana State University Press, 2000.
Hall, Jonathan M. *Ethnic Identity in Greek Antiquity*. Cambridge: Cambridge University Press, 1997.
Hanson, Victor Davis. *Ripples of Battle: How Wars of the Past Still Determine How We Fight, How We Live, and How We Think*. New York: Anchor Books, 2004.
———. *A War Like No Other: How the Athenians and Spartans Fought the Peloponnesian War*. New York: Random House, 2005.
Hegel, Georg Wilhelm Friedrich. *Phenomenology of Spirit* (*Phänomenologie des Geistes*) (1807).
Herodotus. *The Landmark Herodotus: The Histories*. Edited by Robert B. Strassler. Translated by Andrea L. Purvis. New York: Anchor Books, 2009.
Hornblower, Simon. *Commentary on Thucydides*. 3 vols. New York: Oxford University Press, 1991–2008.
———. *The Greek World, 479–323 BC*. New York: Routledge, 1983.
———. *Thucydides*. London: Duckworth, 1987.
Isaac, Benjamin. *The Invention of Racism in Classical Antiquity*. Princeton, NJ: Princeton University Press, 2004.
Johnson, Laurie M. *Thucydides, Hobbes, and the Interpretation of Realism*. DeKalb: Northern Illinois University Press, 1993.
Johnson Bagby, Laurie M. "The Use and Abuse of Thucydides in International Relations." *International Organization* 48, no. 1 (1994): 131–53. https://www.jstor.org/stable/2706917.
Kagan, Donald. *The Archidamian War*. Ithaca, NY: Cornell University Press, 1974.
———. *The Fall of the Athenian Empire*. Ithaca, NY: Cornell University Press, 1987.
———. *The Outbreak of the Peloponnesian War*. Ithaca, NY: Cornell University Press, 1969.
———. *The Peace of Nicias and the Sicilian Expedition*. Ithaca, NY: Cornell University Press, 1981.
———. *Thucydides: The Reinvention of History*. New York: Penguin Books, 2009.
Kennedy, Rebecca F., C. Sydnor Roy, and Max L. Goldman, trans. *Race and Ethnicity in the Classical World: An Anthology of Primary Sources in Translation*. Indianapolis, IN: Hackett, 2013.
Kitto, H. D. F. *The Greeks*. Baltimore, MD: Penguin, 1951.
Koivukoski, Toivo, and David Tabachnick, eds. *Confronting Tyranny: Ancient Lessons for Global Politics*. Lanham, MD: Rowman & Littlefield, 2005. https://books.google.com/books?isbn=074254401X (accessed June 21, 2017).
Kristof, Nicholas. "Et Tu, George?" *New York Times*. January 23, 2007. https://www.nytimes.com/2007/01/23/opinion/23kristof.html?mcubz=3 (accessed March 11, 2021).
Madison, James. "Federalist #10, The Federalist Papers, November 22, 1787." In *James Madison: Writings*, edited by Jack Rakove, 164. New York: Library of America, 1999.
Moore, J. M. "Introduction." In *Aristotle and Xenophon on Democracy and Oligarchy*, translation, commentary, and introduction by J. M. Moore. Berkeley: University of California Press, 1975.
Muraresku, Brian C. *The Immortality Key: The Secret History of the Religion with No Name*. New York: St. Martin's Press, 2020.
Orwin, Clifford. *The Humanity of Thucydides*. Princeton, NJ: Princeton University Press, 1994.
The Oxford Classical Dictionary. 4th ed. Edited by Simon Hornblower, Antony Spawforth, and Esther Eidinow. New York: Oxford University Press, 2012.
Patterson, Cynthia. "Other Sorts: Slaves, Foreigners, and Women in Periclean Athens." In *The Cambridge Companion to the Age of Pericles*, edited by Loren J. Samons II, 153–78. Cambridge: Cambridge University Press, 2007.

Pico Community. "Bush v. Thucydides: Staying the Course." *Daily Kos*. November 21, 2005. https://www.dailykos.com/stories/2005/11/21/166886/- (accessed June 21, 2017).

Pomeroy, Sarah. *Goddesses, Whores, Wives, and Slaves: Women in Classical Antiquity*. New York: Schocken Books, Random House, 1975.

Raaflaub, Kurt A. "Warfare and Athenian Society." In *The Cambridge Companion to the Age of Pericles*, edited by Loren J. Samons II, 96–124. Cambridge: Cambridge University Press, 2007.

Rhodes, P. J. "Democracy and Empire." In *The Cambridge Companion to the Age of Pericles*, edited by Loren J. Samons II, 24–45. Cambridge: Cambridge University Press, 2007. https://doi.org/10.1017/CCOL9780521807937.002.

Ruck, Carl A. P., and Danny Staples, *The World of Classical Myth: Gods and Goddesses, Heroines and Heroes*. Dunham, NC: Carolina Academic Press, 1994.

Samons, Loren J., II, ed. *The Cambridge Companion to the Age of Pericles*. Cambridge: Cambridge University Press, 2007. https://www.cambridge.org/core/books/cambridge-companion-to-the-age-of-pericles/5525AFD992DBC97123E5234C20F58087

———. "Conclusion: Pericles and Athens." In *The Cambridge Companion to the Age of Pericles*, edited by Loren J. Samons II, 282–30. Cambridge: Cambridge University Press, 2007.

Schake, Kori. "The Summer of Misreading Thucydides." *Atlantic*. July 18, 2017. https://www.theatlantic.com/international/archive/2017/07/the-summer-of-misreading-thucydides/533859/ (accessed June 21, 2017).

Strauss, Leo. *The City and Man*. Charlottesville: University of Virginia Press, 1964.

Taylor, John. "Thucydides vs. Victor Davis Hanson." *Antiwar.com*. September 6, 2007. https://original.antiwar.com/john-taylor/2007/09/06/thucydides-vs-victor-davis-hanson/ (accessed June 21, 2017).

Wallace, Robert W. "Plato's Sophists, Intellectual History after 450, and Sokrates." In *The Cambridge Companion to the Age of Pericles*, edited by Loren G. Samons II, 215–37. Cambridge: Cambridge University Press, 2007.

Zagorin, Perez. *Thucydides: An Introduction for the Common Reader*. Princeton, NJ: Princeton University Press, 2005.

Index

Acanthus, 53
Acarnia, Acarnians, 48
Achilles, 16, 69, 97
Acraean Crag, 127
Acragas, 74, 78
acropolis, 13, 16, 19, 21, 25, 29, 36, 40, 46, 84, 87, 88, 138, 139
Adonis, 85
Aegospotami, 139
Aeolian dialect, 26
Aeolian islands, 75
Aeschylus, 25, 27, 72, 73
Aetolia, Aetolians, 48–49
Agamemnon, 16, 69, 143
Agaristie, 86
Agis, 60–61, 62, 104
agora, 15, 17, 27, 33, 58, 71, 81, 86, 87, 99, 136
Agrigento, 70, 73
Alcibiades, 16, 33, 57–62, 78–80, 85, 86, 87, 89, 91, 92, 93, 101, 103–104, 113, 120, 136–140, 141, 142, 148
Alcidas, 43, 47
Alcinous, 46
Alcmaeonides, 86
Alcmaeonids, 16, 24, 34, 58, 86
America. *See* United States of America
Amphipolis, 3, 54, 55, 57, 59, 145
Anaktoron, 85
Anapus River, 105, 126
Anaxagoras, 24

Andocides, 86, 88–89
Andromachus, 86, 89
Antigone, 27, 99
apella (Sparta), 9, 10
Aphrodite, 78
Apollo, 8, 40
Apollo Temenites, 71
Apsephion, 87
Archidamus, 34, 36, 37, 56, 59
archon, 73
Archonidas, 108
Argos, 28, 56, 57, 59–60, 62, 112
Aristogeiton, 14–15
Aristophanes, 41, 42
Aristotle, 16, 24, 148
Artaxerxes, 18
Artemis Orthia, 10
Aspasia, 24–25
assembly, 1, 9, 11, 12, 17, 20, 21, 26, 34, 43, 44–45, 46, 49, 50–51, 54, 59, 73, 74, 75, 76–77, 78, 79, 80, 81, 85, 89, 90, 91, 93, 101, 102, 103, 108, 111, 112, 120, 137, 139, 142, 143, 146, 148
Assinarus River, 128–129
Astyochus, 135–136
Athena, 8, 13, 14, 16, 19, 24, 34, 56, 139
Athenagoras, 91
Athenian thesis, 34, 44, 65n7, 102, 140–145, 149n24
Athenians, character of, 7, 29n3
Athens internal improvements, 21

The Babylonians (play), 42
Bible, 6
Black Sea, 19, 53, 136, 139
Boeotia, 48, 54, 57, 59, 119
boule. See council
Brasidas, 47, 53–55
Byzantium, 19, 69

Cacyparis River, 127
Calicrates, 107
Callicratidas, 139
Camarina, 76, 77, 101–102, 127
Carini, 94
Carthage (Phoenicia), 1, 7, 69, 72, 78, 90, 103
Catana, 73, 74, 92–93, 94, 100, 101, 120, 121, 125, 127, 130
cavalry, 54, 71, 80, 94, 99, 100
Cephallenia, island, 117
ceramicus, 99
Chalcidice, 33, 53, 55
Chalcis, 70
Charides, 86
chariot, 13, 60, 72, 79, 83, 98
Charoeades, 75
Chios, 136
Choerades, isle, 85
Cimon, 20, 21, 40, 141–142
Circle fort, 105, 106, 107, 108
Cleisthenes, 16–17, 21, 73, 88, 142
Cleon, 41–45, 48, 50–52, 54, 55, 56, 59, 75, 112, 141, 144, 145
Clytemnestra, 27
Corcyra, 31–32, 46, 47, 90, 91, 118, 119
Corinth, Corinthians, 28, 31–33, 34, 40, 41, 46, 48, 57, 70, 89, 90, 94, 101, 108, 110, 114, 115–116, 117, 122, 144; Gulf of, 48
council, 9, 12, 17, 21, 46, 57, 59, 73, 86, 87, 88, 119, 136, 143
Croesus, 97
Cylon, 16, 34
Cyprus, 12, 19, 38
Cythera, 40, 56
Cyzicus, 138

Decelea, 103, 104, 113, 120, 135, 137
Delium, battle of, 54, 55
Delos, 5, 19, 28, 40, 141

Delos, Delian League, 5–6, 19, 20, 25, 28, 29, 33, 34, 35, 43, 146
Delphi, oracle, 56, 72
Demagogue, 38, 42, 46, 48, 91, 147, 149n17
demes, 11, 17, 36
Demeter, 33, 83–84, 85, 88
democracy, 2, 4, 11, 14, 16, 17, 18, 20, 21, 23, 25, 29, 38, 40, 43, 44, 46, 57, 73–74, 85, 91, 95–96, 103, 132n50, 135, 136, 137, 138, 142, 143, 145–147, 148, 149n17, 149n19
Demophon, 83–84
demos, 11
Demosthenes (general), 48–50, 51, 52, 100, 112, 113, 114, 115, 116, 117, 118, 120, 122, 124, 125, 126, 127, 128, 129, 141
Demosthenes (orator), 94
Diocleides, 87, 88
Diodorus, 70, 72–73, 74
Diodotus, 44–45, 145
Diogenes, 94, 96
Diognetus, 86, 87
Diomilus, 105
Dionysus, 84
Dorians, 8, 28, 64, 70, 73, 76, 77, 90, 102, 108, 110, 119, 125
Draco, 11
Ducetius, 74

earthquake, 20, 48, 59
ecclesia. See assembly
Egesta, 78, 79, 90, 91–92, 94, 102
Egypt, 12, 28, 37, 38, 97
Eleusis, Eleusinian mysteries, 83, 84, 85–86, 138
Elis, 57, 59, 60
Elpinor, 99
Elymians, 69, 78
empire, 1, 2, 4, 5, 6, 18, 25, 28–29, 33–34, 40, 42, 43, 44, 53, 62, 64, 70, 80, 102, 121, 140, 142–143, 144, 145, 146–147, 148
Ephialtes, 21, 25
ephors (Sparta), 10
Epidamnus, 31
Epipoli, 71, 105–106, 107, 109, 110, 118, 119, 130, 141

erastes and *eromenos*. *See* homosexuality
Eryx, 78
Etruscans, 73
Euboea, 3, 36, 70, 113, 137
Eucles, 108
Eucrates, 42, 44
Euphemus, 87, 102, 144
Euripides, 25, 27, 64, 130
Euryelus, 105, 108–109, 119
Eurymedon, 47, 76, 77, 112, 114, 117, 118, 120, 121
Euthydemus, 112

fear/honor/interest, 34, 144. *See also* Athenian thesis
First Peloponnesian War, 28–29
the four hundred, 136–137

Gela, 71, 76, 77, 78, 90, 102, 127
Gelon, 71–73
gerousia (Spartan), 9
Gongylus, 108–109
Gorgias, 75
Greek dark ages, 7
Gylippus, 104, 108–109, 110, 111, 114, 115, 116, 120, 122, 123, 125, 127, 128, 129, 139

Hades, 70, 83, 84, 99
Hamilcar, 72
Hamilton, Alexander, 5
Harmodius, 14–15
Hegel, Georg Wilhelm, 9
Helen of Troy, 16
The Hellenica, 138
Hellespont, 138, 139
helot, 6, 10, 19, 20, 34, 50, 52–53, 56, 57, 60, 66n43, 104, 115, 117, 129, 139
Heracles, 8, 11, 125
Heraclides, 101, 108
Heraclitus, 40
Herme (statue), 81–83, 84, 86, 87, 88, 93
Hermes (god), 81, 84
Hermocrates, 77, 90–91, 101, 102, 105, 106, 108, 114, 116, 125, 135
Herodotus, 13, 18, 97, 130
hetaera, 24, 27, 94
hetaireia (social club), 88
Hiero, 72, 73, 75

Himera, battle of, 72, 108
Hipparchus, 14–15, 16
Hippias, 14, 15, 16
Homer, 7, 8, 14, 69, 70, 83, 97, 143
homosexuality, 14, 96. *See also* Aristogeiton; Harmodius
Hoplite, 8, 11, 20, 21, 28, 34, 35, 36, 43, 46, 48, 49, 52, 54, 55, 60, 61, 62, 72, 81, 90, 95–99, 104, 105, 106, 110, 114, 115, 116, 117, 121, 122, 124, 126, 127, 137, 142, 147; hoplite phalanx, 8, 52, 54, 95, 96
horses, horsemen, 34, 55, 58, 72, 79, 80, 81, 86, 87, 88, 90, 91, 94, 99, 100, 104, 105, 115, 125, 128. *See also* cavalry; chariot
Hybris, 95, 107, 108, 110, 111, 113, 115, 116, 118, 119, 121, 126, 127, 128, 129, 141
Hycara, 94
Hyperbolus, 42

Iberia, 1, 103
Iliad, 14, 97, 99, 143
Ionia, 8, 24, 26, 28, 70, 73, 75, 76–77, 102, 110, 121

Jason, 16
Jefferson, Thomas, 5

The Knights (play by Aristophanes), 41
krypteia, 10

Labdalum, 105, 109
Laches, 56, 75, 76, 78, 90, 101, 147
The Laches (Socratic dialogue), 147
Lais, 94
Lamachus, 79, 91, 92, 93, 94, 100, 105, 107
Laurium, 25, 40, 87, 104, 141
Leogoras, 86
Leonidas, 5, 18
Leontini, 73, 75, 77, 78, 90, 92, 102
Leotychides, 104
Lesbos, 42, 45, 138
Locri, Locrians, 76, 118
lunar eclipse, 121
Lycurgus (Athenian), 13
Lycurgus (Spartan), 9, 10

Lydia, 12
Lydus, 86
Lysander, 139

Macedon, 11
Madison, James, 17, 146
Malaria, 119
Mamara, Sea of, 136
Mantinea, Mantineans, 57, 59–60, 61, 62, 79, 80, 85, 90, 93, 103, 112; battle of, 60, 62
Mantitheus, 87
Marathon, 19, 20, 40
Medea, 27
Megacles, 13, 16, 34
Megara, 28, 33, 34–35, 53, 57
Megarian Decree, 33, 34–35
Melos, Melian dialogue, 62–64, 144, 145
Menander, 112, 118
Mende, 53, 54–55
Meriones, 97
Messana (Sicily), 75, 76, 92, 101, 108
Messenia/Messenians (Peloponnese), 8–9, 10, 46, 48–49, 50, 52. *See also* helot
Methone, 53
metic, 26, 38, 86, 88, 147
Middle Ages (Europe), 7
Miletus, 121, 136
Miltiades, 20
Minoa, 40
mothax, 104, 139
Mount Taygetus, 10
Mycenaea, 7, 69, 84
Mylae, 75
Mytilene, 42–43, 44, 45, 138, 144, 145

Naupactus, 48, 49, 115–116, 118
navies. *See* trireme
Naxos, 19, 29, 70, 73, 75, 76, 92, 100, 101
neodamodeis, 60
Nestor, 16
Nicias, 38–41, 41, 42, 51, 54–55, 56–57, 58–60, 62, 75, 79, 80–81, 85, 90, 92, 93, 94, 100, 105, 107, 108, 109, 111–112, 113, 115, 116, 117, 118, 120–121, 122, 123, 124–125, 126, 127, 128–129, 135, 140–142, 143, 145, 147; peace of, 56, 57, 58–59, 60, 62, 75, 81, 113, 129

Odysseus, *Odyssey*, 14, 70, 97, 99, 143
Old Oligarch, 38, 40
oligos, 11
olives, 12, 69, 71, 73, 106, 127
Olympic games, 8, 58, 60, 72, 79
Olympic gods, 8. *See also* Aphrodite; Athena; Demeter; Dionysus; Zeus
Ortygia, 71, 107
Osiris, 85
ostracism, 17, 20, 40, 73, 141

Paean, 99, 119, 126, 128
Panathenaea, 14, 15
Panoply, 50, 115
Paralus (trireme), 135
Paros, 20
Parthenon, 21, 24, 25, 139
Patroclus, 99
Pausanias, 19–20, 33, 56
Peithias, 46
Peloponnesian League, 28, 57
peltasts, light infantry, 52, 61, 99, 116, 118, 122, 124, 126–127, 128
Pericles, 16, 21–27, 29, 34, 35, 36, 37, 38, 41, 48, 56, 58–59, 89, 98, 137, 139, 141, 142, 143, 145; funeral oration, 23, 98
Persephone, 33, 70, 83, 84, 88
Persia, 5, 18, 19, 28, 37, 40, 72, 97, 104, 135, 136, 137, 138, 140
Persian War, 5, 18, 19, 20, 33, 36, 40, 56, 102, 142
petalism, 73
Petra, 118
Phaeax, 77, 78
Phidias, 24, 25
Philip II of Macedon, 11
Pindar, 72, 73
piraeus, 36, 37, 88, 89, 135, 136, 137
Pisistratus, 12–15, 88, 142
plague, 37, 40
Plataea, 19, 35, 113
Plato, 21, 96, 147–148
Pleistonax, 56, 60
Plemmyrium, 109, 114, 115, 117
Plutarch, 9, 10, 41, 42, 104, 109, 140
polis, poleis (city-state), 7, 8, 9, 10, 11, 19, 21, 25, 27, 35, 38, 45, 53, 60, 64, 70, 76, 90, 91, 93, 96, 103, 121, 144, 148

Polynices, 99
Potidaea, Potidaeans, 33, 34, 35
prophecies, oracles, 2, 63, 64, 99, 121, 143
Protagoras, 24
proxenos, 20, 103, 142
pylos, 48, 50, 51–52, 53, 56, 57, 59, 103, 129
Pythodorus, 76, 77, 120, 141, 142
Pythonicus, 83, 85, 86, 89

religion, 2, 14, 17, 27, 38, 40, 50, 56, 85, 97, 141. *See also* Eleusis, Eleusinian mysteries; prophecies, oracles; soothsayers
The Republic, 147–148
Rhegium, 75–76, 91, 93
Rome, 1, 2

Salaminia (trireme), 93
Salamis, 5, 18, 19, 40, 72
Scione, 53, 54, 55, 57
Selinus, Seluniti, 78, 90, 92
Sicani, 69
Sicanus, 101
Sicel, 69, 71, 74, 76, 80, 91, 92, 108, 115, 125, 126
silver, 10, 25, 38, 40, 54, 78, 87, 104, 105, 112, 139, 141
Skyros, 20
slavery, 6, 8–9, 11–12, 25–26, 29, 33, 34, 35, 38, 43, 46, 48, 50, 51, 53, 57, 61, 63, 64, 71, 72, 74, 76, 83, 84, 86, 87, 88, 90, 94, 96, 97, 103, 104, 107, 111, 113, 122, 123, 125, 130, 137, 139, 140, 146–147; debt slavery, 11. *See also* helots
Socrates, 24, 25, 33, 54, 58, 139, 147, 148
Solon, 11–12, 17, 97
soothsayers, 40, 99, 121
Sophism, sophist, 24, 43, 74, 75, 80, 121
Sophocles (general), 76, 77, 120, 142
Sophocles (playwright), 25, 27, 99
Sparta, 8–10
Spartans, character, 7, 18, 19–20, 27, 29n3; military training, 10
Sphacteria, 48, 50–51, 52, 56, 59, 60, 77, 81, 109, 112, 113
stasis, 47
strategoi, 21

Sybota, straits of, 31
symposium, 14
Syracuse, political system, 73

Tarentum, 91
Telesterion, 84, 85
Telias, 108
Tellus, 97
Teucris, 86, 89
Thasos, 19, 20, 29
Thebes, Thebans, 28, 35
Themistocles, 5, 18, 40, 72, 142
Thermopylae, 5, 18
Theseus, 8, 11, 20
Thessaly, 94
thetes, 21, 25, 137, 138, 142, 143
"Thirty Years Peace," 29, 31, 33, 34, 60
Thrace, Thracians, 3, 53–54, 113–114, 141, 145
Thrasybulus, 73
Thrasylus, 60
Thucydides, *History of the Peloponnesian War*, 1–3, 54, 55, 125, 129, 137, 138, 140–145
Thurii, 118
Thyres, 40
Tissaphernes, 104, 136
trireme, 31, 72, 81, 83, 84, 89, 90, 93, 109, 110, 114, 139. *See also* Paralus (trireme); Salaminia (trireme)
trophy, 41, 62, 100, 110, 114, 122
Troy, Trojan war, 16, 78, 89, 104, 143
Tyndarides, 74
tyrant, tyranny, 12, 13, 14, 15, 29, 43, 71, 72, 73, 74, 75, 102, 121, 140

United States of America, 2, 5–6, 7, 16–17, 17, 26, 144

walls, battle of, 105–106, 108, 109, 110
Washington, George, 5
women, 13, 24, 25, 26–27, 35, 40, 43, 46, 57, 64, 83, 84, 89, 90, 94, 96, 98, 113, 123, 137, 140, 143, 146
words, 47–48
World War II, Allied Powers, 1; Axis Powers, 1

Xenophon, 138

Xerxes, 72

Zacynthus, island, 117
Zeus, 46, 56, 84, 98, 100, 116

About the Author

Alexander O. Boulton is a retired professor of history from Stevenson University in Maryland where he taught for over twenty-five years. He received his PhD in history from the College of William and Mary (1991). The primary focus of his research is the cultural and intellectual history of the United States. He was drawn to the study of Thucydides for the light that Thucydides' work sheds on the thinking of the nation's Founders and particularly on their ideas on democracy and national identity. He is the author of a biography of the architect, Frank Lloyd Wright (1993), and articles for *The William and Mary Quarterly*, *American Quarterly*, and *American Heritage Magazine*.

www.ingramcontent.com/pod-product-compliance
Lightning Source LLC
Chambersburg PA
CBHW061350300426
44116CB00011B/2059